INTO THE FIELD

INTO THE FIELD:
SITES OF
COMPOSITION STUDIES

Edited by *Anne Ruggles Gere*

The Modern Language Association of America
New York • 1993

Library of Congress Cataloging-in-Publication Data

Into the field : sites of composition studies / edited by Anne Ruggles
  Gere.
    p.   cm.
  Includes bibliographical references and index.
  ISBN 0-87352-398-9 (cloth) ISBN 0-87352-399-7 (pbk.)
    1. English language—Composition and exercises—Study and
teaching. 2. English language—Composition and exercises—Research.
3. English language—Rhetoric—Study and teaching. 4. English
language—Rhetoric—Research. I. Gere, Anne Ruggles, 1944– .
PE1404.I55   1993
808'.042'07—dc20   92-45626

Published by The Modern Language Association of America
10 Astor Place, New York, New York 10003-6981

Contents

Introduction   *Anne Ruggles Gere*   1

PART ONE: THE PHILOSOPHICAL TURN

Being Philosophical about Composition: Hermeneutics and the
    Teaching of Writing   9
Kurt Spellmeyer

Reconnecting Rhetoric and Philosophy in the Composition
    Classroom   30
Brenda Deen Schildgen

The Phenomenology of Process   44
Judith Halden-Sullivan

Self-Reflection as a Way of Knowing: Phenomenological
    Investigations in Composition   60
Barbara Gleason

Polanyi and Composition: A Personal Note on a Human Science   72
Richard J. Murphy, Jr.

Argumentation and Critique: College Composition and
    Enlightenment Ideals   84
George Dillon

PART TWO: POSTMODERN SUBJECTIVITIES

Composition Studies and Cultural Studies: Collapsing Boundaries   99
James A. Berlin

Composition Studies: Postmodern or Popular   117
John Trimbur

Subjectivity and Its Role in "Constructed" Knowledge:
    Composition, Feminist Theory, and Psychoanalysis   133
Irene Papoulis

Creativity and Insight: Toward a Poetics of Composition   147
Rosemary Gates

Composition as the Voicing of Multiple Fictions   159
Derek Owens

Ethnography and the Study of Literacy: Prospects for Socially
    Generous Research   176
David Bleich

Not a Conclusion: A Conversation   193

Works Cited   207

Index   219

Introduction

THIS anthology proposes a new metaphor for the relation between composition and other disciplines. Significantly, *Into the Field: Sites of Composition Studies* does not adopt the common bridge-building metaphor to represent that relation. The idea of bridge building, perhaps best exemplified by the title of Winifred G. Horner's *Composition and Literature: Bridging the Gap*, assumes an unproblematic and unidirectional borrowing by composition. As Geoffrey Squires and his colleagues assert, bridge building, one of two frequent descriptions for interdisciplinary relations, denotes simple appropriations in which the boundaries of both disciplines remain undisturbed.

Offering an alternative to the bridge-building concept, this volume favors "restructuring," the other metaphor named by Squires and his colleagues. Restructuring connotes radical realignments and a critique of the disciplines being restructured, and it suggests that change, disruption, and even challenges to prevailing knowledge emerge from interdisciplinary relations. Because, as George Lakoff and Mark Johnson remind us, metaphors shape our approach to the world, the shift in metaphors that represent the relation between composition and other disciplines signals a major change.

The bridge-building metaphor, which has served composition for several decades, can be used to describe much of the history of composition studies. One early intellectual association, between composition and educational psychology, accurately demonstrates composition's unproblematized adoption of methods and values from another field. Richard Braddock, Richard Lloyd-Jones, and Lowell Schoer's *Research in Written Composition* (1963), which defined composition studies as research on teaching and writing, appropriated the experimental methods of educational psychology, thus opening the way for a large body of research that, according to Stephen North, helped establish composition as a field.

Composition studies formed useful alliances with other areas of psychology as well. In particular, developmental psychology provided both theory and methodology for a significant quantity of work. James Moffett's *Teaching the Universe of Discourse* (1968) drew on the ideas of Jean Piaget to create a plan for teaching writing, one that emphasized progression from egocentrism toward a decentered perspective characterized by the ability to take the viewpoint of others. Other scholars adapted this model to describe the intellectual development of writers.

In a related move, composition studies also borrowed from cognitive psychology. Case studies such as Janet Emig's widely imitated *The Composing*

Processes of Twelfth Graders (1971) adopted the cognitivist's emphasis on the workings of the mind by focusing on the habits and perceptions of individual writers. Linda Flower and John R. Hayes, informed by cognitive psychology's technique of protocol analysis, developed a model of the writing process and described it in several articles. These and other borrowings from cognitive psychology led composition studies to shift its attention away from the products of writing toward explanations of processes that bring writing into existence.

Another bridge was established between composition and linguistics as researchers in composition considered the texts produced by writers. Noam Chomsky developed the idea of transformational grammar, which holds that sentences contain a deep structure on which transformations are performed to arrive at the surface structure. Researchers posited that a text with more transformations is better and more mature than a text with fewer, and, in turn, that the presence of more transformations signals greater syntactic maturity on the part of the writer. This concept of syntactic maturity or fluency, as measured by T units (units roughly comparable to independent clauses), led to the pedagogy of sentence combining, a method to help writers improve their texts by lengthening their sentences.

The bridge between composition and literature has often spanned troubled waters as the two, like stepsiblings thrust together by a marriage over which they had no control, have warily coexisted in English departments. Composition scholars have, with some justification, felt alternately exploited and scorned by their literary colleagues who, in turn, have resented composition's financial power and envied its intellectual liveliness. The recent burgeoning of critical theory has fostered new bridge building between composition and literature. In particular, composition has borrowed from reader-response theory with its emphasis on the active nature of reading and from deconstruction with its description of the radical indeterminacy of language. In addition to focusing on both reading and writing as acts of composing and thereby changing the relation between them, reader-response theory has suggested assignments for writing. Similarly, deconstruction has encouraged writing assignments that avoid closure and that highlight the tropes and figures in writing.

The most common bridge-building exercise has occurred between composition and rhetoric. Indeed, the two are frequently welded together to operate as a single term, even though, as Susan Miller has demonstrated, composition studies has a history and a tradition separate from those of rhetoric. Since 1971, when Edward P. J. Corbett's *Classical Rhetoric for the Modern Student* examined ways to use the traditional canons of rhetoric in a composition class, composition studies has strengthened its ties with rhetoric. This move has added the names of classical figures such as Aristotle and Cicero, and of contemporary rhetoricians such as Kenneth Burke and Stephen Toulmin, to the lexicon of composition studies, revived interest in invention, and led to the development of new strategies for argument.

To the extent that we think of composition as an applied field only, the bridge-building metaphor serves. As Julie Klein explains, bridge building appears "in most applied and mission-oriented [interdisciplinary] projects" (278), and composition in its pedagogical manifestation can be described as both. Pedagogies such as solving problems, combining sentences, responding to drafts, and answering topoi-derived questions—which emerge, respectively, from composition's liaisons with psychology, linguistics, literary theory, and rhetoric—demonstrate how interdisciplinarity conceived as bridge building contributes to classroom applications.

But when we think of composition in terms of both theory and application, as the contributors to this volume do, the bridge-building metaphor proves inadequate. In this fuller expression, composition theory resists boundaries and blurs distinctions between disciplines. Instead of simply borrowing from a given field, it interacts, changing and being changed. Restructuring, the second metaphor for interdisciplinarity offered by Squires and his colleagues, describes this relation more accurately. The restructuring metaphor emphasizes that the essays included here create new perspectives on the field at the same time that they introduce new terms to the discussion of composition. These terms include reconceptualizing the discipline, deconstructing received boundaries, and reconstructing relations between theory and application.

Unlike theorists such as North, the contributors to this collection do not worry about the disciplinary status of composition but enact the metaphor of restructuring by reconceptualizing the field. Questions about the status of composition—whether it possesses the features of a discipline, whether it merits a place in the "disciplined" academy—give way, in these essays, to new ways of talking about composition. Variously represented as an interpretive social science, as processual anthropology, as cultural studies, and as reasoned argument, composition takes on new and complex meanings. These meanings derive from intersections among various fields rather than from a totalizing disciplinary narrative.

Deconstructing received boundaries, another term of the restructuring metaphor set forth in these essays, appears as a consequence of the reconceptualizing described above. This deconstructing occurs as composition interacts with other disciplines and the boundaries between them fade, becoming more permeable. In keeping with the postmodern spirit, composition extends itself expansively, shaping and being shaped wherever writing occurs. Negotiations with literary theorists, for example, about a term such as *rhetoric* demonstrate how distinctions between composition and literary theory become less stable. Similarly, intersections between composition and philosophy around questions of language—What is language? What relation do humans have with language?—show the blurring that occurs between these two disciplines.

Because of this emphasis on permeable boundaries and interactions rather than differences, it may seem strange that the title of this anthology includes the word *field*. In its more common usage, *field* connotes a bounded territory, one that can be distinguished and set apart. Another less common meaning, "a complex of forces," describes the space in which the reconceptualizations attendant to the restructuring of composition and other disciplines occur. *Field* as it is used here, then, refers to a kind of charged space in which multiple "sites" of interaction appear.

The third term of restructuring at work in these essays concerns the repairing of relations between theory and application. While the bridge-building metaphor focuses on application, thereby separating it from theory, the restructuring metaphor accommodates a more complicated relation, one that refigures both educational practices and scholarly research. The interaction of composition and ethnography, for example, combines teaching and research in a common effort to portray the lived experience of students in writing classes. Similarly, considerations of personal voice and subjectivity lead to complex interactions between composition and philosophy.

An anthology is an appropriate form in which to explore some of the forces that operate within the charged space we call a field. By its nature, an anthology allows unity and diversity to coexist; it permits exploration of contradictions without losing cohesiveness. The essays in this anthology do pose contradictions. Among the issues contested are the nature of rhetoric and its relation to hermeneutics, the role of phenomenology in scholarly investigations, the possibility of employing a cooperative and disinterested pursuit of truth, the relation of discursive formations to power, and the dimensions of subjectivity. At the same time, these essays are unified by the metaphor of restructuring. They all rethink dichotomies such as subject and object, reconsider current distinctions such as those between interpretation and production of texts, and retain skepticism about universal agreement. While most of the essays concentrate on issues that can be described as theoretical, many (particularly those by Murphy, Dillon, and Bleich) take us into composition classrooms, and nearly all consider implications for teaching, thereby demonstrating the continuity between theory and practice.

These essays also proceed from a common understanding that composition shapes as much as it is shaped by other fields because questions about the nature of discourse, writing, and subjectivity emerge from mutually defining stances. Evidence of these interactions appears as anthropologists explore writing and its effects on their representations of culture; as philosophers, particularly those of the hermeneutical tradition, reduce the distinctions between producing and interpreting discourse; as feminists ponder the legacies and limitations of (patriarchal) language; as students of cultural studies investigate the relations between discursive structures and the distribution of power.

Many of the essays in this anthology began as papers for convention sessions sponsored by the MLA's Division on the Teaching of Writing, and they retain a concern with pedagogy even as they explore the sites of mutually defining interactions. Part 1 includes six essays that examine dimensions of the philosophical turn or the interpenetration of composition studies and various philosophical traditions, particularly the hermeneutical tradition. In the opening essay, Kurt Spellmeyer considers the history of composition's relation to rhetorical formalism and pragmatism and draws the conclusion that hermeneutical transformations of knowledge can locate unities in composition studies and make connections between formal knowledge and daily experience. Brenda Deen Schildgen approaches hermeneutics from a slightly different angle, emphasizing its capacity to balance interpretation and production of texts, thereby offering ways to realign rhetoric and philosophy. Judith Halden-Sullivan's description of the phenomenology of process develops Spellmeyer's point about hermeneutical transformations by demonstrating that composition students' language bespeaks their condition in the world. Barbara Gleason moves the discussion toward phenomenology by considering self-reflection as a way of knowing, and Richard J. Murphy, Jr., explains how Michael Polanyi's concept of personal knowledge is essential to understanding and justifying the knowledge of practicing teachers. George Dillon's essay, which concludes part 1, provides a classroom enactment of Jürgen Habermas's belief that academic discourse can promote critical reflection that leads to greater autonomy and justice.

Part 2 brings together six essays that contemplate various aspects of subjectivity from a postmodern perspective. James A. Berlin opens this section with an exploration of the collapsing boundaries between composition studies and cultural studies, and he points to the tension between structuralist and culturalist representations of the subject. John Trimbur follows with a caution against a too-ready embrace of postmodernism. He argues that postmodernism, with its potential to reduce the subject from an agent of discourse to a function, can depoliticize and privatize individuals. Irene Papoulis adopts a psychoanalytical-feminist perspective to examine the ways subjectivity participates in the construction of knowledge. Rosemary Gates proceeds in yet another direction as she describes the poetics of composing by a creative subject. Gates concludes that poetics, as enacted by situated subjects, offers a more fruitful approach to composition than does the concept of paradigm. Derek Owens, in a related move, asserts that writers need to develop their own subjectivities—which, he says, should be thought of not as static entities but as shifting areas marked by perpetual metamorphoses—and explains how these processes diminish the boundaries between fiction and exposition. David Bleich's essay closes part 2 by calling for a version of ethnography that honors the subjectivities of those being studied in composition research. This socially generous research, as Bleich terms it, reduces the distinctions between theory and application.

PART ONE

The Philosophical Turn

Being Philosophical about Composition: Hermeneutics and the Teaching of Writing

Kurt Spellmeyer

"JUST beyond our present horizon, I like to think, lie the Delectable Islands": with these words, Victor Turner announced a new era in anthropology, an era ending the protracted fragmentation of his discipline (151). On the one hand, Turner addressed a beleaguered old guard, the structural-functionalists who had lifted anthropology from antiquarianism and travel writing to the level of a rigorous science by adopting as their proper subject not simply "culture" but the specific structures of social interaction distinguishing one culture from the next. On the other hand, he attempted to conciliate the dissenters, "the biological, ecological, structural, semiotic, semiological, 'etic,' 'emic,' ethno-this and ethno-that, kinds of anthropologists"—those who had persistently unearthed everything the old guard forgot, suppressed, or dismissed in its rage for order (151). A dissenter himself, whose careful observation "in the bush," as he put it, made him skeptical of the disembodied precision and symmetry of the structural-functionalist project, Turner believed he had found in hermeneutics—broadly defined as the study of meanings and contexts—an opportunity to reunite the long opposing factions. While he granted that structure was a useful notion, and perhaps even indispensable, he came to feel that it offered only a static, one-dimensional image of social life, which he described as a world of "becoming" or "processuality," a world characterized by change, diversity, and interpretive differences (151–52). There *was* order, but never invariant order; there *were* conventions, but the meanings and uses of these conventions were not the same for all the members of a society. Instead of regarding culture as a collection of rules or a unified body of codes and tenets, Turner saw it as a shifting field of negotiations, conspiracies, alliances, innovations—a world of structure but also always a world in process. At the interface between structure and process, convention and difference, Turner found his Delectable Islands.

If composition had emerged as a field of its own fifty years ago, and if our forerunners had made good its professional claim to the status of a science on the order of linguistics or psychology, I suspect that the readership of this essay would embody just about the same proportions of divisiveness that Turner noted from his vantage point in 1977. And yet, considering the state of the poststructuralist humanities, we may occupy even less common ground than Turner's divided audience, although we probably share at least one trait with them for all our dissimilarities—I mean, of course, a deep suspicion of agreement. Since I, too, have grown accustomed to a determined incomprehension, it would seem more than slightly presumptuous to announce that our Delectable Islands now lie plainly before us, but I would like to suggest that we have, nonetheless, an unprecedented opportunity to imagine what the field of composition might look like should *everyone* turn out to be partly right—should our warring tribes at last have learned enough about language to speak together in the same conversation. How, I want to ask, has this event come to pass? Or has it come to pass at all?

The Crisis of Rhetorical Formalism: The "World" Disappears

Although composition arrived on the academic scene even later than anthropology, we have our own version of Turner's structural-functionalists, "founders" sometimes forgotten in name but remembered in unreflecting practice, who deserve to be thought of as *our* beleaguered old guard. Or, rather, we have several old guards, and the oldest of these I will call the rhetorical formalists. While our predecessors in the 1920s and 1930s seldom agreed about the particulars of "rhetoric," their differences reveal the broader outlines of a basic commonality, best described as a determined evasion of history, an evasion of the present as well as the past. Consider, for example, the following passage from the introduction to *The* Rhetoric *of Aristotle* (1932), a text characterized by Lane Cooper, its editor and translator, as an " 'amplified' rendering" of Aristotle's work for "students of composition and public speaking" (viii):

> The *Rhetoric* of Aristotle is a practical psychology, and the most helpful book extant for writers of prose and for speakers of every sort. Every one whose business it is to persuade others—lawyers, legislators, statesmen, clergymen, editors, teachers—will find the book useful when it is read with attention. And the modern psychologist commonly will find that he has observed the behavior of human beings less carefully than did Aristotle, even though the author keeps reminding us that in the *Rhetoric* his analysis of thought and conduct is practical, not scientifically precise and complete. . . . Yet the attentive student quickly finds that our treatise has the same value to-day as its author had in his day. . . . In detail and in perspective alike lie the reasons

why his treatment of the art of persuasion seems so robust and "modern," when
very recent, ostensibly modern, books are nerveless and trite.   (xvii–xviii)

In this passage—which I cite here as a locus classicus of the rhetorical
tradition's "right wing"—Cooper advances two radically conflicting sets of
claims about Aristotle, namely, that the value and meaning of his work have
remained undiminished with the passing of twenty-three centuries but also,
conversely, that this work is somehow distinctly "modern," distinctly appropriate to the present age. While Cooper acknowledges that the *Rhetoric* is not
"scientific" by the standards of a "modern psychologist," he describes it all
the same as an exemplary work of "practical psychology"—psychology along
modern lines as a study of "behavior," in contrast to Aristotle's disquisitions
on the psyche or soul.[1] These conflicting claims reduce Cooper almost at once
to the absurdity of alleging that the moderns are not modern after all but
"nerveless and trite," whereas Aristotle should be applauded as the real
modern, more up-to-date than any contemporary writer on the subjects he
treated. For the same reason, Cooper must defend his characterization of the
Rhetoric as a work of psychology by discrediting the discipline's actual, latter-
day practitioners: "[T]he modern psychologist commonly will find," Cooper
writes, "that he has observed the behavior of human beings less carefully than
did Aristotle." Though any twentieth-century reader of the *Metaphysics* or
On the Soul would readily see how little Aristotle's psychology—with its
uncertainties about the interplay between human thought and the divine
intellect—resembles the discipline practiced by figures of Cooper's day (like
Sigmund Freud and Charles Sherrington), Aristotle himself still becomes, for
Cooper, the greatest psychologist, whose work not only anticipates modern
achievements but renders them obsolete in advance.

How or, rather, why would Cooper draw around himself such an absurdly
vicious circle? He does so, as I intimated earlier, to escape the burden of
history. Several paragraphs after the passage quoted above, for example,
Cooper peremptorily rejects the view, advanced by Goethe and the classicist
S. H. Butcher, that "we must," as he puts it, "know something about
Aristotle's philosophy outside of the [*Rhetoric*] in order to understand [it]."
Against the historicists, Cooper asserts that "the main positions taken in the
Rhetoric, as in the *Poetics*, are intelligible enough as soon as we grasp the literal
meaning" (Butcher 114; Cooper xix–xx). Intelligibility, however, was not at
all the issue for Goethe and Butcher: the "something" *they* had in mind, or
one of several somethings, was civic life—politics and ethics—and it is
civic life, not psychology, that serves as the starting point for all Aristotle's
researches on human affairs, rhetoric included. To avoid this highly diversi-
fied, highly changeable civic dimension, and with it the possibility that
Aristotle might not furnish the master plan for discourse ever afterward,

Cooper employs the desperate anachronism of representing the *Rhetoric* as a work whose basic assumptions—because they are rooted in "human nature" and the workings of the mind—cannot change over time, as would conclusions premised on the politics of xenophobic, slave-holding city-states in the fourth century BCE (xx).

While the *Rhetoric* by its very nature obliges Cooper to concede a relation between discourse and civic life, he still holds at the greatest possible remove the historicity of each. When he pauses to consider Lincoln's *Gettysburg Address*, he does so primarily in terms of its arrangement, diction, argument, and ethos as deliberative oratory:

> [The *Address*] was an emotional occasion, but [it] reveals no hard effort to stir the emotions; the speech is in this respect appropriate. The *Ethos* of the speech is more persuasive than the Argument. To the maxim, "All men are created equal," objection might be taken. It has not the certainty of a geometrical proposition. Nevertheless the maxims lend a good ethical quality to the speech.   (xxxv)

Despite the invocation of ethos, nothing gets said about the audience or occasion for Lincoln's speech—about his motives in making the oration so brief or about the tepid response from those who heard it. Cooper decontextualizes a consummate instance of political discourse at its most precarious, and when he turns to other kinds of knowledge—"a scientific treatise, such as the *Ethics* of Spinoza, or Dante's treatise *On Monarchy*, or any work on mathematics"— he discusses them only as "chains" of enthymemes (xxvii). Strictly speaking, the specific discursive practices of biology or law, business communication or journalism lie beyond the purview of rhetoric as Cooper understands it. Whereas all such practices are products of history and therefore fundamentally contingent, his version of rhetoric concerns itself with those psychological mechanisms—really psychological laws—unaffected by history: laws determining how we think in general but not how we shall think about this particular issue in that particular circumstance. Beneath the different forms of rationality afforded by modern life—empirical, philosophical, instrumental, economic, religious, and so forth—and beneath the different disciplines, we are invited to find a single informing reason that relies on the syllogism and induction (xxv). But the arguments for this sort of "deep reason," though perhaps unassailable in their logic, run the risk of perfect irrelevance, like the negative theology of the medieval mystics who insisted that God is not a body, or a self, or a person, or a mind, or a memory, and so on. No longer diminished by any similarity to mere humankind, neither could the deity be sought, addressed, admired, implored, or loved. A rhetoric divested of every specific connection to human purposes and experience would be more than elusive, however; it would be unteachable, or nearly so, and irrelevant as well, since it would help not at all in resolving the issues no one can afford to neglect—whether the Congress should reduce the national debt by cutting social services, or whether the Constitution protects the rights of artists like Robert Mapplethorpe, or whether the global climate has begun heating up. To answer *these* questions, a person would require the extra rhetorical knowledge of the specialist, and it is not clear from Cooper's account why anyone should bother to study rhetoric before acquiring more directly useful expertise. But the need for rhetoric becomes still harder to conceive of once we accept its psychological or cognitive basis: if rhetoric discloses the way people actually think, then who, other than the biologically impaired or the mentally ill, would not already think "correctly" without any prior instruction? That Cooper should liken rhetoric to psychology, at a time when any ties between the two seemed far less probable than ever before, plainly shows the extent to which the modern diversification of knowledge—of language into specialized languages, of reason into many different ways of reasoning—had undermined the rhetorical tradition itself; had undermined, in other words, the notion of a unifying public discourse and the belief that free citizens of the polis could reach consensus through reflection and debate. If the Athenian polis had ceased to exist during Aristotle's own lifetime, civic conflicts were resolved by genuine public debate almost nowhere in America after the industrial revolution, which had created a political and economic system, an educational apparatus, and a universe of discourse utterly unlike the ones familiar to Aristotle. While these differences did not quite relegate rhetoric to the company of witchcraft, the reading of entrails, and numerology, they demanded at the very least a rethinking of language in its specific relations to social life—exactly what Cooper and his colleagues were unwilling to undertake.

No more willing, for that matter, were the rhetoricians on the "left"— who are better described, I suppose, as straddling the cautious center, since a bona fide left wing, if we discount Kenneth Burke, never really appeared until the early 1980s. Adams Sherman Hill, John Franklin Genung, and Barrett Wendell all positioned themselves somewhere close to this liberal middle ground, but I regard Wendell as the one whose writings reflect most clearly the values and limitations of all three. Though Wendell belonged to the generation preceding Cooper's, he displayed a far keener awareness of the essentially historical character of knowledge:

Just as we name or nickname people, our ancestors have named and nicknamed the various ideas which in the course of their history they have had occasion to express. Nowadays there are in the world a great many different languages, many of which, now mutually unintelligible, may easily be traced to a common origin; from Latin, for example, have sprung French, Italian, Spanish, Portuguese. But the numerous changes whose accumulation has separated and distinguished these modern languages have all taken place by means of local and increasing differences in use.   (30–31)

Wendell surveyed matter-of-factly the same spectacle of ceaseless change that drove Cooper to reaffirm the permanence of human nature, and this crucial difference is symptomatic of their opposing professional orientations, Cooper a "rhetorician" in the "to the barricades" sense, Wendell a scholar and critic deeply committed to the inseparability of discourse from the particulars of its origins. Yet Wendell no less than Cooper found himself enmeshed in the contradictions of an attempted flight from history. Certain that the prevailing standards and practices of "good writing" could not be justified except by history itself, Wendell nevertheless declined to explain how the prevailing came to prevail. Again and again in his *English Composition* he refers vaguely to consensus as the sole warrant for accepted rules and standards. "Reputable use," he suggests, drawing on Hill, "is the use of no single writer, however eminent; it is the common consent of the great body of writers whose works, taken together, make up what we mean when we seriously use the term English literature" (34). But who does Wendell have in mind when he says "we"? Whose writing counts as literature, and who determines what qualities make it count? On the way to an answer never given, he moves from "reputable use" to "national" or international use, "sanctioned by the common consent of the whole English-speaking world" (35). So great was this world even by 1891, when *English Composition* was published, that the mechanisms for the achievement of consent are hard to imagine, especially if Wendell means the consent of speakers and writers everywhere, as opposed to a single class or coterie. Apparently, though, he does not. After evoking the lofty ideal of an open speech community, Wendell adds that "Whoever uses technical words, or foreign, or local, violates [the] rule of good use. The use of technical words, still more the use of foreign, is commonly a conscious affectation, which any sane man may avoid. The use of local terms is often spontaneous; here lies the chief danger of falling into a style not national" (35–36).

Wendell's commitment to historicism crumbles before the sheer fact of linguistic and cultural diversities that are, as he readily concedes, the products of history itself. Rather than admit that "good English" was indeed the English of "good" people, the "best" people—the wealthy, the powerful, the "educated," the white—he blurs and recolors history to brush out the troublesome inequities by asserting the public character of a discourse never really public insofar as it excluded all but a minority; excluded, if not people (although it did this too, and with a vengeance), then their distinctive voices, the "incorrect" versions of English spoken in the home and the "vulgar" local knowledge of neighborhood, class, and region. While he maintains that "the very essence of good use is that it is not a system of rules, but a constantly shifting state" of conventions, Wendell repairs to an ahistorical formalism remarkably like Cooper's rhetoric in its disembodied generality (38). Eschewing specific injunctions that would soon become outdated, Wendell instead propounds three cardinal "principles of composition": "(1) Every composition should group itself about one central idea; (2) The chief parts of every composition should be so placed as readily to catch the eye; (3) Finally, the relation of each part of a composition to its neighbors should be unmistakable" (40). Whereas Cooper attempted to build his ostensibly Aristotelian rhetoric on the bedrock of human nature, Wendell ends by appealing to nothing more substantial, or more enduring, than the common sense of readers like himself. Less self-deceiving than Cooper about the absence of foundations, Wendell was still as unprepared to address a crisis that no figure of his day (or the next) elected to confront head-on: the disappearance of the "world," the shared cultural script that made it possible to agree, not only about the need for a "central idea," but also about *which* specific features of a paper might "catch the eye" or sustain an "unmistakable" coherence.

Albeit with contradictions of his own, William Butler Yeats monumentalized the advent of this crisis when he wrote in 1919, "Turning and turning in the widening gyre / The falcon cannot hear the falconer; / Things fall apart; the centre cannot hold" (184). What had fallen apart was the nineteenth century's notion of social life, which Yeats no less than Matthew Arnold before him tended to describe using terms like *tradition, custom, ceremony*. The disappearance of the English-speaking "world" begins with its outward geographic expansion, its widening colonial gyre, into the domain of the "savages," where it encountered an overwhelming variety of dissimilar traditions and cultures, each imagining itself to be the real one. Although the "West" sustained a more or less unshaken conviction of its own preeminence, things began to fall apart from the inside as well. The growth of industry and the need for a disciplined, competent work force demanded universal public schooling, which had the unforeseen and (to some) undesired result of equipping social groups hitherto seen but not heard with a knowledge and a language once reserved for the elite. Yet the growth of industry and public education also transformed the nature of knowledge itself, which ceased to possess the internal coherence befitting a single, privileged way of life and became instead a congeries of specialized, often incommensurable knowledges, each characterized by its own practices and discursive constraints. With the balkanization of discourse, Wendell's faith in a common language and common rules of usage looked more and more farfetched, just as his admonitions against "technical words" and "local" terms served to mark him as the last representative of an earlier, less complicated, and vastly less capable era. With his invocations to the Philosopher, Cooper looked just as absurdly passé.

In their retreat from change, or more precisely, in their failure to see it, the rhetorical formalists bore a close family resemblance to near-contemporary anthropologists like E. B. Tylor and J. G. Frazer. Inventors of an overarching, transhistorical, and ambitiously cross-cultural style of analysis—which Clifford Geertz calls "the old key-to-the-universe" approach (*Interpretation* 4)—Tylor and Frazer ultimately concealed much more than they managed to reveal, for the reason Geertz himself identifies: "To make the generalization about an afterlife stand up alike for the Confucians and the Calvinists, the Zen Buddhists and the Tibetan Buddhists, one has to define it in the most general terms, indeed—so general, in fact, that whatever force it seems to have virtually evaporates." As with "religion, so," Geertz adds, "with 'marriage,' 'trade,' and all the rest of what A. L. Kroeber aptly called 'fake universals' " (*Interpretation* 40). Geertz goes on to claim that later anthropologists, no longer persuaded by the too-easy answers of the great syncretists, have been obliged, without disowning altogether the likelihood of larger commonalities, to look more carefully at each society's minute particulars—each community's, each village's, each caste's, each tribe's (37). And so, for that matter, should have the generation of teachers following Cooper's, but this recognition of difference on the local level, seemingly always about to occur, was delayed for more than fifty years.

After the Fall

In composition as in anthropology (we should remember that Geertz wrote his remarks on the particulars in the mid-1960s), the disappearance of the "world" did not immediately engender a hermeneutics or even a retreat to some version of Deweyan pragmatism, but it prompted instead the search for a new empirical grounding, a science of language that would circumvent, by direct appeal to "what works," the need for any broader justification, historical or otherwise. As H. H. Remmers and his colleagues at Purdue University observed in a 1934 pamphlet, *Concerning Freshman Composition—Tangibles and Intangibles of Achievement*, writing teachers could employ the new methods of standardized testing to measure "degrees of knowledge before and after college treatment" and to determine "whether freshman composition may be a contributor not only of knowledges and skills that are measurably measurable but also of less tangible mental and psychological increments" (3). The Purdue assessment team followed the now all-too-familiar route of "objective" error analysis as an indicator of general improvement, and the error guide they devised for this analysis lists forty-three different infractions grouped under the headings of punctuation, grammar, spelling, sentence structure, and diction. Grammar errors include "agreements, miscellaneous" as well as "conjunctions and prepositions: confusion of the two." Under sentence structure, the authors include "vague *so* clause," "offensive repetitions—wordiness," and one especially eclectic category: "Errors of logic . . . Contradictions [and] Undeveloped thoughts" (7–8). Missing from this list, as the researchers themselves point out, are what they call "intangibles," although for them this term denotes nothing more than the skills, dispositions, and incidental general knowledge not susceptible to measurement by their test, among which they number "increased ease, enjoyment, and rapidity in writing," "greater knowledge of current events," "increased tolerance of others and of others' ideas," and "development of a sense of proportion about people and things" (27–28).

But what about other qualities of students' writing as such, independent of both their proficiency with "mechanics" and their edification as moral beings? I am thinking now of the qualities we admire in the writers we read—the ability to examine a complex issue, to "converse" with other writers, and to extend the horizon of understanding that unfolds between writer and writer, text and reader. These "intangibles" the Purdue team neglected altogether because such qualities cannot be "measurably measured" within the simplistic confines of error analysis—which is simplistic to the point of absurdity, if we consider the degree of tacit knowledge and expert judgment writing actually entails, just as it would be an absurdity to call Faulkner a "more proficient" writer than Flaubert because he composed longer sentences and employed a larger vocabulary. No less than Cooper's psychologism and Wendell's fanciful notion of "good use," the scientific study of language entails its own vicious circularity, reflected in the conclusions drawn by Remmers and his team. "It is evident," they write, "that those abilities which are most objective in their manifestation and therefore most easily measured—spelling and punctuation—show the greatest amount of growth" (10). At least as much as the Purdue test measured the improvement of student writers, it measured the ability of the test makers to measure something, anything, regardless of its relative importance to experienced writers and readers. Like many standardized tests today, the "instrument" used at Purdue did not allow the researchers to distinguish between a deficiency in the student and a defect in assumptions underlying the test itself, or between a student's failure to "improve" and the test designer's failure to consider other areas of improvement, areas less amenable to "objective" measurement.

Insofar as we must all make comparative assessments of writing by one set of standards or another, I am unwilling to portray the effort at Purdue as an example of sheer self-deception. All the same, the Purdue study indicates a basic problem with the attempt to devise a truly "empirical" program for language assessment, since language is not a "thing" like oxygen or a projectile falling to earth at so many feet per second, nor is writing a routine instrumental behavior like fastening plastic wipers to the windshield of a car as it rolls along the assembly line. Instead, language is the cultural and historical framework by virtue of which we know that oxygen is something we breathe, instead of something we speak or eat, and that projectiles fall to earth, as opposed to sliding or walking or singing. Although we encounter the day-to-day world through the mediation of language—and although this mediation permits us to perceive the world as "objectively" real, independent of our "subjective" impressions—language itself cannot be known with any similar objectivity, since we are always "inside" it, unable to get out altogether and take a neutral, timeless, distanced look.[2] By the same token, writing is never simply an unreflecting action but a reflective activity, the strenuous, precarious task of sustaining a dialogue between the images of the world preserved by language and the writer's own experience of this same world at one particular moment, in one particular place.

"Better" writing for Remmers and his colleagues was necessarily more "correct" writing in a narrowly technical sense, more predictable, less open to risk and infusions of cultural diversity. At a time when "science" had become the master trope of almost every discourse, the members of the team at Purdue never felt compelled to explain why their version of "better" writing was genuinely "good," instead of unambitious, infantile, banal, and irrelevant. Forty years too early for post-Kuhnian science, Remmers and his colleagues still associated research on language with an inductive method that builds step-by-step from observations whose truth everyone could accept on the evidence of the senses. Not only did they believe that their research would hold true in all contexts but they expected it to possess virtually infinite replicability, since each new induction would be just as "objective" as the first. Perversely enough, however, this method of assessment both shaped and diminished the products it assessed, making them more uniform and predictable—more like incarnations of a single "model paper" endowed with its own, infinite replicability—although replicability is exactly what writing must *avoid* to be writing at all. Ordinarily we refer to prose that merely restates the language of previous writers as "quotation," "paraphrase," "summary," or "plagiarism." Every writer, of course, borrows something from past achievements and must work within the historical limitations of a genre, but sheer replication is never apropos because writing addresses itself primarily to the not yet written. At the very minimum, the writer must have "something to say," which means saying something further, different, better. Whereas objective inquiry on the positivist model advances by incorporating more and more evidence of the same kind, writing actually proceeds through a deliberate series of problematizations—shifts of perspective that demand a rethinking of past achievements, even down to the level of founding assumptions. What gets lost amid Remmers's lengthening columns of hash marks tabulating fragments, danglers, and incomplete thoughts is any sense of language as a way of deliberately seeing and acting on a world that is recast through seeing and acting themselves. While no one invents language ex nihilo, while no one speaks without institutional constraints—and while, in addition, the speaking self is to some degree a linguistic "construction"—the act of speaking or writing always exposes past knowledge to the ordeal of the present, exposes the general to the burden of the particular, and the conventional to the test of the extraconventional. Precisely because writing reconceives the given, it involves still another activity overlooked by the proponents of objective assessment—I mean, of course, persuasion. Beginning with difference, and proceeding through difference, writing constantly seeks to overcome difference retrospectively by presenting the writer's insights to an audience whose assent must be secured. Not a skill, not an art, persuasion is the struggle, perpetually on shifting terms, to establish a domain of intersubjectivity.

If the objective testing designed by Remmers and his colleagues could neither rise to the complexity of this struggle nor promote among students a greater willingness to undertake it, then we would do well to ask what other purposes their efforts might have served, since the criteria they selected, though far from arbitrary, are also far from value neutrality. Writing can be measured by any number of standards, but the ones adopted at Purdue betray the lineaments of a larger trend in social life during the 1920s and 1930s—the same trend that engendered a radical restructuring of the curriculum itself: the pursuit of "efficiency." It was efficiency that rose to preeminence in works like Eugene Wera's *Human Engineering* (1921), which I cite here as typical of countless others. "At the present time," Wera notes, "we see social life divided into divergent group lives. Each of these groups has its distinctive public opinion, creed, ideals, moral standards, and leaders" (349). Wera reasons that continued progress in the face of this growing "complexity" requires a "shift" of "social control from the hands of amateurs into those of trained men, in order to realize a systematic integration of the members of society and [to] exercise rational direction on the active pursuit of willing, social progress—the most valuable form of life for an industrial people" (351–52). Not only does Wera presume that differences of experience and culture constitute a social liability but he believes that a resolution must be imposed from the top downward, by specialists who will steer the entire body politic. Toward this end, he proposes that universities organize departments of "social engineering . . . directed by sociologists, engineers [like Wera himself], business men, hygienists, educators, economists, moralists, city-builders" (352–53). As engineers of language, writing teachers in the early decades of this century carried to their classrooms the paradigm of an administered society (as did their colleagues in literary studies), a paradigm dividing experts from amateurs, specialists from clients. Just as language became the focus of practices designed to ensure uniformity, so the students themselves became the subjects of what Remmers and his associates frankly refer to in their pamphlet as a "treatment."[3]

The "cult of efficiency"—as Raymond E. Callahan has named it—gradually lost its purchase over the popular imagination, but the old alliance of science, pedagogy, and "treatment" survived this decline and even flourished once again at the end of the 1970s. In "A Cognitive Process Theory of Writing," for example, Linda Flower and John R. Hayes portray their approach, with its concern for what "really happens" during the writing process, as a reliable way of answering the kinds of questions that the rhetorical tradition failed to resolve decisively. From their point of view, the long-standing problem with rhetoric was precisely that the conclusions it reached were predetermined by its initial assumptions. The rhetorician who looked at a particular writer's work for evidence of, say, engagement with an audience, or else indifference to that audience, almost always found it. Cognitive psychology, by contrast, invited composition theorists to set off on a holiday from the vagaries of interpretation. It promised to ground the study of writing in the neutral observation of composing behaviors, the subconscious routines through which writers conceptualize their goals and pursue them, successfully or otherwise ("Cognitive Process" 366–67).

But this new attempt to get behind culture and language presupposed the existence of an invariant "real world" writing situation—rather than writing for business, or for history class, or for one's mother—as well as a standard definition of success. To observe the writer in such a perfect vacuum, moreover, the cognitivists had to screen out interpretive variations at both "ends" of the writing process: not only did Flower and Hayes ignore the specific social and experiential factors that enable or obstruct individual writers but, at the same time, they overlooked the diverse forms of reason and expression— the diversity of "codes"—that are, as Robert Scholes contends, always available to any discipline or to any discourse community (162). Beginning with this diversity, David Bartholomae conjectures in "The Study of Error" that the problems of basic writers might owe less to cognitive derailings than to the cultural distance between those writers and ourselves. The language such writers use and the texts they construct might not be incoherent but ordered by a coherence at variance with the language we regard as correct. "The task for both teacher and researcher," Bartholomae concludes, "is to discover the grammar of *that* coherence . . . the 'idiosyncratic dialect' that belongs to a particular writer at a particular moment in the history of his attempts to imagine and reproduce the standard idiom" (313). In a similar spirit, Patricia Bizzell has argued that the problems of beginning writers owe less to their internal "monitor," as Flower and Hayes describe the higher-order writing behaviors that go on inside our heads, than to a simple ignorance, not only of discursive conventions but also of the fact that such conventions exist at all (see "Cognition," esp. 223–29). Whereas Bartholomae faults the cognitivists for overlooking the importance of the cultures brought by students from the home, Bizzell calls attention to the normative role of subcultures inside the university itself.

These critiques fail, however, to address a larger methodological contradiction. In keeping with the empirical spirit of their research, Flower and Hayes explicitly deny that a writer can be trusted to furnish accurate information about his or her own composing processes, since they reason that retrospective accounts are often distorted by prior training ("Cognitive Process" 368–69). To bracket out such biases, they record the spontaneous commentary offered by their subjects during the process of writing, and, from this record or "protocol," they purport to reach objective conclusions about the effectiveness of the writer's behavior. While Flower and Hayes celebrate the writer's ability to solve problems, they also deny the trustworthiness, and indeed the relevance, of the writer's own self-understanding. If their therapeutic effort to help students overcome hidden cognitive limitations superficially resembles Freudian analysis, its purpose is radically dissimilar. Whereas Freudian therapy attempts to bring to consciousness the patient's unconscious life, thereby restoring a lost power of self-determination, the one thing excluded from the cognitivist method of behavior modification is conscious life: the ideas the writers actually entertain, the connections they want to establish, the transformations they undergo when their assumptions become problematic—all of which can be inferred from another record, not the protocol but the writers' actual texts.[4]

Flower and Hayes's reduction of writing to an ensemble of automatic behaviors brackets out meaning, brackets out content, brackets out language and culture, and replaces them with a model of pure instrumentality—the task of solving problems posed by others, in a manner that these others determine. And this instrumentality, as Linda Brodkey charges, "not only decontextualizes writing, but quite literally transforms the individual who writes into a writing machine" ("Modernism" 412). Although the flow charts and diagrams that ornament the cognitivist literature recall the kinds of schematizations characteristic of work in the social sciences several decades earlier, they could not be less relevant to writing as consciously practiced by writers. Because the goal of cognitivist "therapy" is success in school and in the world of business, as opposed to critical reflection or empowerment in any social setting larger than these, the issue of the writer's self-awareness and motivation has no importance whatsoever. As long as workers get the job done, after all, who cares what they think?

Round Three: The Real Structural-Functionalists Make Their Appearance

Regrettably, but perhaps also unavoidably, a faltering of the scientific ethos since the early 1980s still did not produce on any significant scale the hermeneutic or ethnographically "thick" research conducted by Bartholomae and his associates—research that seeks, in other words, to reconstruct the writer's *conscious* efforts to achieve understanding and to appropriate authority within the constraints of a culture or institution (see, e.g., Coles and Wall; Salvatori). Instead, dissatisfaction with the various old guards, rhetorical as well as scientistic, created a true structural-functionalism, the so-called social-epistemic rhetoric, which also largely ignored the hermeneutic dimension of knowledge even while its advocates believed they had finally brought this dimension to light. In the pathbreaking article "Social Construction, Language, and the Authority of Knowledge," widely regarded as the manifesto of the constructionist movement, Kenneth Bruffee renews a long tradition by dismissing the achievements of *his* predecessors as epistemologically naive. Whereas empiricists like Flower and Hayes presuppose that writing is the product of behaviors accessible to objective scrutiny, Bruffee describes perception, expression, and identity as functions of the social contexts in which they occur. For Bruffee, knowledge is a body of "community-generated and community-maintained artifacts," and the "entities we normally call reality . . . thought, facts, texts, selves . . . are constructs generated by communities of like-minded peers" (774). In these terms, it makes no sense to speak of any universal cognitive process of writing or of an unproductive dissonance between cognition and convention, private sensibility and public speech; rather, each "community" has its own distinctive mode of cognition, its own characteristic "flow chart" for problem solving. Psychologists do not think first and then practice psychology: strictly speaking, the discipline of psychology preordains the nature of thought for its practitioners.

Whatever we perceive, then, is a construct, something constructed by communities, and whatever we have learned derives not from experience but from a process of initiation into those rituals of community life that create both selves and worlds. This reasoning, however, omits a crucial step: the step between the premise that perceptual schemata give shape to experience and the conclusion that communities make them. If everything is a construct, nothing can be constructed; if individuals are created by communities, then who creates the communities themselves, and in response to what forces? There is clearly more to the world we inhabit than any tradition of knowledge at any moment in its history can account for—so much more that the word *knowledge*, as Bruffee defines it, becomes effectively meaningless, a knowledge that dictates, without ambiguity, without resistance, the character of both its subjects and its objects. Were it not for differences between individuals, and for miscarriages in practical application, knowledge might indeed be communal and self-referential just as the constructionists believe. But regardless of how carefully we draw the boundaries of a community, regardless of how like-minded its members may seem, these members will sometimes find themselves at odds over fundamental issues.

The history of any discipline is a history of just such discordant moments because knowledge can never entirely escape its historical and institutional blindnesses, and our own everyday practice takes these blindnesses into account. When we write about a poem or novel, for example, we assume that something will still need to be said even after our work is completed. We know that other writers, equipped with other knowledge, will reveal some portion of the remainder that our temporal and material limitations have concealed from us. To broaden our understanding of the material at hand, we might turn to less familiar disciplines and even to approaches radically different from our own. We presume that a world exists beyond our constructions, and as soon as we lose this sense of a larger world, this uneasy intimation that something is inevitably missing, we become both the prisoners and the jailers of our communities, dogmatic opponents of change and difference. Worse yet, once we deny the reality of an outside to our knowledge, we have nothing further to say, since a discourse always moves, in the words of Hayden White, " 'to and fro' between received encodations of experience and the clutter of phenomena which refuses incorporation into conventionalized notions of 'reality,' 'truth' or 'possibility' " (4).

By defining communities as associations of "like-minded peers," Bruffee fails to recognize that difference is not simply an adjunct to the production of knowledge but an indispensable precondition for social life itself. This failure becomes more conspicuous when we move from the level of theory to actual practice, as Bruffee does in an essay published several years before "Social Construction":

> In order to learn to write, we must learn to become our own representatives of an assenting community of peers with whom we speak and to whom we listen in our heads. This audible or inward talking-through of our tasks as we do them with a community of knowledgeable peers is itself, in fact, what becomes eventually what we have been calling "the writing *process.*" The *product* of writing results when internalized instrumental social speech (talking-through) is reshaped, revised, and edited to become a composition, a term paper, a dissertation. ("Writing" 168)

As Bruffee portrays the writing process here, we do not represent ourselves and our social interests within the community; rather, we represent the community within ourselves. By "inward talking-through"—by internalizing conventions of social action, the community's collective behavior—novices learn to replicate that behavior as though they were "knowledgeable" also. But critical reflection on the assumptions and practices of the community, like self-representation within it, is notably absent from the process. Although "instrumental social speech" can be "reshaped, revised, and edited," it remains no less instrumental than the cognitivist model of successful problem solving: a speech without living speakers (who not only act but reflect on their actions) and a community without real commonality and consensus. If anthropologists like Victor Turner, Renato Rosaldo, and James Clifford have anything to tell us, it is that consent emerges from dissent, the play of oppositions that makes knowledge accessible to a variety of social interests.

Because teachers in our society have emphasized performative competence so one-sidedly and have attempted to instill this competence so mechanically, as Bruffee does with his heuristic of "inward talking-through," the intimate relation between dissent and sociability has remained a kind of family scandal, akin to having Florence Nightingale *and* Jack the Ripper at the base of one's family tree. Well before the constructionists revived the decorum of concealment about this scandal, teachers held as an article of their neo-Lockean faith that imitation must precede what they conceived of as innovation. First we "learn" by doing, and then we can ask questions. As the philosopher Karl-Otto Apel contends, however, imitation already entails interpretation. Apel might argue that Bruffee's social constructionism fails to comprehend fully the social character of meaning because it retains a model of knowledge "transmission" carried over from the naive realism it claims to supplant.[5] Whereas this older epistemology understood the perception of objects to be unaffected by conventions, Bruffee still assumes that the conventions themselves can be perceived or acted on without mediation, since he supposes that they dictate unilaterally the character of seeing and knowing. And yet, if, as Apel holds, our experience of conventions is also mediated by our particular circumstances—historical, social, economic—then learning begins not with imitation but with communication, not with action but with the achievement of intersubjective agreement (37). We ask questions *before* acting or doing, first to determine what a certain action means for each of us individually and then to decide what it could mean for all of us together.

Along these same lines, Apel's colleague Jürgen Habermas argues that conventions of practice are merely the record of past intersubjective deliberations, past arguments about practice, which cannot determine in a lawlike manner the direction of future activity. As an alternative to a tradition of social analysis focused solely on conventions of practice, Habermas has developed a two-tier model that accommodates the dialectical interplay between communicative deliberation and ongoing disciplinary work. The ongoing work, which he refers to broadly as purposive-rational action, employs the practical, calculating reason typified by Flower and Hayes's goal-directed behavior as well as by Bruffee's instrumental social speech. Through communicative action, by contrast—through the expression of dissent and the pursuit of new terms and frameworks—individuals preserve a common horizon of understanding when their differing experiences challenge prevailing norms of practice (*Reason* 10–11, 285–86). Precisely because experience can challenge—and change—the norm, communicative action reaches past the discipline proper into the cultural "lifeworld" of society as a whole (*Reason* 13–14; *Lifeworld* 113–52). Implicit in Habermas's schema is the recognition that a disciplinary practice, on the part of either individuals or entire communities, does not make sense in itself and cannot be studied exclusively from an insider's point of view. The purpose of medicine, for example, is not the practice of medicine, any more than the purpose of government is the administration of government, whatever politicians happen to believe. Habermas suggests that these specialized activities are meaningful only within the context of a larger process of society's self-formation, the pursuit of a life worth living. It might be argued, indeed, that even the hardest of the hard sciences derive their legitimacy from this same appeal to the "outside." As Geertz says of the communicative dimension underlying one area of specialized practice, "Science owes more to the steam engine"—to the way of life from which the steam engine emerged—"than the steam engine owes to science" (*Local Knowledge* 22).

Charting the Islands

For rhetoricians—though not rhetoricians like Cooper and Wendell—the idea that the construction of knowledge always implies a certain vision of the good life can scarcely come as a surprise. When Aristotle describes the human being as a *politikon zōon*, he means that our activities, their endless multiplicity notwithstanding, derive from, and aspire to fulfill, an ethical sensibility we share with others. So convinced is he of a relation between the sociocultural whole and its quotidian parts that he calls politics the "master art," the art whose aim is a collective good that subsumes the other, relative goods beneath it—those short-term versions of the good pursued, for example, by doctors, bridge builders, or teachers of composition (*Ethica* 1094a–b15). Aristotle would regard as an absurdity, then, the modern notion that writing is an instrumental skill essentially unrelated to the character of the writer or to the writer's successful participation in the affairs of the polis.[6] Though he concedes that writing is "useful" *tout court*, he cautions at the same time, "To be [forever] seeking after the useful does not become free and exalted souls" since judgments based on utility alone soon lose sight of the larger good, the larger "art," which always involves both social engagement *and* self-cultivation, rather than an uncritical acceptance of the status quo (*Politica* 1338b1–10).

Aristotle, in his better moments, holds not that humankind exists to serve knowledge—whether practical, productive, or theoretical—but that knowledge exists to serve humankind. It exists, that is, to bring about the full development of each individual's entelechy, or innate powers, according to the society's shared conception of human nature itself. From the *Ethics*, the *Politics*, and indeed the *Rhetoric*, no teachers could draw less philosophical support than those who are ready to sacrifice meaning for instrumental adroitness, and diversity for standardization.

Aristotle's epigones, nevertheless, have often failed, or have simply refused, to perceive the obvious: that our common ethical sensibility died with preindustrial Europe (if it existed even then) and that nothing short of a return to the political, nothing short of a return to the ideal of the polis with its all-inclusive, unrestricted debate, would bring the need for rhetoric—for dialogue and understanding—back into view. The rhetoricians least true to Aristotle's project were those like Cooper, who kept trying to dismiss such a return as superfluous on the grounds that the master (or, in Wendell's writings, Western civilization) had already figured everything out. An approach more consistent with Aristotelian rhetoric, whose subject is to discover the available means of persuasion in *"each particular case"* (*Rhetorica* 1355b; my emphasis), would recognize disparate readings or misreadings of a text, no less than the different dialects spoken by students outside the classroom, as reflections of different cultural "scripts"—widely different visions of a life worth living. Such an approach would also attempt, as a prelude to the search for a shareable notion of "life," to make explicit the connections (and the disconnections) between formal knowledge and day-to-day experience. For teachers of writing, however, this project must take a complicating turn, since they will need to become more adept not only at pursuing the connections for themselves but also at assisting student writers in their progress toward the same hermeneutic sophistication. Aristotle, I suspect, would be the first to agree that until our students have begun to consider knowledge in its relation to specific forms of life—their own first of all—they will remain the passive recipients of our "treatments," instead of playing their rightful parts as reflective, socially critical practitioners, the closest modern-day equivalents to the free citizens of the polis.

And just as we might imagine a new rhetoric devoted to the study, critique, and reconciliation of competing social "worlds," so might we welcome certain novel kinds of quantitative research: not research claiming to furnish an account of what "really happens" apart from your take on the data or mine, or studies that pretend to know their human subjects better than these subjects can know themselves. Composition as an interpretive social science would enlist the various research traditions in the project of reconstructing, always admittedly from an outsider's viewpoint, the self-understanding of its subjects, but instead of doing so for the purposes of therapy, it would seek to promote unobstructed communication between readers and texts, writers and writers, writers and teachers.[7] Hermeneutic and "philosophical," our reformed metaempiricists would start from the conviction that no one simply "behaves," manipulated and ventriloquized by psychological imperatives, but that we all consciously *act* in response to experience and reflection, even if the historical sources of this action, no less than its subconscious motives and ultimate consequences, fall outside our immediate circle of awareness. And precisely because professional perspectives on such action are always fragmentary, always limited by the observer's own circumstances, those who conduct interpretive research on writing would be obliged to test, as often and as thoroughly as possible, their determinations (from case studies, statistical samplings, and participant surveys) against what student writers have to say for themselves on the page. While the self-understanding of novice writers is no more definitive than anyone else's, their voices, heard in counterpoint to ours, can challenge methods, assumptions, and hidden agendas that have hitherto authorized profoundly disabling—and profoundly dishonest—"constructions" of the student and the student's language. Not only would hermeneutic researchers guard against the reduction of writing to unreflecting skills and decontextualized rules but they would ask questions about their own procedures and the contexts that occasion their work. Witnesses to the deepening failure of Wera's new order and the weltanschauung of "human engineering," they would ask how, and by whom, their data are used, and for what institutional purposes.

If we renew our discipline along these lines—if we begin to value knowledge in general, and our own knowledge in particular, as a "text" always open to revision and multiple "readings"—then we will become, at least, more truthful about ourselves: better able to account for the persistence of difference and dissent within *our* specialized community, as well as for the transformations that every discipline undergoes, to a greater or lesser degree, with each new conference and publication. Despite my initial misgivings, I would like to conclude by suggesting that these transformations of knowledge, in their rhetorical, sociological, and discursive aspects, might be thought of as *our* Delectable Islands, the subject we began searching for in the days of Barrett Wendell. Within this capacious framework, the research of many old guards can be put to new uses after all, even if these uses sometimes stray far afield of the founders' intentions. To survey language as we need to now, from the broader, hermeneutic perspective, is not to emulate the "social sciences" of a generation past, when the stress fell on the second term; still less would our practice take its cue from somewhat harder versions of research, such as linguistics or psychology. Composition on the terms I have argued for here would more closely resemble what Turner calls processual anthropology. As a form of engaged, politicized inquiry into speech and writing, a processual composition would continually struggle to recall the larger, always changing dimension of public life. Through this struggle of recollection, our field might discharge its institutional task—teaching students how to write—while at the same time affirming the possibility of a knowledge without domination and a commonality without coercion.

Rutgers University, New Brunswick

NOTES

[1] Not only do I regard as indefensible Cooper's conflation of Aristotelian rhetoric with psychology but I would make the same charge against James S. Baumlin and Tita French Baumlin's updated version of this view, via Jacques Lacan and others (see esp. 248). That Aristotle does not conceive of rhetoric as a branch of psychology is clear from *De Anima*, where he notes, "[P]erceiving and practical thinking are not identical . . . for the former is universal in the animal world [while] the latter is found in only a small division of it." Although "perception of the special objects of sense is always free from error," it is "possible to think falsely as well as truly, and thought is found only where there is [a] discourse of reason" (427b5–15). Psychology describes the invariant operations of the cognitive faculties, but rhetoric is concerned with pragmatic strategies for deliberation about matters that do not admit of certain or unchanging knowledge.

It is, moreover, well known that the *Rhetoric* belongs with the *Ethics* and the *Politics* as subjects of what Aristotle calls "the philosophy of human life," which involve neither scientific knowledge (*theoria*) nor productive skill (*technē*) but the exercise of free choice and practical wisdom (*phronēsis*) in response to real-world issues: in response to "such things" as those that fall "more or less, within the general ken of all men and belong to no definite science" (*Rhetoric* 1354a1–5). Whereas *theoria* and *technē* furnish certain knowledge, *phronēsis* governs the *disposition* of this knowledge in the contingent—and political—realm of day-to-day human affairs (see Guthrie, esp. 331–46).

[2] It is easy, of course, and even commonplace nowadays, for us to treat language as another one of Alfred Kroeber's "fake universals" by imagining that words predetermine the self, society, and the world rather than sustain a three-way "conversation" among them. Although we cannot know the world except *in* and *through* language, we are not obliged to conclude, therefore, that we can know nothing except language. In my view, teachers of writing who accept this idea have set off with their predecessors on a flight from history—or, rather, from our many different histories. Whatever else the everything-is-language argument might do, it gives the teacher a new, totalizing alibi for ignoring social differences. Who needs to listen to students when language is always the speaker?

[3] Composition and "human engineering" share many primary sources. Wera, who also uses the term *treatment* as a synonym for cultural normalization, quotes from Alexander Bain's *Mental and Moral Science*, in a chapter outlining management strategies for "the proper assimilation of workers" (Wera 325–28). But perhaps the single most important shared text is Herbert Spencer's *The Philosophy of Style*, first published in 1852 and reprinted in 1892 with an introduction and notes by Fred Newton Scott. An apostle of social Darwinism who applied the laws of thermodynamics to "mental energies" as well as labor, Spencer greatly influenced the literature of the efficiency movement, but quotations from

his writings also appear in textbooks like Genung's *The Working Principles of Rhetoric* (esp. 23–25) and, somewhat later, in Strunk and White's *Elements of Style* (23).

[4] Freud is not a behaviorist like B. F. Skinner—or, for that matter, like Flower and Hayes themselves—precisely because his version of analysis demands the patient's conscious, willing participation, a requirement that explains his refusal to work with psychotics. The analyst's task, as Freud explicitly maintains in *An Outline of Psycho-analysis*, is to "strengthen the weakened ego" as the first stage in a process of "extending . . . its self-knowledge" (56). Without reflection, there can be no cure.

[5] See, in this regard, Apel's contention that Ludwig Wittgenstein's account of "language-games" cannot adequately explain why all "games" necessarily change over time. In Apel's view, Wittgenstein acknowledges the existence of both conventions and a real world, but he fails to consider the role of conscious subjects who are able to change the "game" as they play it (1–38, 147–72). See also Giddens 1–48.

[6] In Aristotle's terms, a composition pedagogy concerned solely with technical proficiency would be well designed for the training of slaves but entirely inappropriate to the education of free people. Aristotle holds that free people must take the cultivation of "moral virtue" as their principal concern, since the life of the polis depends on this cultivation absolutely, but he observes that the artisan, by contrast, "only attains excellence in proportion as he becomes a slave"—in proportion, that is, as the artisan submits to a "special" and limited form of slavery (*Politica* 1260a35–40). Slaves ask "how"; free people ask "why."

[7] For the theoretical orientation behind the practice of an interpretive or hermeneutic social science, I recommend the following works (listed in order of publication): Berger and Luckmann, *The Social Construction of Reality*; Giddens, *Central Problems in Social Theory*; R. J. Bernstein, *Beyond Objectivism and Relativism*; Fay, *Critical Social Science*; Clifford, *The Predicament of Culture*; and Rosaldo, *Culture and Truth*. Among the many possible examples of hermeneutic social science practice, I suggest Willis, *Learning to Labour*; Shostak, *Nisa: The Life and Words of a !Kung Woman*; Heath, *Ways with Words*; Moffatt, *Coming of Age in New Jersey*; and Foley, *Learning Capitalist Culture*.

RECONNECTING RHETORIC AND PHILOSOPHY IN THE COMPOSITION CLASSROOM

Brenda Deen Schildgen

> No text and no book speaks if it does not speak the language that
> reaches the other person.
> —Hans-Georg Gadamer, *Truth and Method*

COMPOSITION, as practiced and supported by current pedagogical research, reconnects rhetoric and philosophy. Composition research in pedagogy, combined with the social attitudes and interests of teachers, demonstrates the exercise of fundamental hermeneutical principles, and the composition classroom has thus become a site for the discovery of practical philosophy and its realignment with rhetoric. The connection between composition and philosophy was initially made in ancient Greece at the time rhetoric emerged as a discipline. For Aristotle, rhetoric included three elements: argumentation (or *inventio*, the invention of arguments and proofs), a theory of style (*elocutio*), and a theory of composition (*compositio*). The discussion of the first, argumentation, takes up two-thirds of the *Rhetoric* and constitutes the foundation of rhetoric. Argumentation links rhetoric and demonstrative logic and therefore aligns rhetoric with philosophy (see Ricoeur, *Rule* 9).

Despite this link, the history of discourse presents us with two distinct traditions, rhetoric and hermeneutics, opposed to each other as a theory of production and a theory of comprehension (Todorov). The theory of production emphasizes the argument or style by which rhetoric is reduced to persuasion and distinguished from philosophy. It defines rhetoric as either persuasion or dialectic, on the basis of dominant cultural tastes or interests. The theory of comprehension separates poetics from dialectic or logic, and literature from theology and philosophy. Current composition theory and practice are engaged in realigning philosophy and rhetoric because composition defines rhetoric to include both production and interpretation of texts. In fact, the contemporary epistemological focus of composition theory and pedagogy—the related roles of readers and writers—reconnects rhetoric and hermeneutics. This essay explores the way current composition theory and practice demonstrate the interconnection of rhetoric and hermeneutics as developed in the work of Hans-Georg Gadamer.

Hermeneutics, that is, the theory of interpretation, translation, or under-standing, is as ancient as rhetoric. Rhetoric is the creation of meaning in written or spoken form, whereas hermeneutics is the "art of bringing what is said or written to speech again" (Gadamer, *Reason* 119). Both require the use of language and involve dialectic as well as a context for their exercise. The antagonism between philosophy and rhetoric as expressed in Plato's *Gorgias* is addressed again in the *Phaedrus*, where Plato endows rhetoric with a philo-sophical justification. The argument of the *Phaedrus* informs Aristotle's *Rheto-ric*, which presents a philosophy of human life as determined by speech rather than a technical doctrine about the art of speaking. Aristotle, and the humanistic tradition of rhetoric he engendered, advanced the idea that knowledge is socially constructed through language. For Aristotle and the Renaissance Aristotelian revival, hermeneutics and rhetoric were interrelated. Philip Melanchthon (1497–1560), "Teacher of Germany," revived Aristotle the rhetorician and transformed rhetoric from "the art of making speeches to the art of following discourses with understanding which led into hermeneu-tics" (Gadamer, *Reason* 123). For Melanchthon, Aristotle had "tied together the subject of dialectic, physics, and ethics, and applied two things which brought light to his teaching: method and propriety of speech" (Melanchthon 76). Furthermore, Melanchthon noted that Aristotle, like the rhetoricians, knew that one must interpret point of view to understand discourse; therefore, to determine the meaning of texts, one must recognize that they are not neutral but validated by their own context and claims to understanding (Gadamer, *Reason* 125).

Modern hermeneutics developed in conjunction with Melanchthon's re-newal of Aristotelianism precisely because the ability to produce discourse has the same claim to universal understanding as the ability to understand and interpret written discourse. Contemporary hermeneutics philosophers, such as Paul Ricoeur (*Rule*), Hans-Georg Gadamer (*Truth; Rhetorik; Reason*), and Ernesto Grassi, attempt to realign philosophy and rhetoric, dialectic and rhetoric, and hermeneutics and rhetoric as interrelated intellectual activities used in the discovery and creation of authentic meaning effected in language. One of Gadamer's basic ideas, nurtured in the rhetorical tradition, is that "there is no understanding of things apart from language, and no understand-ing of language apart from things" (Weinsheimer 232).

Gadamer's systematic approach to understanding accepts that "interpreta-tion begins with fore-conceptions that are replaced by more suitable ones" (*Truth* 236). The existence and reality of these subjective foreconceptions or presuppositions constitute an important alignment between composition or rhetoric and philosophy. In both intellectual activities, the subject writer or subject interpreter brings his or her intentions, biases, and prejudices to the creation or re-creation of the text. These foreconceptions, however, challenge understanding because, as Gadamer points out, "inappropriate fore-meanings

. . . come to nothing in the working-out" (*Truth* 237). In other words, the interpreter is asked to recognize the reality of his or her own foreconceptions that rule the meaning he or she may elicit at first from an object of scrutiny. But this recognition is merely the first stage in coming to understand. After further scrutiny, dialogue, and self-correction, the initial "meaning" or "conclusion" may be corrected or changed. As Gadamer says, "The prejudices and fore-meanings in the mind of the interpreter are not at his free disposal. He is not able to separate in advance the productive prejudices that make understanding possible from the prejudices which hinder understanding and lead to misunderstandings" (*Truth* 263). Through a systematic and method-ological inquiry, the interpreter will come to identify inappropriate and appropriate responses.

The basis of Gadamer's hermeneutical theory is that "the ability to under-stand is a fundamental endowment of man, one that sustains his communal life with others and, above all, one that takes place by way of language and the partnership of conversation." Though this appears to be a simple proposition, Gadamer also recognizes what he calls the "insurmountable barrier" in the linguistic exchange between people, which lies at the heart of the hermeneutical enterprise ("Text" 21). Gadamer's *Truth and Method* is a sustained attempt to surmount this barrier. A later seminal essay, *Rhetorik und Hermeneutik*, emphasizes the relation between interpretation and construc-tion of discourse and, as a consequence, points to the connection between teaching students to write essays and reading (interpreting and responding to) student essays. Many of the current practices in composition pedagogy demonstrate the methods and principles of hermeneutical inquiry as developed by Gadamer. Three topics of his philosophical method in particular, *foreconcep-tions*, *dialogue*, and *fusion of horizons*, are effectively used in current composition pedagogy.

Foreconceptions is Gadamer's term for the entire range of cultural and histori-cal attitudes, whether tacit or conscious, that we bring to bear on an object as we scrutinize it. *Dialogue* is the ideal conversation that occurs when a subject (an inquiring reader or teacher who responds or interprets) communes with an object of inquiry (e.g., a literary text, a historical event). The *fusion of horizons* takes place when the subject becomes conscious of his or her own prejudices and simultaneously recognizes the subjectivity of the object he or she interprets and the necessity to accommodate the "otherness" of this object in an act of communicative or listening understanding.

Some of the presuppositions underlying the current composition classroom are fertile grounds for assessing the interconnection of hermeneutical practice and the teaching of writing. These include the following convictions: (1) The student text has the same claims to understanding as any other literary document. (2) Conventions tend to regulate written discourse, but the history of our literature applauds adaptation, correction, transgression, and even violation of the conventions of genre, style, and language (diction and grammar). (3) Intentionality exists on both sides of the interpretive act. That is, both writers and readers have conscious and unconscious intentions when they read and write, and these intentions direct the creation of the text and the interpretation of the reader. (4) The student who writes an essay is a writer in control of his or her own literary enterprise rather than an automaton who reproduces according to an established code. (5) A literary text communicates when another person understands it. But this dialogue requires both reader and writer to be open to the possibilities of the text's communication and conscious of cultural affiliations, norms, and conventions that may differ from one person to another, or from one social environment to another, and that therefore might make either party vulnerable to misunderstanding the text under discussion. (6) Cooperative group work may facilitate the interpretation and understanding of a text.

Foreconceptions

When we probe the attitudes, convictions, and prejudices we as teachers of composition bring to the classroom, we are applying the hermeneutical practice of identifying foreconceptions to the teaching of composition. What assumptions do we have about the conventions of diction, style, and form and about ideologies? To what degree do we expect the student essay to conform to these conventions? And how willing are we to question our own preconceptions about the efficacy of conventions? Are we open to transgression against these conventions? Furthermore, since student writers often interpret a literary work before they write their essays, the validity of their interpretive acts are also at stake. Are we willing to consider the potential differences in interpretive conclusions? These are the kinds of concerns teachers might entertain when evaluating their foreconceptions before closing the possibility of communication with the student text. Such questions do not undermine the authority of the reader; on the contrary, they recognize the authority of the object (student text) and the subject who constructed it, thus enhancing the authority of the teacher.

Gadamer's ideas about foreconceptions in the creation of written discourse and about responses to it in a hermeneutical exercise are relevant to the teaching of composition. In both interpretation and construction of a text, we cannot rely completely on these foreconceptions; rather, we are forced to examine their legitimacy, their origin and validity. We must understand our own linguistic usage; we must allow the text to impose its own world on us as we ask questions of it and of ourselves; and we must examine our own presuppositions, particularly as they control and direct our reading and writing habits. Finally, to approach the subject of inquiry as reader or writer, we must be open to its possibilities, because to understand we must be outside ourselves.[1] To approximate some truthful understanding in the construction of a text (rhetoric) and the reconstruction of its meaning (hermeneutics), we must be aware of our own bias, "so that the text may present itself in all its newness" and "be able to assert its own truth against one's own fore-meanings" (Gadamer, *Truth* 238).[2] The working definition of *truth* offered here resonates with current composition teaching practice and with Aristotelian rhetoric. It is preserved in the rhetorical tradition through the idea of argumentative "contingency" and construction of meaning by language. Context, circumstances, and intentionality define *truthfulness*.

The self-scrutiny required to identify foreconceptions in writing and reading is an epistemological effort to make the reader or writer conscious of what is tacit and to subject what is conscious to examination. This activity, which helps us understand prejudices and evaluate their validity, is directed toward both "usage" and "content," that is, linguistic conventions and the ideas being expressed.

According to Gadamer, every text presents us with the task of scrutinizing our own linguistic prejudice. In a shared language, linguistic usage would appear to be easily understood, but Mina Shaughnessy and others have shown that it not only reflects cultural differences but also supports prejudices about them (see also Labov, *Language*; Shores). As linguistics research and composition pedagogy and practice have proved, the way we use the syntax of our language is a gauge of education, cultural attitudes (high, low, popular, and indifferent), affiliations (ethnic, class, gender, and status), and personality traits (rule followers vs. rule breakers; system manipulators, challengers, or adherents), so we cannot take syntax for granted.[3] Nor is it the only area for potential difference between writer and reader. Lexical variety may also be a measure of difference. Vocabulary and common usage can vary according to social and economic status, gender, ethnic identity, profession, and cultural affiliations. For example, professions and subgroups within professions share vocabulary that few outside their community would understand (see Michaels and Ricks).

A second topic of foreconceptions that also points up the differences between writer and reader is "content." Gadamer speaks of "breaking the spell of our fore-meanings" that determine our understanding of a text (*Truth* 237). There is indeed an element of incantation and cult in the underlying assumptions that privilege our foreconceptions. The right words and syntax, that is, the words and syntax we expect from the traditions of our professions—what Dwight Bolinger refers to as a "sociolect" (126)—must appear in the text or it will not mean what we anticipate it to mean.[4] The text must speak the magic words that conjure recognition in its audience, showing the membership of both text and audience in the cult.

In the act of interpretation, however, we rarely encounter such a rapport between the reader and the text. On the contrary, the hermeneutical exercise begins with the recognition that incantation will not work, because the text cannot speak. Conversation has ceased; ritual is gone. To some degree, every reading act poses this problem. The text presents itself, and we respond to its communicative gestures with questions, doubts, apathy, or joy. The text may or may not yield meaning, or its meaning may not be compatible with our foreconceptions, so that its sense eludes our understanding. The text impedes our facile conclusions. Yet, the text depends on the reader to render it, and it will only speak through its reader. The danger of subjectivism in this process is, needless to say, overwhelming, and the opportunism of imposing selfish or self-immersed demands on the text is likewise pervasive. Our reading process is not an objective endeavor but a product of our prejudices, which to a great degree predetermine what we will uncover. We do not approach the object of our inquiry as a tabula rasa, evaluating the evidence in all its purity; rather, we approach it with a panoply of foreconceptions. Gadamer does not move from this observation to dismiss these foreconceptions as illegitimate, but he is interested in recognizing that they exist and that interpretation must be directed by knowledge of their substantial contribution to our process of understanding.

Dialogue can begin to take place as these foreconceptions are acknowledged, that is, as the teacher who is reading a student essay begins to realize that the paper in question is the product of the student's foreconceptions, just as the teacher's foreconceptions direct how he or she reads or interprets the paper. After Gadamer analyzes the foreconceptions that inhibit understanding, in his beginning step toward dialogue, he moves to the linking question:

> [W]e may ask how we can break the spell of our fore-meanings that determine my own understanding. . . . [W]hat another person tells me, whether in conversation, letter, book, or whatever, is generally thought automatically to be his own and not my opinion; and it is this that I am to take note of without necessarily having to share it. But this presupposition is not something that makes understanding easier, but harder, in that the fore-meanings that determine my own understanding can go entirely unnoticed.   (*Truth* 237–38)

To bridge this gap between the object's point of view, position, or communication and one's own prior conceptions on a topic or mode for expressing the ideas requires openness to the object's possible truth and the concession of some authority to one's object, even if only temporarily. Such openness may dictate not a redefinition of what constitutes the ideal and the true but a momentary abandonment of one's own prejudices about truth. In other words, openness to the possible truth of a text or someone's claims seems again to involve an openness to the possible challenge these present to one's own prejudices (Warnke 97). Thus, in the composition classroom, teachers must be conscious of their own convictions about writing, able to scrutinize the limits and possibilities of these attitudes, and willing to concede that these convictions are open to question, correction, and adaptation, particularly as a consequence of the experience with the written projects of others.

This process of self-scrutiny leads to Gadamer's point that "there is no such thing as a fully transparent text or a completely exhaustive interest in the explaining and construing of texts"; therefore, all perspectives about reading or interpreting are subject to alteration (*Reason* 105). As a result, we realize we are not just investigating a given written text but actually tracing the interests that guide our approach to it.

Dialogue

With the self-discovery of foreconceptions and the simultaneous recognition of alternate conceptions in the object, the subject is ready for dialogue with the object under scrutiny. Reflection on the teaching activity and the dialogue between writer and responder may prompt the reader to adjust his or her attitudes about the conventions that regulate both the teaching of writing and the essay itself, thus contributing to a modification of the rhetorical tradition. These modifications could include a new understanding of what constitutes rhetorical and hermeneutical practice as well as more modest changes, such as new approaches to reading or assigning essays, heightened awareness that each creative act is unique, and the consequent pedagogical adjustments of that realization. The circular movement—from a subject whose approach to an object is ruled by foreconceptions to a subject in dialogue with an object that becomes a subject itself as a consequence of the conversation—results in a consensus, a reappraisal of tradition, and the reform or modification of attitudes and interests. This re-formation of foreconceptions through analysis of one's own self-understanding is never complete, for it moves perpetually through "experience, interpretation and revision" (Warnke 29). We can readily see that current composition pedagogy recommends this movement.

To suggest a method for talking about a subject, Gadamer identifies Platonic dialectic as the art of conducting a conversation and forming concepts to work out a common meaning. In other words, dialogue involves language as we experience it in a composition classroom, as the medium of exchange, as the process of question and answer, giving and taking, and talking at cross purposes while attempting to see one another's points. It is not monological and therefore not without nuance, affect, or possibility for misinterpretation, difference, or congruence. It "performs that communication of meaning which, with respect to written tradition, is the task of hermeneutics" (*Truth* 331). That we must use language to communicate or to have a dialogue confirms the interrelation of philosophy and rhetoric. Dialogue consists in trying to discover the strength of what is said rather than in discovering weaknesses; the conditions of the conversation that occur in a dialogue clarify understanding. In a genuine conversation, Gadamer asserts, one side concedes or submits to the other in an effort to get inside the other's viewpoint. It is this viewpoint—what the person says, not the person individually—that is at question, although the two often have much in common.

A dialogue attempts to overcome the differences between the subject and the object of inquiry. In the dialogue, a transformation of original positions ensues. But one neither imposes one's own point of view in this process nor accepts the views of the object without question; rather, one may come to recognize personal deficiencies and failures of understanding, as well as a willingness to learn. The subject and object (and the subject who creates the object) often share many assumptions, because both may be products of a common tradition that is not static but dynamic, in an open-ended historical motion. Because of this shared tradition, dialogue is not only possible but essential to understanding. In the openness of dialogue, subjects may move beyond their original points of view, the products of their foreconceptions, and a new understanding may adjust, change, or advance tradition. In the composition classroom, the dialogue aims for a successful conclusion in which both reader and writer understand the subject matter explored in the student text, but this understanding goes beyond the views of the writer and the reader because both have explored their own initial assumptions, prejudices, and objectives. Thus hermeneutics makes possible the discovery of tradition in which each new act of interpretive construction contributes to the development of that tradition.

When such a dialogue takes place in a composition classroom, the teacher's first step is to recognize that foreconceptions restate and maintain established traditions in teaching practices and then to scrutinize and evaluate those traditions. Many students and teachers share foreconceptions about what constitutes a well-written essay. According to many freshman rhetoric books, essays must be organized, clear, succinct, grammatical, and original. This is the tradition in which student and teacher tend to operate. However, when subject and object, reader and writer have compatible foreconceptions, both exercise the same prejudice in the act of understanding,[5] so no dialectic actually exists, and tradition at this point potentially turns into conservative preservation of the status quo, which may be oppressive. When one partner is merely performing for the other's expectations, dialogue cannot occur. The composition classroom, therefore, must be built around the idea of potential conflict, where dialogue takes place and eventual consensus is possible. In the classroom, the process of coming to consensus lays open the possibility of ideological collusion, a danger that must be confronted and addressed. The most serious criticisms of Gadamer's method have focused on this problem, as I discuss later.

In fact, even though student and teacher may share some ideas about what constitutes "good" writing, more often than not a gap exists between teacher expectations and student essay. This gap is central to Gadamer's idea about the dialogue that follows recognition of foreconceptions. When the writing lacks what a teacher's foreconceptions demand, the first response on both sides should be to scrutinize the expectations and their validity. In other words, both the teacher and the student writer should examine their own claims to efficacy in responding to and creating the text. This first step toward openness on both sides would lead to a dialogue that recognizes the valid subjectivity of both writer and reader. The teacher-student conferences introduced in the last twenty years—proceedings that emphasize reading and responding and favor identifying the characteristics of student writing rather than judging or grading—reflect this aspect of the Gadamerian method.[6] The use of writing groups in the teaching of composition has also established a social and pedagogical environment for exploring literary premises and expectations, as well as for confronting and discussing stylistic and ideological differences (see Gere). Revision occurring as a consequence of these verbal exchanges can show that a genuine dialogue has taken place if both reader and writer demonstrate adjustments in expectations. A consensus has been reached.

Fusion of Horizons

For composition teachers, the fusion of horizons between teacher and student writer begins with the acknowledgment that both have perspectives through which they see and understand their worlds and their activities. For each to understand the other's world involves constructing a shared language that both can use to communicate. It requires openness to the possibility of "truth" on either side as well as to the possibility of accommodating diverse linguistic habits or ideological positions. Thus the responder to a student essay is not the recipient of information or the judge of the quality but the "catalyst" of a communicative exchange (Warnke 68). The catalyst metaphor describes the student writer of the essay for whom the act of creation is a response to, and a result of, an interpretive act. At the same time, the writer participates in a process of "personal change" while inciting change in an intended audience. For the teacher, the act of interpreting the student essay is the catalytic experience that promotes understanding of the essay, invites reassessment of his or her convictions about the acts of creation and interpretation, and reinforces historical precedents for the mode of expression and understanding (rhetoric and hermeneutics).

"Horizon," according to Gadamer, is the

> range of vision that includes everything that can be seen from a particular vantage point. Applying this to the thinking mind, we speak of narrowness of horizon, of the possible expansion of horizon, of the opening up of new horizons etc. The word has been used in philosophy since Nietzsche and Husserl to characterise the way in which thought is tied to its finite determination. . . . A person who has no horizon is a man who does not see far enough and hence overvalues what is nearest him. Contrariwise, to have an horizon means not to be limited to what is nearest, but to be able to see beyond it.
>
> (*Truth* 269)

Recognizing different horizons, unshared by interpreter and object of interpretation, helps establish a method for bringing these horizons, with all their differences, together. Projecting a horizon is a "phase in the process of understanding" in which interpreters maintain the horizon of their own time or situation as they reconnoiter with the horizon of another time or situation. To abandon one's own situation in favor of the other is to assent to what Gadamer calls the "self-alienation of a past consciousness" (*Truth* 273). Empiricism and positivism, with their claims to objectivity, their single-method approach to knowledge, and their myth of the unbiased researcher, have obscured the reality of these differences. Gadamer's method not only recognizes such differences but attempts to establish a means whereby they can be entertained in the process of coming to understand.

The fusion of horizons occurs when a dialogue has actually happened. This concept underscores that the interpretive act has at least two sides and that imposing a single horizon denies the subjectivity of not only the object of inquiry but also, in essence, the inquirer. Such a concept presupposes a frozen "truth" not subject to time, historical dynamics, structural revolution, or personal adaptation. Every encounter with what Gadamer calls "tradition"— the range of attitudes and interests that regulate the explorer and the exploration or the interpreter and object of interpretation—involves a tension between the text in itself, in its own environment, and the reader in his or her own environment. To cover up this tension is a naive attempt at assimilation; interpreters should aim to bring it out in order to identify the different horizons. Thus Gadamer rejects the idea that difference does not exist between subject and object or that sympathy can be conjured to eradicate the subject as he or she becomes immersed in the object's subjectivity. Quite the contrary, he wants to acknowledge the validity of the different horizons between subject and object and to move from there to a methodology for fusing these disparate worlds.

This fusion is not a process whereby the interpreter becomes the other (i.e., the text as subject that the reader empathizes with as creator). Rather, it is the recognition of the subjectivity of the object of scrutiny and a conversation with it, in which both sides engage the subjectivity and reach an understanding. In this process, the interpreter makes the text speak. The understanding that follows is temporal since it is never complete and always subject to revision as it changes in response to intellectual, psychological, and social encounters. Through this self-scrutiny and recognition of the subjectivity of the object of interpretation, a kind of consensus about the text can take place. New experiences help the inquiring subject redefine his or her understanding of the past and the conventions attached to it and to approach the future with revised attitudes.

The realization of the differences in horizons allows dialogue to begin to take place. These multiple differences include time, gender, race, culture, ethnicity, ideology, social and economic status, religion, and even physiological or age variations. Unlike Gadamer, Jacques Derrida considers difference a rupture between past and present, writer and reader, and object and subject; it is therefore the basis for subjective re-creation. Interpretation is not possible because the "object" is dead (*Grammatology*).[7] There can be no conversation; instead, subjective, creative play takes its place. Gadamer sees difference as essential to dialectical or opposing views that prepare the way for dialogue, change, and reconstruction. "Sameness," or the reflection of the interpreter's convictions in the object of study or interest, is monological and static and therefore not open to growth and change.

This danger of falling into soliloquy or self-mirroring in the act of interpreting converges with composition teaching. The greatest teaching disappointment is receiving a student paper that not only regurgitates the ideas advanced in class but also follows the most rigid format for essay production. Here there is no dialectic, dialogue, or conversation, only an echoed monologue, regardless of how skillfully it is rendered. In this replication, conversation is foreclosed as both teacher and student are denied the opportunity for reflection and change.

When a mutual exchange occurs in the interpretive transaction, however, both sides cede authority to the intended object, which they now acknowledge as a subject for whom scientific objectivity is not a possibility. In the challenge to each partner's prejudices, convictions are not overthrown; rather, they are recognized, scrutinized, and placed in the perspective of the larger horizons. Taking the task at hand seriously—that is, reading and interpreting the student text as well as constructing the text—is, in the most fundamentally simple way, learning to respect the claims of both the student text and the valorized tradition of rhetoric advanced by the teacher. In the fusion of horizons, neither side necessarily adopts the position of the other; agreement need not always occur. Far from tragic, this effort of understanding emphasizes reflection on another viewpoint and the development of ongoing and open-ended discussion of both the topic at hand and the mode of conducting the discussion (i.e., rhetoric; see Elbow, *Embracing*).

Consensus in the fusion of horizons, therefore, involves methodology instead of ideas or forms. It is understanding that happens and not necessarily agreement about the truth content of the ideas or the form of their expression. But this notion of consensus is open to criticism in the hermeneutical process as deployed in teaching composition and as expressed in Gadamer's work, because in both the danger of collusion between teacher and student, inquirer and object of inquiry, or subject and subject of scrutiny is always present. Jürgen Habermas objects to the exercise of tradition in the interpretive act because it potentially makes Gadamer a conservative supporter of recalcitrant ideologies (*Logik*; "Hermeneutic Claim").[8] Gadamer's insistence on the validity, or "truth value," of the object of study appears to justify the "truth" content of any idea. Furthermore, his point that agreement about meaning emerges from dialogue overlooks, according to Habermas, potential complicity in politically or socially oppressive ideologies. It also ignores, in Habermas's view, the degree to which our common cultural attitudes and interests may be deluded. Teachers conscious of this potential for collusion with their students must recognize the power relations in the classroom, in which students may experience fear, anxiety, and other forms of insecurity in concert with a desire to ingratiate, while teachers might tacitly impose a cultural hegemony.

Gadamer's idea of "fusion of horizons" emphatically does not imply agreement with the underlying ideologies on either side of the dialogue; instead, it identifies those ideologies in an effort to understand, change, or reach consensus. Interestingly, Derrida rejects the idea of consensus on the grounds that understanding cannot take place.[9] Habermas rejects it because it may cement structured and systematic distortions. For Habermas, the problem with Gadamer's notion of consensus is that its psychodynamics do not address endemic social and political coercions and conspiracies fostered in tradition. Habermas identifies as a further problem Gadamer's claim that the universality of hermeneutics is beyond all doubt (Gadamer, "Text" 21). In asserting openness as necessary for understanding, Gadamer appears to have advanced a method whose universalist pretensions exclude other methods. Most self-reflective teachers readily agree that such an assertion contradicts their experience in the classroom, for no single method has ever proved universally successful.

At the root of the criticisms of "universal" claims in methodological efficacy is the question of whether the method uncovers traditions in order to subvert or applaud them. From Habermas's view, Gadamer's assent to a consensual model for human understanding suggests acquiescence to ideological positions that under certain circumstances should be overthrown. But Gadamer does not believe that traditions are free-floating, idealized "truth"; they are products of social-historical circumstances that are discovered during the process of interpretation, as is their distinctiveness from current or approved attitudes. He leaves open the door for adjusting and changing traditions when circumstances change. For him, the issue is neither subversion nor applause but understanding. As a model for describing the interpretive act taking place in a composition classroom, his method proves to have much in common with current pedagogical practices. Nevertheless, a potential problem remains when the power relations between teacher and student are coercive or conspiratorial instead of cooperative or consultative. The politics of the educational edifice and the social arena, and the entrenched social reality of privileged and unprivileged, must stand in the foreground rather than on the horizon during the exercise of understanding in a pedagogical setting. Teacher and student must become conscious that the postmodern classroom is not an objective environment without passion or disinterest but a place where all the underlying and contested ideologies of our times are put into play. As useful as Gadamer's method might be for facilitating dialogue between teacher and student, its application must be guarded by awareness of and commitment to the democratic values that make any universalist claims subject to suspicion. Because the United States has a tradition of public education, the democratic convictions of equality, fairness, openness, and interest in cultural diversity have fostered the underlying social and political foreconceptions of many rhetoric teachers. The challenge is to realize this tradition and practice it. The reconnection of philosophy and rhetoric evident in contemporary composition classrooms and represented in Gadamer's hermeneutical method may prove useful in this activity.

University of California, Davis

NOTES

[1]Mina Shaughnessy's *Errors and Expectations* represents a powerful example of teacher self-evaluation of foreconceptions in composition pedagogy.

[2]Georgia Warnke provides a useful definition of what Gadamer means by truth: "Throughout his work . . . he emphasizes the necessity of distinguishing between two forms of understanding: the understanding of truth-content and the understanding of intentions. The first form of understanding refers to the kind of substantive knowledge one has when one is justified in claiming that one understands Euclidean geometry or an ethical principle, for example. Here understanding means seeing the 'truth' of something, grasping that the sum of the squares of the two sides of a right triangle is equal to the square of the hypotenuse, that the validity of Euclidean geometry is relativized by the discovery of other forms of geometry or that murder is wrong. Understanding in this sense involves insight into a subject-matter or, as Gadamer puts it, an understanding of *die Sache* [the thing]. The second sense of understanding, in contrast, involves a knowledge

of conditions: the reasons why a particular person says that murder is wrong or the intentions behind someone's claiming that a geometrical proposition is true. This kind of understanding thus involves an understanding of the psychological, biographical or historical conditions behind a claim or action as opposed to a substantive understanding of the claim or action itself. What is understood is not the truth-content of a claim or the point of an action but the motives behind a certain person's making a certain claim or performing a given action" (7–8).

[3] See Dwight Bolinger, *Language: The Loaded Weapon*, for a collection of essays on the many uses and abuses of language. In particular, "Stigma, Status and Standard" (44–57), "A Case in Point: Sexism" (89–104), and "Power and Deception" (105–24) explore the sociology of language use in America in recent years; see also William Labov, *The Study of Nonstandard English*.

[4] See Bolinger, "The Jargonauts" (125–37), in *Language*. A "sociolect" is "one of the most important active media for transmitting certain kinds of social awareness through the culture" (126). Bolinger quotes Geoffrey Nunberg, "Slang, Usage-Conditions, and l'Arbitraire du Signe" (305).

[5] Gadamer's understanding of *prejudice* starts with his observation that a prejudice of the Enlightenment was "the prejudice against prejudice itself." He insists that prejudice has neither a negative nor a positive value, since it does not mean "false judgment"; rather, prejudice is the operation of "tradition" in the interpreter, the recognition of which is the first step toward understanding (*Truth* 238–53).

[6] George Hillocks calls this method of instruction the individualized mode and suggests that future research "might profitably examine the effects of real tutorial situations in which diagnostic and corrective procedures are used systematically" (131).

[7] Derrida goes further than Gadamer in challenging Cartesian thinking, rejecting the possibility of any idea of immanence in a text. Instead, he advances "deconstruction" or nonidentity and nonunderstanding. See Dallmayr.

[8] See chapter 4 of Warnke's *Gadamer*, "Hermeneutics and the Critique of Ideology," for an extensive discussion of the major critical arguments against Gadamer's work (107–38). Habermas's main criticisms are that what "we are trying to understand may systematically obscure its connections to social relations of power and domination" and that the way we appropriate what "we are trying to understand . . . may itself reflect the influence of ideology" (Warnke 140).

[9] In a debate with Gadamer in Paris, Derrida comments, "A third question also has to do with the underlying structure of good will. Whether or not psychoanalytic afterthoughts are brought into the picture, one can still raise questions about that axiomatic precondition of interpretive discourse which Professor Gadamer calls 'Verstehen,' 'understanding the other,' and 'understanding one another.' Whether one speaks of consensus or of misunderstanding (as in Schleiermacher), one needs to ask whether the precondition of Verstehen, far from being the continuity of rapport . . . , is not rather the interruption of rapport, a certain rapport of interruption, the suspending of all mediation?" ("Three Questions" 53).

THE PHENOMENOLOGY OF PROCESS

Judith Halden-Sullivan

THE INEFFABILITY of language grounds both composition studies and hermeneutic phenomenology and makes composition the source of compelling philosophical inquiry. The field of composition and the path of hermeneutic phenomenological thinking intersect at essential junctures: What is language? What is a human being's relation to language? How does thinking make this relation apparent? How do writing and its interpretation help characterize human beings as both historical and temporal? A diverse discipline that embraces structuralist, deconstructive, psychoanalytic, Marxist, and feminist critiques of rhetorical theories and texts, composition studies confronts all these questions that interrogate its engagement with language. But, coming to prominence in a technological age, the field persists in imposing on an entity a scientific interpretive design: making the thing under discussion controllable for the human interpreter.

Control and command are not the intentions of phenomenological investigations. Instead, in hermeneutic phenomenology, language as the saying of Being—as that which makes all worlds apparent and possible—addresses people. Human beings dwell within language, the "house of Being," and respond in their "saying" to Being's call, manifesting what presents itself to them in language. The paths of phenomenological thinking often seem circuitous, approaching the entity under discussion as it stands out in thought in ways that are rarely straightforward. Thus, in trying to disclose the nature of something, the hermeneutic phenomenologist Martin Heidegger enters into a nontraditional and perhaps enigmatic discussion of language. He teases readers out of their "common" thoughts, insightfully revealing what may be disguised as the commonplace. Such language can also show the philosophical dimensions of a term frequently and comfortably used in composition studies: *process*. In a hermeneutic phenomenological context, this notion invites the uncovering of truth, an a priori function of the human being; the disclosing of a world and its structures, which further elucidates the ongoing event of being human; and the interpreting of disclosures that expose truth, the world, and the human mode itself as both historical and temporal. Within these processes, composition studies, insofar as it continually involves language, finds its essence.

This essay is not the first to apply Heideggerian theories of language to composition studies. The most thorough and elegant description thus far is Lynn Worsham's 1987 *Pre/Text* article entitled "The Question concerning Invention: Hermeneutics and the Genesis of Writing," which provides a context for my remarks. Worsham begins with an extensive critique of current composition theory's technological focus. Within the confines of a scientific worldview,

> [w]riting becomes a technology, a study of systems of methods as means to various ends, which include self-realization or expression, the creation and discovery of knowledge, the promotion of the democratic process and economic prosperity. Writing appears before us, in short, as an answer, not as a radical form of questioning. To the extent that we conceive of writing technologically, the profession of composition studies participates in a process in which human potential is mobilized and rendered available as a resource for the production of specific social ends. (210)

Worsham elaborates on the technologically based problem-solving approach to writing; mastery and control, notions suggestive of current invention procedures; and the propositional character of truth inherent both in modern topoi theories and in assessment of invention methods that seek out comprehensiveness and adequacy. Her critiques discuss Richard Young, Alton Becker, Kenneth Pike, Janice Lauer, and Ann Berthoff—all of whom share, if, like Berthoff, inadvertently, a scientific predisposition to the writing process and its purposes. Worsham then proposes

> an alternative approach to thinking about invention, one that may serve to put us back into an experience of questioning, not *what* but *how*. At the very least, this approach may lead someday to a future for composition in a hermeneutical understanding of writing, one in which no method will guarantee that process yields product, one that will recognize neither truth nor knowledge apart from an endless process of concealing and revealing. (218)

Launching into the "genesis of another topology," Worsham seizes on Heidegger's notion of the "topology of Being" and defines it as "how human being is placed in the world and the different modes in which human being exists and encounters things." Topology, however, "should not be regarded as a system or an instrument by which to get an atemporal and conceptual grasp on the meaning of human being but as a guide to the places, the topoi, where truth happens as an event in human existence" (219). Worsham then describes Heidegger's "three topoi," three places where human being resides and "where the meaning of human being happens": *Befindlichkeit*, or the disposition or state in which one may be found; *Verstehen*, or understanding—to exist "understandingly"; and *Rede*, or language—a making manifest in words disclosures of a world. In a powerful synthesis entitled "Re-placing Writing," Worsham concludes with the implications of Heidegger's hermeneutic phenomenology for composition theory. Three are of particular concern for this study. First, Worsham asserts that "[o]nce we enter the question that brings writing into being as *writing* . . . we risk the on-going transformation of ourselves and our world" (235). But what would such writing be?

> It would be a kind of writing that seeks not so much the conceptual and abstract but the sensuous and emotional. It would seek not the truth of propositions but the rigor of possibility and the nuance of the impossible. It would seek not the distance of generalization and objectivity but the nearness of involvement.   (236)

And finally, such writing would make apparent our relation to "the earth and to the world," revealing "a sense of homelessness, a sense of alienation, and lack of belongingness to the earth and to the world that cannot be had through concepts and theories" (236).

The value of Worsham's contribution to a hermeneutic phenomenological reorientation toward the "places" of invention cannot be questioned. My interpretation of process, however, has a more fundamental emphasis and features a closer link between Heidegger's ontology and its implications for composition studies and the teaching of writing. Specifically, two key terms in Heidegger's analytic of the human mode of being elude Worsham's full attention. The first is *openness*. Worsham states that "mood or state-of-mind constitutes our openness to the world, our attunement to the world" (222). Openness and the uncovering co-original with it offer an a priori grounding to Heidegger's ontology that demands further explication. The second term that needs more exploration is *saying*. Heidegger, Worsham reports, "locates the essence of language in the phenomenon of speaking" (226); she goes on to remark that "[s]aying or speaking is a listening, listening to what is housed within language, listening to what language gives us to say" (227). Indeed, the primacy of saying in all its forms and its relation to Being demand fuller articulation. By focusing on what she interprets as the "topoi" of *Befindlichkeit*, *Verstehen*, and *Rede*, Worsham exposes her own predisposition to retrieve the rhetorically appropriate from Heidegger's ontology. She bypasses opportunities to return to structures that constitute the human mode of being and its larger connection with worldhood and Being, and, consequently, she fails to manifest more precisely the "nearness of involvement" she rightly contends would characterize writing that is the "topology of Being" (236). I address two concerns here: the phenomenology of the human mode of being and the relation between human speakers or writers and their language. Composition's emphasis on the ways writing manifests writers' thinking of worlds forever grounds the field in these concerns. Reciprocally, these phenomenological concerns bring to the fore issues hotly debated in composition studies: process, students' authenticity, and teachers' authority.

Heidegger's hermeneutic phenomenology prompts a rethinking of process. It asks that composition studies recall the processes inherent in the beings of writers and readers, the relation of those writers and readers to language, and what that language reveals. In a hermeneutic phenomenological context, human beings are continually *at the disposal of the language* they receive; they act on it. Indeed, writing as a form of received language cannot be examined as an entity divorced from the processes of the mode of being that make it possible. Composition, then, in its most essential form, is the study of the human mode of being. But what is it to be human? In Heidegger's estimation, the response to this question finds its clue in the simultaneity of being human and being open to "truth." The human mode of being, in Joseph Kockelmans's words, "is openness in the direction of the other"—turning toward things and human beings in the world. Unlike stones or plants, human beings "ek-sist": they stand "open" to the world and can apprehend it as a totality of relations ("Language" 13, 9). Their understanding of the world is "equipri-mordial"; that is, it occurs simultaneously with their openness: understanding "is to be conceived of not as a concrete mode of knowing but precisely as that which makes all concrete modes of knowing possible." Because openness and original understanding are "given" assets, human beings are born already "being able" to know, and this inborn trait "opens and frees [them] in the direction of [their] own Being [and] in the direction of the world" ("Language" 13, 14). What do they learn? For Heidegger, human beings' most important lesson is that they live "in the truth."

Living in the truth is the essential foundation for Heidegger's examination of human existence. So that his description of human being phenomenologi-cally addresses its subject as itself in itself and does not suggest earlier analytics of human existence, Heidegger calls the being he examines "Dasein," literally "being there." He claims that "Dasein is in the truth" (*Being* 263). In his phenomenology, Heidegger adheres to the revealment theory of truth as *aletheia*, or nonconcealment—the uncovering or showing of something in itself. He goes on to identify the human mode of being with disclosure of the world, pointing out that "Being-true as Being-uncovering is a way of Being for Dasein." For Heidegger, truth and meaning "are" only insofar as the human mode of being (Dasein) "is"; human beings must be there to uncover them. He continues:

> Circumspective concern, or even that concern in which we tarry and look at something, uncovers entities within-the-world. These entities become that which has been uncovered. They are "true" in a second sense. What is primarily

"true"—that is, uncovering—is Dasein. "True" in the second sense does not
mean Being-uncovering (uncovering), but Being-uncovered (uncoveredness).

(*Being* 263)

Human beings are the creatures who disclose the truth because the state of
revealing things is their condition. In turn, that which human beings reveal
assumes the secondary role of the thing "Being-uncovered." Heidegger argues
that, while human beings are not "introduced 'to all the truth': in every
case, the disclosedness of [their] ownmost Being" is part of their essential,
existential makeup (*Being* 263). Through the "circumspective concern," human beings can bring to light both their world and themselves. The language
of writing, as the saying of Being, discloses human openness to the truth,
showing in every nuance the writer's being-in-the-world. Therefore, composition's concerns for writing and the behaviors that engender it bespeak this
field's fundamental engagement with truth: pursuing and evaluating *what*
students' writing and teachers' interpretations of it show in particular places
and times and *how* both students and teachers stand open to truth.

From a phenomenological perspective, composition studies must also take
into account factors that mitigate a human being's exposure to truth. Heidegger describes what it is to be human as the four "basic structures" of Dasein.
These four observations share a circularity in their relation to human understanding and being in the truth: people could not live as the ones who disclose
without these structures, nor could they comprehend these four considerations
if they were not the disclosive beings in the truth. Heidegger's first structure
is "care." Human beings disclose what they turn their attention toward, what
they care about: this disclosing "embraces the whole of that structure-of-
Being which has become explicit through the phenomenon of care." Heidegger defines *care* as the "source" of the human mode of being (*Being* 243, 264):

Care, as a primordial structural totality, lies "before" . . . every factical "attitude" and "situation" of Dasein, and it does so existentially *a priori*; this means
that it always lies *in* them.   (*Being* 238)

Human beings can reveal entities that they care about, but this illuminating
process of involvement with things also discloses the person who performs it.
Human beings are concerned and interested in their world; they must be to
survive in it. Their care takes many forms, from casual concern for physical
objects to love to fervid political commitments or simply "the cares of life."
People are not released from care "but held fast, dominated by it through
and through as long as [they are] 'in the world.' " This generalization is
ontological and a priori, "already underlying in every case," like human
openness and understanding (*Being* 243, 244).

Along with care, another factor Heidegger describes that has bearing on human exposure to truth is "thrownness." Human beings are cast into a real world of things, a world they do not choose. "In thrownness," Heidegger claims, the human mode of being "is already in a definite world and alongside a definite range of definite entities within-the-world. Disclosedness is essentially factical" (*Being* 264). The world exists and people are simply "thrown" into a place and time. Their first familiarity with their world comes through contact with things—the physical or ontic character of their everyday experience. Regardless of their lack of choice, human beings *have to be*. With being thrown into a world, then, comes an unasked-for task or, as Heidegger defines it, a responsibility: being human. Although people find themselves in a world not of their own creation, they are charged with creating themselves in this place, in this milieu of things, within whatever totality of meaning their place has.

In addition to being care-ful and thrown, a person is also an unfolding "projection"—a "disclosive Being towards its potentiality-for-Being." People can care about the entities that they are thrown among and that they disclose, and they can project possibilities for the being of both themselves and things from a variety of perspectives. Selves and things come to light in different ways. As the mode of being that is understanding, Dasein "*can* understand *itself* in terms of the 'world' and others or in terms of its ownmost potentiality-for-Being." While people cannot actualize all potentialities at once, they can be flexible enough in their perspectives to always look beyond what they are to what they can be. Only human beings can project themselves and "stand out" in various ways according to their understanding of their "potentiality-for-Being" (*Being* 264).

At times, however, standing out in the world seems a burden: worrying about being an authentically human "self" is too cumbersome in a workaday world. Heidegger notes, "The average everydayness of concern becomes blind to its possibilities, and tranquilizes itself with that which is merely 'actual.' " This narrowed perspective occurs because, according to Heidegger, human beings are "falling" (*Being* 239, 264). They fall into certain acceptable ways of defining the world and themselves and, consequently, do not consider projecting themselves in different, nonapparent ways. Heidegger asserts that people are "lost" in their world or, as Heraclitus suggests, estranged from that with which they should be most familiar (Kirk and Raven 187–88). Human understanding is obscured by the pronouncements of the "they" world—the public opinion that predominates in its own popular interpretation of the world. Entities are disguised or partially hidden, or they seem like other things that they are not. Heidegger comments, "*Because Dasein is essentially falling, its state of being is such that it is in 'untruth' * " (*Being* 264); it is "especially prone to succumbing to the danger of what is common" (qtd.

in Kockelmans, *Truth* 149). But still a person's task is to be human: to "ek-sist" and disclose while being thrown into a complex, "factical" world of mingled truths and untruths.

Heidegger's analytic returns composition studies to its source: the processes of the human mode of being—caring, being thrown, projecting possibilities, falling, and standing out. Heidegger asks that the three theories of process popular in current composition studies be intertwined. In its engagement with the fullness of "ek-sistence," Heidegger's analytic accounts for the concerns of the expressive theory, which emphasizes a student's spontaneity and authenticity; the cognitive theory, which develops models of thinking or ways of negotiating the world; and the social theory, which interrogates the social constraints that shape writers' composing behaviors (Faigley, "Competing Theories" 527–28). From a phenomenological perspective, these three theories of process bring into focus the need for integrating the "basic structures" of students, teachers, and theorists. Composition journals reveal the condition of teachers and theorists with particular clarity. Students' being-in-the-world, however, demands equal articulation.

Students are historical-temporal beings intimately connected to a world that makes itself present through them. Worsham also asserts this idea (226) but fails to elaborate on the specific implications of world-relatedness for student writing. Students' "saying," from its being in the truth and in the world, is legitimate and authentic. Instructors of writing often clearly perceive what their students' work is *not*; as one manifestation of the saying of Being, student writing should speak to instructors for what it *is*—a revelation of their openness to the world. Students disclose in their speaking, writing, gestures, and behavior the otherness of their encounter with the world: the nearness of their involvement with—care for—the simplest things that constitute the milieu into which they are thrown. Teachers must desediment their cynical conceptions of appropriate saying to acknowledge students' worlds as valid. Describing the importance of heavy-metal music, "house" dancing, movies, and television programs—as evidence of care and thrownness—embodies authentic saying. Students are a thinking of the truth of their world. Disclosures of care, thrownness, projection—and, at the same time, what is revealed through *Befindlichkeit, Verstehen,* and *Rede*—are all grounded in this essential openness. Students' nearness makes manifest in their saying the topology of Being that maps not just their place, as Worsham argues, but their connection to the world, to what has presented itself to them in thought. This openness and the way it is revealed must not be subordinated to the closure of received traditional expectations of articulation. For example, students should have equal time to determine, reflect on, and evaluate their intentions, constraints, and evolving modes of articulation; student-generated criteria should have a place alongside the demands of academic discourse.

Language is a gauge of students' world-relatedness, their relation to Being. What do they care for? How do they think about the things of their world—what they have been thrown into? How do they know what they know? These questions are not just cues for invention but ways of thinking about what care and thrownness indicate: the unasked-for responsibility of being human. In the writing classroom, giving students the opportunity to uncover their thrownness and articulate their connections to the world is a key assignment that encourages students to reflect on their own authenticity and autonomy. Writing invites the interplay of these processes that a priori openness makes possible for all human beings: of caring and not caring for the entities with which a human being is cast alongside at birth; of building, dismantling, and rebuilding conceptions; of rethinking the world logically, abstractly, emotionally, poetically. In addition, writing that recognizes essential openness does not draw dichotomies between affective and cognitive experiences—as Worsham does between the "sensuous and emotional" and the "conceptual and abstract" (236)—but invites the play of all thinking that encounters Being in its fullness. This fullness integrates the sensuous, the emotional, and the intellectual, unbinding the systematization and dichotomies inherent in Western rhetoric's conventions. In Heraclitean terms, writing and teaching in the traditional composition classroom often seem estranged from that Being with which they should be most familiar.

Writing reveals the integration of the processes inherent in being human, and, in turn, writing is at the heart of the discipline of composition studies. But what is the relation of composition studies to language—to that which manifests the human mode of being by speaking to it of its being-in-the-world? Thus far, as Worsham makes apparent, the trend in composition studies has been to conceptualize language as, and reduce it to, an instrument used to control and bring order to the world. Language acquisition and growth are cultivated to promote efficient management of experience:

> Although [composition theorists] now talk about language as the center and ground of human being and making, although we recognize that human being and experience are verbal constructs, we simultaneously turn this new substratum into an instrument and resource, our ultimate instrument and resource, for formulating solutions and making answers. What makes epistemic theories of writing so powerful and popular, in fact, is that they manage to take language out of our hands, so to speak, and acknowledge its centrality and at the same time place language in our hands as our principal instrument for the production of knowledge and selfhood. Once language is recognized as our quintessential instrument, what appears to be a new subject position for human being opens up: The intellectual property manager, whose business is to mobilize all beings in the creation of knowledge as a commodity, to oversee the distribution of that knowledge, and to adjudicate over rights to knowledge.
> (Worsham 217)

Composition studies shows an alarming tendency first to disregard the nature of being human and second to subvert the relation between human beings and language. In the context of hermeneutic phenomenology, writing—the wellspring of composition studies—is the site for recognizing *what* it is to live as a human being and *how* language defines that being over time. The direction of the relation between human beings and language distinguishes Heidegger's later works. The radical reorientation toward language that his key term *saying* implies brings into question, as Worsham has shown, composition studies' own relation to language.

To speak, people must first listen carefully to what the world has to say. Standing out and open, human beings are the world's ready listeners and speakers. The world, as a totality of things and meanings, addresses human beings; their language, then, articulates the structure of the totality that the world offers. Kockelmans, paraphrasing Heidegger, explains:

> Language simply *is* Being itself formed into word. But this assertion entails that in the relation between Being as language and *Dasein*'s speaking, the language of Being retains full primacy. Man's authentic speaking is a responding to "the silent voice of Being." . . . The result is that language seems to be at the disposal of *Dasein*, when actually the reverse is the case. It seems as if *Dasein* invented language, whereas in fact it discovers itself only in and with language. It also follows that *Dasein* in its speaking can come to the truth only when its own listening and speaking are directed toward the saying of Being.   (*Truth* 149)

What does careful listening to "the silent voice of Being" reveal to people? How does the Being of the world reveal itself? It becomes known through logos—a term Heidegger retrieves from the pre-Socratics—which is the world presenting to human beings any entity under discussion. Heidegger claims in *Being and Time* that the original meaning of logos has been covered over and " 'translated' (and this means that it is always getting interpreted) as 'reason,' 'judgment,' 'concept,' 'definition,' 'ground' or 'relationship' " (55). Identifying the primary significance of logos as "discourse," however, Heidegger claims that logos "means rather . . . : to make manifest what one is 'talking about' in one's discourse. . . . Discourse 'lets something be seen' . . . : that is, it lets us see something from the very thing which the discourse is about . . ." (*Being* 56). Heidegger's sense of logos entails an active engagement with, an openness to, what the world presents. The logos gives the human mode of being the source of its articulation. It addresses human beings. Their careful response in their own saying makes apparent the directive of logos.

Speaking and writing are two sites of logos where the directive of Being toward the human mode of being is revealed. But what is the logos of the discourse of composition studies? What directive addresses professionals, the responses to which fill composition journals? What does the language of composition studies make manifest? And, in turn, what is the logos of student writing? One answer to all these questions is that for both composition studies and student writing the logos is the human mode of being as it presents itself in discrete worlds over time in written expository and persuasive prose. Essentially, both discourse communities share the same logos. The logos of composition studies is particularly self-reflexive—observations about language *in* language that reveals and persists within the directive of that historical logos. Currently, as Worsham argues, the equipmental character of language predominates in composition studies, bespeaking distance from and control of an entity. But how logos makes itself manifest to the human mode of being changes with the passing of generations: the structure of things and their meanings that constitutes the totality of the world changes over time. Things come to have different meanings; things come to suggest completely different worlds. For example, even in a relatively short time, the notion of process has fluctuated from Louise M. Rosenblatt's processual, transactional theory of reading to the problem-solving strategies espoused by Linda Flower and John R. Hayes to this phenomenological reconsideration. Change is guided silently by the ontological "dif-ference": that unseen middle ground that metes out the measure of all things and grants them a world and, conversely, grants worlds their appropriate things, granting their abiding mode of being. Ontological difference becomes apparent in people's saying of the logos over time and throughout history:

> Being sends itself in different epochs in different ways and, thus, the original saying of the language of Being addresses [humankind] in each epoch in a different way. . . . [The] ontological dif-ference comes-to-pass effectively in all realms of meaning characteristic of that epoch (. . . concerned dealings with things, science, technology, art, social practice, religion, etc.).
>
> (Kockelmans, *Truth* 158)

Because of the shifting sway of the ontological difference and human beings' own historical condition, articulation of logos must be encountered freshly, and this is no easy task.

As "the place where language speaks," human beings "must learn to hear and listen to what the language of Being has to say" (Kockelmans, *Truth* 147). Heidegger's use of the word *speak* in no way implies a contemporary sense of "communicating": people can communicate and "say" very little, while they may remain silent and "speak" profoundly. In his later reflections on language, Heidegger retrieves the sense of *saying* from the Old Norse word *saga*, which means "to show: to make appear, set free, that is, to offer and extend what we call World . . ." (*On the Way* 93). As I noted earlier, the world "says" something, and, in turn, disclosure shows something, lets something appear for its conversants.

The meeting ground for the saying of Being and the human mode of being is the process of thought: thought, which as Heidegger defines it "cuts furrows into the soil of Being," brings the world nearer to people (qtd. in Kockelmans, *Truth* 161). Thrown into a structured world that has preceded them, human beings think the Being of the world—listen to what the world "says," what the world "offers"—and then respond in their utterances to it. As Kockelmans points out, "It is obviously not Dasein's task to construct the 'house of being'; Dasein merely brings it to completion by its thought, which also is the thought of Being" (*Truth* 151). From infancy, human beings move toward this completion, immersed in language that offers them their world in structured form. They comfortably use the language they receive, but, since part of their existential makeup is to be "fallen" into a premade and complete world, does language *speak* to them freshly and do they *respond* to it "authentically"?

When, as Being's articulators, human beings cling to the common or traditional articulation of meaning made apparent within their own historical context, they may be forgoing the opportunity to listen for themselves to Being's address and overlooking the possibility of an "authentic" response to its saying—both hallmarks of fully realized being-in-the-world. This kind of originality born of uncovering, listening, thinking, and then saying is all too frequently the province of only philosophers and poets, and it need not be so. While teachers of writing demand a certain originality from their students, perhaps the field of composition studies should demand authenticity for itself: practitioners should interrogate their own discipline like philosophers and listen to their world like poets to uncover another thinking of language, another logos.

Within the field of composition studies, essential uncovering, saying, and interpreting disclosures of truth, world, and the human mode of being are nowhere more dynamic than in the writing classroom. Composition and hermeneutic phenomenology find their most compelling common ground there because the classroom is the place for intimate reflection on language's address. Students in writing classrooms bespeak their condition, not so much as mirrors reflecting an external world from which they stand apart, but as voices of their world's being, emitted from within that world. Their thinking reverberates with their attachment to objects, family, friends, community, ethnicity, gender, race, tradition—their involvement with the totality of the world in which they find themselves. Revealing their engagement with the world and, in turn, with Being, their language should make them realize the extent to which they can participate and belong. As Worsham also claims, their language is a gauge of not just literacy but the broad possibilities for seeing the world as it presents itself (236). This recognition takes on great significance for teachers of "nontraditional" students; the students I teach, for example, have yearly family incomes of less than $15,000. For the most part, the first language they possess is an oral one: my students often do not read and write in their first language, even when it is Spanish. This is not to say, however, that the language they speak does not make perfectly vivid their experience in the world: as long as they remain in the discourse community that is their neighborhood, they are fluent. But when they venture outside those neighborhoods, their language disallows their full participation.

The world of academe, for instance, is alien to my students until they assimilate its structures, its matrix of interrelations—*if* they do. At its best, college offers students the language to build bridges between worlds; at its worst, college makes palpable for students the depth and width of the chasm. In particular, students must be receptive to the primacy of language and what it shows or they may not recognize the interdependence of, and the distinction between, the ontic and the ontological in daily life and the usefulness of both ways of coming to experience. Less experienced students are well-versed in the language of the ontic in relating everyday experiences (what they did, what they have, where they went, and so on), but they have a great deal of difficulty identifying the ontological—the meaning of things in their lives. When asked what they *think* about something—particularly topics related to their own experience, such as city housing, child care, or employment possibilities—they know they "feel" one way or another about the subject, but many have a troublesome time articulating in language why they see things as they do. The difficulty is not that they do not know or that they simply lack the argumentative training needed to support a claim. Instead, they are intelligent people whose language fails them: the words do not come to articulate what they have experienced and felt. Because "[l]anguage, by naming beings for the first time, first brings beings to word and to appearance," this deficit is a crucial one (Heidegger, *Poetry* 73). Less experienced with saying, these students lack a close association with *any* language that would help them reveal their own insights; hence, their repertoire of responses seems limited. Teachers inculcated in standard English usage and rhetorical traditions of development and organization sometimes judge these students as remedial—substandard learners whose expression needs "fixing." What they need, however, is experience: to be addressed by language in rich and complex ways and to respond to it.

In my freshman composition course, for example, I use a thematic approach to writing that focuses on choosing right action. I borrow from both traditional, canonical texts and a range of noncanonical works, including selections from Aristotle's *Ethics*, Dante's *Inferno*, and Milton's *Paradise Lost*, and I conclude the course with Spike Lee's controversial film *Do the Right Thing*—a daunting assortment for my students. In both simple and complex ways, my students respond by making it clear who they are and how they stand in relation to the measures of right action these intricate texts support. My colleagues have successfully introduced diverse thematic texts and assignments in *basic* writing courses to give students over to an "experience with language." The focus of instruction is to have students acknowledge their language not in relation to its correctness but in its primal connection to them and their world.

The writing classroom, then, is the ideal place to gauge and appreciate students' openness, uncovering, and saying. The demands of the writing classroom crystallize students' authenticity. Language, in making manifest the being of their world, gives students both possession of that world and possibilities for their own being in a world beyond the barriers of their secure but closed thicket of experience—a place that they, even by their own exclusion, do relate to and are immersed in. Without fluency in language, they stand mute: they can experience their world, but, without articulation, they cannot make it fully present to either themselves or anyone else. To impress on students an ongoing involvement with the rigors of paying attention, listening, thinking, and then responding for their own sakes as human beings, for their own freedom to fully participate in a world: this is the education these phenomenological concepts suggest and the autonomy they invite. Language makes this place, their home, manifest, and this dwelling can be as proportionally large as their capacity for thinking of the whole world in which they find themselves. If composition teachers empower students at all—and this issue is of great contemporary interest—it is not by giving them control over the universe of discourse but by revealing to students how language controls them, directs them, interrogates them, *is* them. Students' empowerment springs from their projective and care-ful thinking of Being: they can choose how to respond to language's profound address.

Students are active histories in the making. Therefore, learning and teaching, by their dynamic connection to these temporal beings, are historical and, in turn, hermeneutic. The political ramifications of the scene of language teaching—in particular, teachers' authority—are argued in composition journals and at conferences. How teachers interpret the beings who populate their classrooms shapes what they let happen in those classrooms. Teachers should be sensitive to their own historicality and its constraints on their understanding of their students' work, as Brenda Deen Schildgen clearly points out in this volume. Where teachers stand within their world affects what they see as possibilities for students' learning. If the instructor's task is to help students think of their own place and their own possibilities, perhaps class discussion could focus on how students know what they know—on the hermeneutics of their own thinking. What history has influenced them? What influences them in their daily lives? What has shaped their thinking? How does work in the classroom mold their thinking? How do they relate to their family? to their community? to their country? How do they see themselves fitting in? Where do they stand? Can they move toward defining the context in which they find themselves and the influences that constrain their thinking? Hermeneutic activities—such as tracing the meanings a word or concept has had for a group of people over time or interpreting the meaning of things and events in both the present and the past—could confront students with the question of meaning in their own lifetime and in the lifetimes of other historical peoples. Such simple activities, mainstays of many disciplines, could help students know where they stand in time and in relation to their world. And in an age where pluralism is the goal of a balanced curriculum, this type of activity defines not just historical distinctions but cultural ones as well.

Hermeneutic phenomenology, however, also points up those basic structures that unify in their essence a diverse student population. Students need to feel integrated into a larger, meaningful totality that shapes their lives and minds. And, since both teachers and students are processes of uncovering and articulators of Being's address, meaning is always new and freshly negotiated. Apparent in this newness is the recognition of a continuous generation of possibilities: students should realize that their historical context is not their prison house but an available horizon of choices from which they can partly shape their own being-in-the-world. This realization becomes poignant for nontraditional students who, because of their situatedness, rarely detect inconspicuous opportunities for themselves to participate in a larger world.

Does this Heideggerian interpretation of Dasein's relation to language simply reinforce traditional classroom practices? Not quite. These phenomenological concepts also indicate that, while possessing the home that language builds is important to students, educators must learn that possessing this dwelling does not necessarily mean *controlling* it. Authority, methodology, and systematization—predisposing students to certain kinds of order or imposing control over students' saying—have limitations. Students should have unencumbered experiences with their own thinking; journals, not surprisingly, help in this effort. An implication of these phenomenological points is the limitation of preconceived methods—the reduction of foundationalism. When teachers impose a sense of order on a subject, when they try to control it for the sake of expedience, they remove themselves from a closer experience with the subject as it is. Of course, to be a teacher is to understand fully the necessity of order, of choosing what students will study and how; we cannot teach coherently without a rationale. While the authority we assume and the methodology we use serve practical classroom goals, we must carefully assess their power to supplant students' thinking. When adopting methodological approaches, teachers can overlook students' direct experience with the language of their texts. Perhaps teachers intervene too much early on in students' writing processes, undercutting students' own articulation for the sake of guiding them to more "traditional" and acceptable forms of expression. In the end, whether students share their thinking in peer-critiquing sessions for student writing or in teacher evaluations, they will be asked to meet the demands of the interpretive community. Students face the task of determining just how they want to relate to the community in which they find themselves. How should they remake their thinking? Who should influence their choices? Why? How do they choose to stand out? When students critique themselves and their condition and recognize the validity of their opinions in relation to the standards of the discourse communities they occupy, they can achieve a sense of empowerment.

In making their thinking manifest for themselves and others students should both answer the needs of their community, for they are part of a world, and realize how they stand out in relation to the world of others. "Ek-sisting" is not easy, but we must always remember and recall to our students the primacy of their own openness, their own reception. Obviously, the first consideration in a more human and humane teaching rationale would be not to inculcate but to lead students to understand the traditions of discourse in which they find themselves. Perhaps the dilemma of preconditioning students' responses cannot be overcome, but we can have a greater respect for students' authenticity and be more comfortable with their all too frequent confusion. Students must learn to indulge in the recursive and frustrating processes indicative of their being-in-the-world: they must return to, rethink, and remake anything of value in their reading and writing.

In recognizing that uncovering and saying are fluid—indeed, slippery and elusive—modes of being, composition studies invites what was once left suppressed: mystery. For students, teachers, and scholars, standing open to the world and listening intently to the "songs" it reveals are risky interpretive practices. To acknowledge oneself as a process—as a being whose job, as it were, is to report from the milieu the connectedness of the surrounding world—is a mysterious position indeed. Therefore, the phenomenologist's role demands a kind of negative capability: that of being immersed in the world's confusions without what Keats might call an irritable grasping after fact, reason, or a presupposed order. Keats's negative capability is phenomeno-logical in its emphasis on receptivity and an active, thoughtful acceptance of the world—an energetic pursuit of the mysterious process that reality unfolds, which human beings can never fully grasp but only uncover and say again and again over time. Mystery and the confusion in response to it are not causes for alarm: they signal a return to the familiar condition of being human—of discovering the topology of Being as it presents itself. But, contrary to what Worsham suggests, tracing the otherness of what addresses the human mode of being does not alleviate alienation from the world and the earth. The dilemma is that human beings are both *comfortable* in the thicket of their received world and estranged from that with which they should be most familiar, from what they articulate daily: Being. Completely engaged in the ineffability of language, composition studies must return students and teachers alike to the processes of their own being-in-the-world and the richness of their own thinking of Being that undoes all common expression; it must, that is, help them articulate where they stand and how they stand out.

LaGuardia Community College, City University of New York

Self-Reflection as a Way of Knowing: Phenomenological Investigations in Composition

Barbara Gleason

AS A philosophical and methodological perspective on composition, phenomenology has received increasing attention in the past decade. When Janet Emig discusses phenomenology as one of three "governing gazes" for research on reading and writing, she defines the phenomenological gaze as one that "examines how the world is experienced" and "the nature of that world for the perceiver" ("Inquiry Paradigms" 162). With this description, Emig provides a generally recognizable definition of phenomenology, one that many theorists would be likely to accept. Beyond this level of generality, however, lie numerous interpretations of phenomenology, a story that originates with the philosophical speculations of Edmund Husserl and continues with revisions of his phenomenology by Martin Heidegger, Jean-Paul Sartre, Maurice Merleau-Ponty, Paul Ricoeur, and many others. Among philosophers, these revisions of phenomenology, which emphasize experience or consciousness, eventually give way to the social scientists' concern with "structures" of language and culture.

If we trace the evolution of phenomenology, we discover a fascinating history of ideas that reveals the twentieth-century epistemological shift from a focus on consciousness to a focus on language, text, and interpretation. In effect, this shift in focus turns on arguments that all experience/consciousness is permeated by language (structures) to such a degree that it must be understood as language or as some kind of text (Ricoeur, *Hermeneutics*). While we can observe this trend in the work of many scholars, Jacques Derrida's "reading" of Husserl in *Speech and Phenomena* is a particularly obvious example. Derrida challenges Husserl's distinction between private speech and public speech, arguing that (public) language always inhabits private thought/speech and therefore that private thought/speech really does not exist. This argument, of course, also disputes the notion that we can access our own thoughts (as they exist apart from language or as they exist as products of individual minds rather than as products of culture or language). From the perspective of deconstruction (as a philosophy laid out by Derrida), it would not make sense to talk about reflecting on one's own thinking or on experience; in fact, it would not even be appropriate to speak of reflecting on language since language, which has a will of its own, is not subject to the control of language users.[1] Thus does phenomenology (as philosophy of consciousness) position itself in opposition to deconstruction (as philosophy of language), with each leading to separate, highly consequential conclusions about the act of writing, the writer, and, indeed, the field of composition.

As we consider the implications of a phenomenological approach to understanding composition and our own practices within the scope of this field, it is essential to continually foreground the basic tenet that we can access our own thoughts through self-reflection, a practice that may best be understood as an art. In acts of self-reflection, we make our own thoughts (or experience) the object of our attention.[2] For Husserl, this capacity for self-reflection is fundamental to cognition:

> Living in the *cogito* we have not got the *cogitatio* [mental act] consciously before us as intentional object; but it can at any time become this; to its essence belongs in principle the possibility of a *"reflexive"* directing of the mental glance towards itself naturally in the form of a new *cogitatio* and by way of a simple apprehension. In other words, every *cogitatio* can become the object of a so-called "inner perception." (111)

As Husserl goes on to discuss consciousness and our ability to reflect on acts of consciousness, he develops an important distinction between the processes involved in contemplating one's own mental acts and those involved in grasping realities that exist apart from, or that transcend, one's experience. Despite his belief in the accessibility of both kinds of realities, Husserl holds that acts of consciousness (feelings, attitudes, perceptions, expectations, etc.) are most available to us via self-reflection, thus making consciousness the most favorable focus for phenomenological forms of inquiry. To begin such an investigation, a person might compose highly personal descriptions of actual experience, much like those Donald Murray has produced on writing and conferencing. Eventually, however, these cases of individual experience give way to descriptions that foreground properties common to all such experiences or, in Husserl's terms, descriptions that capture the essence of a general category of experience or mental act.

While Husserl and others consider self-reflection to be inherent to cognition, some theorists have also described it as one of several types of intelligence. When approached from this perspective, the capacity to be aware of one's own thoughts can be considered both a sort of intelligence and an art: a capacity that comes to some more naturally than to others but that can be developed (at least in some degree) by almost everyone.

For Howard Gardner, "intrapersonal intelligence" is but one aspect of a broader category, "personal intelligence," which is juxtaposed to other intelligences (linguistic, musical, logical-mathematical, spatial, and bodily-kinesthetic). Although Gardner limits intrapersonal intelligence to the domain of "affect," his depiction of this capacity introduces the idea of self-reflection:

> The core capacity at work here is access to one's own feeling life—one's range of affects or emotions: the capacity instantly to effect discriminations among these feelings and, eventually, to label them, to enmesh them in symbolic codes, to draw upon them as a means of understanding and guiding one's behavior. In its most primitive form, the intrapersonal intelligence amounts to little more than the capacity to distinguish a feeling of pleasure from one of pain. . . . At its most advanced level, intrapersonal knowledge allows one to detect and to symbolize complex and highly differentiated sets of feelings.
>
> (239)

If Gardner's definition is broadened to include thought as such (whether by means of introspection or retrospection), his concept of intrapersonal intelligence includes the capacity for self-reflective thought.

Although introspection is fundamental to human cognition, it often meets with a good deal of suspicion when proposed as a valid way of knowing: Is introspective analysis appropriate for the study of cognition? We might respond by examining actual phenomenological descriptions for signs of legitimacy as we filter them through the lens of our own experience. A successful phenomenological description awakens in others recognition of a common experience since the validity of such descriptions is in part self-evident, as Max Van Manen explains:

> The essence or nature of an experience has been adequately described in language if the description reawakens or shows the lived quality and significance of the experience in a fuller or deeper manner. . . . [I]n the words [of a phenomeno-logical description], or perhaps better, *in spite* of the words, we find "memories" that paradoxically we never thought or felt before.   (10, 13)

The best phenomenological descriptions invoke "memories," or re-cognitions of experiences, in a way that allows for fuller understanding and appreciation of these memories as instances of a general type.

Other concerns about introspection are that during the process of self-reflection, the object of these reflections (experience or consciousness) changes in essential ways; that introspective accounts of experience may suffer from lack of completeness; and that the depth of these accounts may be inadequate for purposes of research (Sternglass 1–43). Since Marilyn Sternglass has addressed these problems extensively (see *The Presence of Thought*), I limit my own response to the first concern, that in thinking about our own mental acts we alter them in essential ways. Discussions about introspection and self-reflection advance this claim relatively often; however, as Husserl points out, the claim is itself based on the notion that someone can actually reflect on thought effectively enough to make this claim:

> He who merely says, I doubt the significance of reflexion for knowledge, maintains an absurdity. For as he asserts his doubt, he reflects, and to set this assertion forth as valid presupposes that reflexion *has* really and without a doubt (for this case in hand) the very cognitive value upon which doubt has been cast, that it does not alter the objective relation, that the unreflective experience does *not* forfeit its essence through the transition into reflexion.   (209)

In addition to Husserl's challenge to the logic of this assertion, a study of a great many verbal reports of thought reveals that verbalization of cognition (except in perceptual-motor tasks and visual encoding) does not change cognitive processes (Ericsson and Simon).

As we in composition and rhetoric have become more concerned with philosophical perspectives (that is, with the epistemological and ontological underpinnings of teaching and research practices), self-reflection has become increasingly significant as a way of knowing. Since we are unwilling to deify any one approach or method, we must continually seek to distinguish among philosophical and methodological perspectives and to position ourselves within the geography of the field. Several studies have aimed to uncover differences in philosophical perspectives, including James Berlin's and Lester Faigley's analyses of pedagogies, C. H. Knoblauch's analysis of rhetorical statements, and Janet Emig's analysis of inquiry paradigms (see Berlin, *Rhetoric*; Faigley, "Competing"; Knoblauch, "Rhetorical"; Emig, "Inquiry Paradigms"). With this heightened awareness of perspective, it is difficult for us to avoid examining our own philosophical assumptions as professionals in composition. Do we, for example, subscribe to a social constructionist epistemology or to some form of realism? And how do these philosophical leanings affect our teaching and research? The basis for this type of thinking is self-reflection, which brings self-reflective thought into the limelight of a field whose "central purpose has been to make room for . . . many voices, to imagine a multi-vocal, dialogical discipline that reflects in its actions its theoretical opposition to a unifying, dominant discourse" (Bartholomae, "Freshman English" 49).

Along with fostering the development of a professional identity, self-reflection plays a vital role in the teaching of writing and serves as a rich, though largely untapped, source of knowledge about reading and writing. As writing instructors, we have long felt the need to observe intentions, creative moments, acts of reading, and other types of mental acts, both our own and those of our students. In working with our students, we can often make inferences about their thinking on the basis of conferences and written products. For instance, we may see that a student is having difficulty making a specific type of logical relation (e.g., cause and effect) and then use this knowledge to help the student further. Indeed, we commonly recognize that an essential part of teaching writing is teaching students to think, even though there are differences of opinion about what this means (see Lauer; Berthoff).

How might we approach instruction in thinking? One strategy, teaching the use of heuristics, can make students aware of their own thought processes. In fact, most forms of "process" pedagogy focus primarily on invention (which requires students to attend to their own thinking), and many theorists have argued that metacognition (or metalinguistic awareness) is central to literacy, that people capable of reflecting on their own thought (and language) may attain the highest degrees of literacy. In arguing for the broadest possible definition of literacy, Robert Pattison proposes that "we allow each age to express literacy for itself, within the broad guideline that literacy must always refer to consciousness of language and skill in deploying this consciousness" (6–7).

When this emphasis on self-reflection emerges in pedagogy, we find students contemplating their own past experiences and writing descriptions that are more or less consciously phenomenological in purpose. The composing-process assignment and the practice of writing literacy autobiographies can both be understood as exercises in self-reflective thinking.

In a recent textbook, Peter Elbow and Pat Belanoff tell students, "[M]eta-cognition gives you power over your future learning and over yourself." Elbow and Belanoff explicitly refer to self-reflection as fundamental for writers: "Writing about writing . . . because it consists of self-reflective thinking . . . is the most cognitively sophisticated writing" (*Community* 181). Essential to their pedagogy are exercises in self-reflective thinking that require student writers to transform experience into words and to provide readers with a vicarious experience, much as the phenomenological description is intended to do:

> In a nutshell: if you want to get your reader to experience something, *you* must experience it. If you want your reader to see something, then put all your effort into *seeing it*; give all your attention to having a hallucination. Don't worry about words; worry about seeing. When you can finally see it, just open your mouth and start the pen moving and let the words take care of themselves. They may not be elegant or well-organized words; you can take care of that

problem later. But if you are actually seeing what you are describing, your words will have some of that special quality that gives your experience to the reader. (*Community* 78–79)

This pedagogy of experience features deliberately phenomenological exercises and an emphasis on self-reflective thinking that continues throughout the book.

In "Unit 4: Experience into Words: Description," Elbow and Belanoff invite students to practice experiencing an object and to write descriptive reports of their experiences. This exercise relies on the important distinction between *an object* and *the experience of that object*. In phenomenological descriptions, an awareness of this distinction allows the observer to focus on perceptions of the object (its perceived properties) rather than on previously known theories about the object, theories that may interfere with a person's ability to know the object on its own terms. Without explicitly explaining this theoretical background, Elbow and Belanoff advise students as follows:

[F]ix your eyes steadily on your object and describe it so that listeners *see* it. . . . The main traps you can fall into here are storytelling, memories, and feelings: talking about when you got the pen, who gave it to you, your attachments to it, and so forth. Save all that for another time and keep yourself focussed solely on the physical attributes of the object. (*Community* 80–81)

Students who acknowledge a difference between their perceptions of the pen (or any object) and their feelings about, or memories of, the pen may more readily appreciate their ability to choose among the many available types of cognition and to control their own cognitive acts. Elbow and Belanoff direct students to describe the experience of the object and not to tell a story about the object.

William Wallis has developed a similar pedagogy for his classes at a community college in Los Angeles. Wallis takes students through a sequence of tasks, each requiring students to write descriptions of an experience of some object. Working with both native and nonnative speakers of English, Wallis frequently uses a statue of Venus to draw students' attention to symbolic content and the relation between one's culture and the ability to "read" cultural artifacts. When students of diverse backgrounds describe the physical properties of the statue, they produce recognizably similar accounts of their perceptions. As they move on to the meaning (or value) of the object and then to their individual attitudes (like, dislike, curiosity, surprise), it becomes evident that experience has both an objective and a subjective dimension, each of which constitutes an essential aspect of cognition. As Wallis uses this pedagogy from semester to semester, he finds that students at all levels of instruction can become adept at self-reflection and integrate this ability into their development as writers and readers.

While not all teachers aim to teach self-reflective thinking, most engage in some type of self-reflection in class, in conferences, and as readers of student texts. Indeed, many teachers are now arguing for a more cohesive perspective on research, theory, and pedagogy, one that grounds theory in practice rather than the reverse. Dixie Goswami, a well-known advocate, has articulated a motivation for teacher research:

> Increasingly, teachers feel the need to ask research questions themselves and to verify their intuitions. Instead of being the objects of specialists' observations and evaluations, they want to observe, document, and draw conclusions for themselves—and they want to do so throughout their professional lives.
>
> (347)

As teachers turn more and more to their own experience as an authoritative source of knowledge, they may become acutely aware of their own observations and make these observations objects of their inner perceptions. This focus on experiential knowledge does not mean that teachers forget what they know of theories and research; however, theories and research may not carry quite as much weight as they might when individual perception and introspection are viewed suspiciously as invalid, unreliable, or too subjective. In contrast to the traditional scientist, many teacher-researchers share with the phenomenologist a greater confidence in individual perception and introspection as sources of knowledge (for samples of teacher research, see Goswami and Stillman; Perl and Wilson).

This confidence extends equally to work less directly associated with teacher research. Studies on acts of reading and composing are highly appropriate for phenomenological investigation, which typically begins with self-reflective analysis of particular types of mental acts. One area of phenomenological inquiry, reading and responding to student texts, has recently become so active that many interpretive perspectives are now vying for attention. Margaret Himley, in a distinctly phenomenological approach that draws on Patricia Carini's work, devises a method she calls "deep talk" (see her *Shared Territory* and "Reflective Conversation"). Rather than produce individual descriptions of the reading experience, Himley suggests that teachers collaboratively read and talk about student texts. This process engages teachers in a communal discussion of pedagogy and opens up understandings of the general experience of reading student texts. Himley's method involves reading a student text aloud, paraphrasing sections of that text, making observations about it, and summarizing its features.

One advantage of this collective reading experience, Himley argues, is that it promotes a deeper understanding of the reading process, in part because these "reflective procedures provide time for readers to come at a text from multiple perspectives, to engage with and dwell in the materiality of that text, to construct a writer cued by textual choices, to remember one's own writing experiences and to imagine the writer's current one" ("Reflective Conversation" 16). Other advantages of the method are the pleasure of shared time with a text, a welcome relief from the isolation of grading student essays, and the opportunity to develop a community of teachers and readers. Himley's method allows for a sharing of experience that can deepen the insights available to the individual reader. She has also added a social dimension to an approach that some would criticize for being solipsistic.

In developing a conceptual schema for reading, Louise W. Phelps has sought to identify specific types of reading experiences by distinguishing different ways of seeing student texts ("Images"). Drawing from her graduate students' descriptions of reading their students' work, Phelps outlines four general attitudes that define reading experiences and four related understandings of student texts:

	Attitude	*Object of Reading*
1.	Evaluation (summative)	Closed text
2.	Process (formative)	Evolving text
3.	Developmental	Corpus of writing (portfolio)
4.	Contextual	Text or context (situation or field of discourse)

Although these attitudes toward the student text could describe the teacher's development—that is, the way experience makes a teacher read student texts differently—they are actually meant to show the *discipline's* development in understanding this reading experience.

This particular research is most salient in calling to mind phenomena of which all experienced teachers are at least tacitly aware. Experienced teachers immediately recognize the essential differences between reading a text as finished product and reading a text as a phase in a formative process. As Van Manen writes, "[T]he description reawakens or shows the lived quality and significance of the experience in a fuller or deeper manner" (10). This reawakening and invitation to deeper insight validate the phenomenological description as a successful project. Moreover, in this sensitive portrayal of teachers as readers, we find the first comprehensive introduction to an entire domain of inquiry that Phelps has termed "pedagogical hermeneutics":

[T]he study of pedagogical hermeneutics as a field where students and teachers engage in dialogue and conflict has the same radical potential for enlarging our horizons that we felt in early composing process research.   ("Images" 64)

Although she is not the first to discuss the reading of student texts, her analysis enlarges our understanding of this domain as no other scholarship has.

Along with the works of Himley and Phelps, a third phenomenologically oriented study of reading, by Joseph Williams, sets out to understand error as it is experienced by the reader. Errors, he contends, can be experienced differently (perhaps not even as errors) by various readers. Williams demonstrates this point exquisitely by inserting one hundred "errors" in his own text and inviting readers to find them.

Analogous to grammatical error is social error, which occurs in the flux of human interaction. Williams notes that grammatical error can be viewed as a process, rather than a discrete entity, as

> part of a flawed transaction, originating in ignorance or incompetence or accident, manifesting itself as an invasion of another's personal space, eliciting a judgment ranging from silent disapproval to "atrocious" and "horrible."
>
> (153)

In essence, Williams views error as a flawed transaction between reader and writer, as a cue signaling something about readers' and writers' expectations (e.g., a reader as grammarian or writing instructor with idiosyncratic preferences that influence the reading of student texts). Williams's use of examples reinforces this attitude, for readers can continually monitor their own responses to grammatical faux pas such as *irregardless*, *like* substituted for *as*, *impact* and *enthuse* used as verbs, faulty parallelism, and the use of the conversational *well* in scholarly prose.

Williams's essay, entitled "The Phenomenology of Error," offers a fresh perspective that is rich in implication for writing instructors. Teachers who view errors as flawed transactions may wonder whether communication breakdowns are related to students' writing maturity and linguistic competence or to both the teachers' and the students' linguistic and cultural backgrounds. Instructors may even find that some students who deliberately flout convention can ably articulate their reasons for doing so.

The phenomenological spin on all this is Williams's call for readers to understand error in the light of their experience. New questions arise: What is experienced as error? How serious is a particular error perceived to be and why? Are some errors experienced more universally as error than others are, and, if so, why? These and other questions may usefully enter into a writing instructor's thinking during evaluation of student texts; in addition, the teacher enters into self-reflective considerations of the act of evaluating itself. This act of self-reflective thought is likely to enhance the teacher's art as a reader of student texts.

Supplementing these three studies are many self-reflective investigations of composing, both by professional writers and by composition instructors (see, e.g., Waldrep). The most clearly phenomenological work is Phelps's "Rhythm and Pattern in a Composing Life," an inquiry into Phelps's own experience with composing over time. In the process of conducting her investigation, Phelps brackets, or sets aside, two dominant assumptions about composing: the first is that composing generally refers to the particular act of producing a text; the second is that composing is best, or even solely, understood in the dimension of time. By bracketing these two theories, Phelps allows us to see composing as a way of living, as a process woven into the fabric of routine daily activities and writerly practices. Once described, this encompassing view of composing becomes beautifully obvious (i.e., it invokes re-cognitions of experiences while deepening our understandings of these experiences in essential ways), even while we recognize this as an experience that many of our students have not had. For these students, there is no composing life *per se* but, rather, (an often painful) activation of strategies for short-term task completion.

As an illustration of phenomenological inquiry, this re-cognition of composing demonstrates the possibility of setting aside theories about some phenomenon in order to experience it on its own terms, as advocated by Husserl. In reflecting on her own composing, Phelps never forgets the production of texts or the temporal dimension of composing; she simply chooses to put these issues aside for a while to arrive at a better understanding of composing. With this deliberate act of mind, Phelps demonstrates the possibility that Husserl has called bracketing:

> What I am trying to do here—a beginner's effort—is to intensify that self-reflective attitude to approach the level and quality of phenomenological description, which involves not only intuiting, analyzing, and describing particulars of composing in their full concreteness, but also attempting to attain insight into the essence of the experience. A primary obstacle to this goal is the conceptual baggage I carry—the labels, concepts, distinctions, and assumptions I have absorbed from existing rhetorical or composing theory and the teaching tradition. In order to clarify my intuitions and open myself patiently to the truth of my own experiences, I need to bracket or hold in abeyance two aspects of my composing that carry a heavy burden of prejudices. Formulating and maintaining those brackets has been the most difficult and rigorous task in composing this account, requiring constant vigilance.
>
> (Phelps, "Rhythm" 243–44)

Husserl concedes that it is difficult, sometimes impossible, to set aside assumptions and theories. But he does not say that it is always impossible, especially for someone with a trained mind, someone like Phelps, who knows both her own habits of mind and new cognitive strategies that she can employ. If asked, Husserl would likely contend that this type of self-reflective thought is an art that can be developed through time.

Another telling aspect of Phelps's self-study is her effort to identify essential qualities of her own composing. While she makes no claim about the composing lives of others, Phelps does find, in her own work, an "essence" consisting of principles that generally define her experience of composing over time. This raises an interesting issue about universals that can best be expressed as a question: Are there "universals" of individual experience, that is, principles that define the repeated experiences of one person? In other words, is this one type of universal?

Phelps's study is unique in identifying defining principles rather than sequential steps in a process, an approach Phelps explains as a deliberately phenomenological form of inquiry:

> Much earlier than my intuition of the dialectic of generative and discursive impulses, I recognized "generating," "structuring," and "focusing" as the three most distinctive molar experiences of my composing life. . . . By rigorously striving for the suspension of textual particularity and temporality I succeeded in conceiving these as abstract, unordered phases or "moments." . . . I am using "moments" in the phenomenological sense, not as temporal points (though they have complex temporal implications) but as contextual elements of concrete experience that can be conceived separately only by abstraction.
>
> ("Rhythm" 246)

This passage clearly indicates Phelps's use of phenomenological strategies in her conscious attempt at this sort of inquiry. Both the endeavor to define the essence of her composing and the deliberate bracketing of assumptions make this a very close approximation to a study of the kind Husserl would advocate.

While Phelps's self-study aligns itself with a Husserlian approach, Phelps shares with Himley and Williams a confidence in introspective analysis as a way of knowing. Any object may become the focus of reflective thought, including both phenomena that are immanent to experience and phenomena that transcend experience. From Husserl's perspective, our own cognitive acts, for example, of composing and reading, are most accessible to reflective thought, but we can also reflect on error and on student texts, as Williams and Phelps have demonstrated. Moreover, there are different ways of conducting and presenting self-reflective investigations, some more formal than others. Much research suggests that teachers need not be well versed in the philosophical issues to conduct this type of study, that even beginning teachers can reflect on their own practices and on issues they identify as important in their classrooms. Indeed, one potential value of self-reflection is that it may facilitate teachers' development in such areas as conferencing and the reading of student texts.[3] Another virtue, the linking of philosophical speculation and descriptive studies of experience, is particularly important since composition and rhetoric aim to integrate different levels of understanding or inquiry and various ways of knowing.

While some scholars find the epistemological issues most intriguing, others are more concerned with the actual practice of self-reflection and with descriptive-analytical studies of experience. In fact, there is a tension between these two branches of phenomenology: the consideration of abstract issues versus the careful analysis of experientially grounded descriptions. While such tension can result in some forms of cognitive dissonance, it can also prove to be the most rewarding aspect of working within this philosophical tradition. Layers of understanding become intricately interwoven as we strive to negotiate the immediate world of experience with timeless questions about knowing and being.[4]

City College of New York

NOTES

[1] See, for example, Derrida's discussion of an inherent violence in language in "A Discussion with Jacques Derrida." Here, Derrida claims that while one may imagine a nonviolent linguistic gesture, one cannot control one's own language to produce a purposefully nonviolent language: "Non-violence, or pure non-violence, cannot be calculated, but perhaps it can happen" (11).

[2] The terms *consciousness, mental act,* and *act of cognition* all signpost the Husserlian emphasis on the study of consciousness; the term *experience* was substituted for these earlier terms by many existentialist phenomenologists. All those terms can be found in the phenomenological literature today, and I have not used them to indicate particular philosophical leanings in specific contexts. Instead, I use the more general term *experience* except when I wish to call attention to mental experience or to a specifically Husserlian approach to phenomenology.

[3] Both Phelps and Sternglass have used self-reflective methods to facilitate the development of teachers. See Sternglass, *The Presence of Thought*.

[4] For my investigation of phenomenology and composition, I am deeply indebted to a community of scholars at the University of Southern California. I would especially like to acknowledge my professors Dallas Willard and W. Ross Winterowd and my colleagues Mark Wiley, Barry Freedman, and William Wallis.

POLANYI AND COMPOSITION:
A PERSONAL NOTE ON A HUMAN SCIENCE

Richard J. Murphy, Jr.

THE SUN did not rise until 8:30 on those early January days. In the predawn darkness, I could hear the high heels of village women hurrying down cobbled streets to a bus stop at the bottom of the square. By 9:00, I was settled at the table by the window, looking out on the moors above Grassington, with another cup of tea and Michael Polanyi's *Personal Knowledge*.

I had not expected to be reading on those mornings. I had come to England to write a draft of a book on the teaching of writing. Once there, however, like many travelers, I found myself dislocated. Then, only days after arriving, I was suddenly called home by my father's death. When I got back to Grassington, I could not write. Instead, I turned to Polanyi, whose book I had for years been urging myself on scrap-paper notes to read and had at the last moment thrown into my bag.

Situating Polanyi

If I begin talking about Polanyi by speaking about myself, I take my cue from the first pages of *Personal Knowledge*: "As human beings, we must inevitably see the universe from a center lying within ourselves. . . . Any attempt rigorously to eliminate our human perspective from our picture of the world must lead to absurdity" (3). It is no exaggeration to say that my knowledge of Polanyi is inseparable from that room in the north of England and a memory crowded with life and death.

The window of the flat overlooked a busy square—shoppers with grocery baskets for meat and vegetables, walkers come for the footpaths in the Yorkshire Dales National Park, herds of sheep being moved down to a lower field in preparation for spring lambing. My room was full, too. Of sadness. Of promise. Of intimation. The word *intimation* is Polanyi's. It describes not only the book I was unable to write but my feeling of approaching ever nearer to it as I read:

> In the absence of any formal procedure on which the discoverer [can] rely, he
> is guided by his intimations of a hidden knowledge. He senses the proximity
> of something unknown and strives passionately towards it.   (395–96)

For almost twenty years, in four different colleges, I had been teaching
freshman writing. For the last several years, I had been supervising graduate
students who were teaching freshman composition at Radford University.
With their encouragement, I was trying to write down what I had been
teaching. One chapter on generating ideas in writing was complete in draft,
as were others on the architecture of groups, syllabus design, and the first
day of class. But I did not believe my own words and did not know why. I
cited Elbow, Emig, Knoblauch and Brannon, Macrorie, Mohr, Murray, and
others—writers whose books I had asked the graduate students to read, books
that had made a difference in my teaching. But I did not quite believe my
citations either. What had seemed vital in my work felt passionless in my
written words.

So I gazed out the window and read Polanyi and remembered, as he did,
the strange mix of experience that had brought me there. Describing the
situation of his own knowing and experience, Polanyi says:

> I must admit now that I did not start the present reconsideration of my beliefs
> with a clean slate of unbelief. Far from it. I started as a person intellectually
> fashioned by a particular idiom, acquired through my affiliation to a civilization
> that prevailed in places where I had grown up, at this particular period of
> history. This has been the matrix of my intellectual efforts. Within it I was to
> find my problem and seek the terms for its solution. All my amendments to
> these original terms will remain embedded in the system of my previous beliefs.
> Worse still, I cannot precisely say what these beliefs are. I can say nothing
> precisely. The words I have spoken and am yet to speak mean nothing; it is
> only *I* who mean something *by them*.   (252)

Polanyi's words called up the matrix of my own beliefs. I started as a person
fashioned at least in part by the schools I attended and the teachers with
whom I studied. I felt what school was, imagined what teaching was, built
up for myself an ineffable system of beliefs, and yet could not, cannot, say
precisely what they are.

When I was in the ninth grade at Saint Joseph's High School in Mountain
View, California, Father Olivier taught us music in the basement of an ancient
four-story stone building. In a room with impossible acoustics—concrete
floor, steam pipes running across the ceiling—he tried to lead us in singing
Gregorian chant. His hair was jet black. The whitest French cuffs I had ever
seen extended perfectly beyond his cassock sleeves. I watched him, enraptured,

the day he sat in one of our scarred wooden desks, head resting against one hand, eyes closed, and listened all through class to Beethoven's Sixth Symphony.

Years after I began teaching English at Moreau High School, a former student told me something I had not known: that what made him want to listen and learn in that sixth-period, tenth-grade class was not the essays we read about Hiroshima or about Gordon Cooper, astronaut; not Jackson's "Lottery" or Steinbeck's *Pearl*; not the sentences we diagrammed or the books he read in class on Fridays to the accompaniment of Jimi Hendrix or Crosby, Stills, and Nash. One day, early in the year, before I even knew the students' names, a boy had dropped his pencil accidentally on the floor. It rolled to my feet. I bent to pick it up and give it back. "I'd never seen a teacher do that," my former student told me. It was enough to make him trust and try, seeing a teacher, as he said, "be kind like that."

In my first year of graduate school at Berkeley, for a course in medieval literature, I wrote a paper on the allegory of *Piers Plowman*. I did not know what allegory was or quite what I meant to say, and this was my first paper as a graduate student. The class met early on Tuesdays and Thursdays around a large seminar table, and the teacher sat silhouetted against a window of morning light, his face in shadow, two finely sharpened pencils before him on the table next to his copy of the text. I stayed up late finishing my paper, showed it to no one, and knew it could not be very good.

"Do you expect to get a PhD here?" he asked quietly the day I went by his office to pick up my graded work. I must have nodded dumbly, said something, but all I can remember is the softness of his voice and his hard words: "You'd better learn how to write."

During my last spring in graduate school at Berkeley—my dissertation by now already approved—the English department nominated me to be its summer fellow in the Bay Area Writing Project. Jim Gray, the project director, greeted me with a laugh like we were old friends, pressed Ken Macrorie's *Uptaught* into my hands, and dragged me down the hall to meet other members of the staff. After eight years of nearly silent scholarship, I had not been in the Bay Area Writing Project twenty minutes before I was made to feel that I had come home. That summer—with a roomful of other teachers—I heard for the first time about James Britton, got down on the floor to finger-paint, joined my first writing group. One week a little contest was staged for us: we were to take a short piece of good published prose and graft a paragraph to it, so like the original and so seamless that its artifice would be invisible. I won. The prize: Mina Shaughnessy's *Errors and Expectations*, a book just published by an author I'd never heard of.

"Oh, there are so many stories," my father said, as he struggled, in the last years before he died, to tell me about his life. "Have I told you this one?" Stories within stories, in infinite regress, an effusion: as I read Polanyi and thought about the teaching of writing, the room filled with them, his and mine, braiding together.

One summer near the end, he came to visit. He brought sixteen pages of writing about his childhood and youth, nonchalantly handed them to me, and then sat in the chair by the window and watched me read. They were full of fragments I had never heard: the squirrel he had caught as a boy and let get away by half chance to race around the kitchen, terrifying his tyrannical grandmother; the living room window being removed, casing and all, after the wake of his grandfather, in order to get the corpse-filled casket out of the house; the evening they all heard an explosion from his father's bedroom upstairs and ran up to find him smiling at the window, shotgun in hand, having blasted an owl off the barn roof in the dusk; his stepmother reading aloud the weekly subscription of *Argosy* on Saturday night, the family assembled in the kitchen, she sitting in the center on a stool.

My father held his breath as I read, held it until I thanked him and told him how his writing had moved me. Then he explained that he had brought it because I was, as he liked to tell his friends, "his son the writing teacher."

All our knowing is personal, Polanyi says. Intimately personal. We know with minds and bodies, reason and belief. To logic we add our assent. Science is driven by surmise. Every claim we make to truth implies our acceptance of a community of others who we believe will acknowledge the truth we assert. We know the world—facts, machines, poetry, gossip, institutions, other persons, everything—by projecting ourselves into it, by what Polanyi calls "indwelling." In the postcritical twentieth century, Polanyi's is an ode on our mortality: all our knowing in and of the world is an intimation of reality.

I knew it immediately. Reading *Personal Knowledge* in that gray January, I felt with instant conviction the truth of Polanyi's claims for the world of the classroom and for my life as a teacher, as a person.

Knowing and Teaching

In recent years, within the field of composition, a number of attempts have been made to understand and justify the knowledge of practicing teachers. Polanyi's conception of personal knowing is essential to this undertaking, particularly his emphasis on the passionate nature of our knowing, that is, on intimation.

Stephen North's *The Making of Knowledge in Composition* attempts a spirited defense of the knowledge of "practitioners"—writing teachers who are in the classroom, doing their work, while the new field of composition studies defines itself around them. It is not a fully successful defense. The approach North takes in his portrait of the field simplifies the problem of what teachers know and artificially complicates the way they know it. Some readers find the polemical, even feisty, stance he adopts toward his subject and audience more annoying than compelling. Still, by scrutinizing the ways knowledge claims are being made in contemporary composition, North has exposed them as political, an analysis that permits him to dignify the knowledge of teachers. For teachers are, after all, at the center of the field, and their knowing exerts an "epistemological gravitational pull" on all the other kinds of knowledge being made (371).

North's defense of teachers depends in part on his arresting reading of composition's recent history as a field. The "birth of modern Composition, capital C," North says, occurred at the moment the field decided to "replace practice as [its] dominant mode of inquiry." To establish its own place in the academy, "Composition" had to exert "authority over knowledge about composition: what it is, how it is made, who gets to say so and why." In other words, the field had to turn to something that "looked like acceptable, formal, academic inquiry," inquiry "modeled in method and rigor on research in the sciences" (15, 17). Quoting J. N. Hook's 1962 lament that "in English teaching we have relied too long on our best guesses," North concludes that the reorientation of composition meant in effect that "practitioner knowledge . . . would have to be supplanted" (16).

Turning to modes of inquiry that look academically respectable, however, had only an indirect effect on the status of composition teachers. North's analysis traces a more direct and deliberate effect as well. To compete successfully with mathematics and science teaching for federal dollars in the early 1960s, composition declared itself in a state of crisis. In 1961, the NCTE declared that the teaching of literacy was in a "state of chaos," that the nation thus faced a "critical problem," and that what was needed was a "national effort to solve it." But the point North emphasizes is that the report also identifies teachers as the cause of the problem: "Poorly prepared teachers of English have created a serious national problem" (qtd. in North 323, 324).

North cites frequent restatements of this general theme: teachers are thoughtless, illiterate, as stupid as barnyard geese, and appallingly ignorant (326–28). In addition, teachers are intractable. Not only do they lack adequate knowledge but, when given it, they do not seem willing or able to use it properly. Instead, teachers seem satisfied with what Clinton Burhans has called "myths": "beliefs accepted uncritically, [requiring] neither evidence nor proof, neither research nor theory. Indeed, [teachers' beliefs] are impervious over long periods of time to rational inquiry, reasoned argument, or the claims of conflicting research or theory" (qtd. in North 330). North's sprightly restatement of all this criticism indicates his own (opposite) sympathies: "In other words, Practitioners not only have ideas about how to do things, but they actually believe in them" (330).

The task, then, for teachers in the field of composition, as North defines it, is "to defend themselves—to argue for the value of what they know, and how they come to know it" (55). Their defense involves knowing the limits of the authority other knowledge makers in the field can claim—historians, experimentalists, philosophers, and so on. North devotes most of his book to assiduously uncovering and examining these limits. But teachers must also understand the nature and limits of their own knowing, and North is much less successful in suggesting what that knowing is or might be.

The structure of North's analysis, for example, leads him to set up teacher knowledge as a "mode of inquiry" and to outline the "steps" of practice as inquiry:

1. Identifying a Problem;
2. Searching for Cause(s);
3. Searching for Possible Solutions;
4. Testing Solution in Practice;
5. Validation;
6. Dissemination.   (36)

North quickly admits that this account of practitioner inquiry is much tidier than most teachers would recognize. He concedes that teachers tend not to be "methodologically self-conscious" or too concerned with "strict methodological uniformity" (36). Still, North misrepresents teacher knowledge by calling it a "mode of inquiry" at all (as if it were like the other modes he analyzes) and by listing an artificial series of "steps" (as if it proceeded by some clearly formalizable system toward a clearly recognizable end).

Further, in defending teacher knowledge, North leaves out the personal knowing at its core. In his sketch, the end toward which practitioner inquiry aims is lore: "the accumulated body of traditions, practices, and beliefs in terms of which Practitioners understand how writing is done, learned, and taught." Lore is communal, a vast body of knowledge shared by teachers from generation to generation. As such, teachers understand it as a "shared *institutional* experience." North admits that "the individual, finally, decides what to do and whether (or how) it has worked—decides in short what counts as knowledge" (22, 28). But nowhere does he explain how the individual makes these decisions or how teachers know or believe what they do.

In *Composition as a Human Science*, another serious defense of writing teachers, Louise Wetherbee Phelps directly acknowledges the personal dimension of teacher knowledge. With dazzling aplomb, she articulates her argument in the arcane terms of contemporary philosophy. Not one particular teacher appears in her pages, but she argues nevertheless that composition is a human science, a "science of the spirit," in which theory and practice are inseparable. The knowledge sought in the field of composition is "understanding," the application of theory to concrete human situations, or what Hans-Georg

Gadamer (following Aristotle) has called "phronesis" (*Composition* 8, 215). Thus, for Phelps, the knowledge of composition is always knowledge in action, mediated by a knowing person.

This defense is necessary, Phelps explains, because in composition a deep conflict has arisen between theory and practice. The "leaders of reform" in the field have insisted on "rigorously developed knowledge." Eager to establish a "scholarly ethos" for the young discipline, they have insisted on the power of theory to inform teaching, and they have explicitly set out to correct the "incoherent, inconsistent, unreflective beliefs and maxims" of untheorized teaching practice (*Composition* 205, 206). The targets of their corrective action are teachers. Phelps's account of this conflict is another version of the story North has already told: teachers are skeptical, anti-intellectual, even "reactionary"; they "fear and distrust the abstract and they constantly, stubbornly assert the priority of the practical and concrete over 'theory' " (*Composition* 206). What Phelps's book elegantly undertakes is the theoretical defense of this stubborn resistance to theory. It is a sober celebration of the wisdom of practice.

Several different lines of thought lead Phelps to the same end. Among them, she highlights the postmodern notion of the self as "inseparably embedded" in a life world of facts and meanings, thought and action, that precedes the reflection of science and philosophy (*Composition* 23). One particular version of this idea is Paul Ricoeur's assertion that, as Phelps puts it, "philosophy is itself grounded in the prereflective, in concrete human existence and the symbol or poetic word: 'all has been said *before* philosophy, by sign and by enigma,' and it is the symbol itself that gives rise to thought" (*Composition* 92). For John Dewey, too, Phelps says, "experience is itself prereflectively intelligent." In experience, we think and act, guess and guess again, form expectations based on the past and then check them against the present. The experience of every day is thus for Dewey "the laboratory in which philosophical concepts are tested," "the source for the refined methods and products of philosophy," and the testing ground "where reflective concepts can be experimentally verified" (*Composition* 209, 210).

Perhaps the most important concept in Phelps's argument is Gadamer's "phronesis." All the other contemporary theorists whose ideas she brings together point toward one conclusion: knowledge is inseparable from its application in particular situations, and application cannot be strictly technical. Because situations are fluid, the application of knowledge in them requires dynamic acts of knowing—problem recognition and solution, analysis, judgment, tact—none of which can be predetermined. Gadamer gives Aristotle's term *phronesis* to this kind of situational knowing, and Phelps extends it explicitly to teaching. In the composition classroom, she says, "no prescriptions are possible," and teachers' actions are guided by their practical knowhow in what is right and good (*Composition* 215, 217).

As sophisticated as Phelps's defense of teacher knowledge is, it does not fully satisfy. For one thing, her own prose contains some of the impenetrable jargon she admits makes theory suspect. Those who resist theory, she says, frequently do so because they do not believe it is *felt*; its voice does not seem authentic. Too often in Phelps's book—even for readers who appreciate its aims and achievements—theory seems so removed from the classroom as to be irrelevant. Moreover, Phelps's defense of teachers seems finally somewhat reluctant. She began, she explains, by trying to defend theory in a field resistant to it. Only in the end, as a "last irony," she says, did she turn to defending the practical knowing of teachers "against the oppression of theory" (*Composition* xi).

Perhaps because of this reluctance, Phelps does not take her argument far enough. She does not draw out the implication Polanyi would urge us to see in practical wisdom: that our knowing—even of theory—is personal. Phelps does explain Polanyi's ideas about science: "[T]hat scientific practice is rife with unformalizable elements, many of them inaccessible to consciousness and some of them crucial to the claim of rationality." She also extends Polanyi's ideas to the practical experience of teaching: just as intuitive conviction prompts intellectual inquiry, so "the choice to select and enact Theory rests on personal confidence, a sense of rightness and fitness, the gamble that one's tentative commitment will be confirmed by experience" (*Composition* 13, 222). Still, strangely, Phelps ends by asserting that "teachers must respect the possibility that Theory can get at truth." It would be anti-intellectual, she says, for them to trust too much to their own reflection, even when that reflection is undertaken "within a collaborative context, a community in which observations and ideas are shared and tested against one another" (*Composition* 240, 239).

But this conclusion is regressive. Phelps has already painstakingly demonstrated that the "truth" of theory only exists as it is known and applied in situations. She has shown that the practical reflection of teachers is intellectual, is indeed theory itself. What she needs to admit is that all theory when known—as Polanyi says of all knowledge—is fundamentally tacit, ineffable, felt, and passionately believed.

Both North's and Phelps's arguments, in other words, need to be supplemented by the conception of tacit knowing that Polanyi develops in *Personal Knowledge*. In the act of knowing, Polanyi says, we do not focus on what we do. Our knowledge is instrumental, serving the purpose of our action. Our minds are subsidiarily aware of the elements of our act, of their sequence and relation to one another (as we are aware of the heft and texture of tools). But we know these things only tacitly, without fixing our attention on them. What we concentrate on, instead, is the integration of all these elements as a whole. We direct our focal awareness at the end toward which we are acting and toward which we are coordinating (without attending to them) all the separate, intricate elements of our act (*Personal Knowledge* 55–56). Polanyi describes other tacit features of our knowing as well. Acts of anticipation, integration, or intimation are equally inexpressible. We sense the solution to a problem before we can say what it is. We recognize a human face without being able to explain what makes the whole we know. We read and interpret maps of many kinds—models, diagrams, two-dimensional illustrations—and apply them to the objects they represent by an essential but inexpressible insight (88–89). These are familiar examples of our knowing in general: all the knowledge that can be expressed is embedded in a tacit dimension forever beyond saying. Or, as A. N. Whitehead put it, "There is not a sentence which adequately states its own meaning. There is always a background of presupposition which defies analysis by reason of its infinitude" (qtd. in Polanyi 88n1).

Polanyi does not often use teaching as an example, but our knowledge in the act of teaching writing is always tacit in the ways he describes. Whenever we conduct a class, we focus on its dynamic elements. We present specific instructions, prompt or field questions, follow the winding thread of discussion, all the while attending subsidiarily to the plan we hope to realize, even if that plan is to permit the class to assume its own direction and shape. Our working days are full of intimations that guide our practice—the sense that a course is going well or not, for example, or the hunch that we should change a familiar essay or journal assignment to accommodate the needs of these specific students. Every time we diagnose or evaluate a student's writing, we integrate particulars in much the way Polanyi describes our seeing a face and recognizing its complex multiple parts as constituents of some coherent whole. When we read or write a syllabus, we do so with the same insight Polanyi claims we use in interpreting maps—the tacit awareness of unspecified relations among texts, assignments, the dynamic texture of class meetings, and the calendar of the term.

But the reason our knowing is personal involves more than its subtle tacitness. (In fact, as computer simulations of human intelligence become more sophisticated, much of what Polanyi calls "tacit" may turn out to be very quick computations of exactly specifiable elements.) Polanyi argues for the *felt* in the tacit, the *intimate* in the intimation. Our knowing is personal—and not finally formalizable—not simply because it is inarticulate but because we know it. What we know requires an act of personal investment: we know it because we dwell in it. What we know requires an act of assent: we know because we believe. Any statement of our knowledge minus that indwelling faith is incomplete, and no statement can be at once a statement *and* a statement of our belief in it. For Polanyi, that is, our knowledge is fundamentally passionate, and the passion is forever beyond words.

This is what North leaves unacknowledged and what Phelps admits and then denies. This is what was missing from my incomplete manuscript on teaching. This is what filled my room overlooking the Grassington square, as I sat reading Polanyi and remembering: the passionate knowledge of a person.

The Calculus of Intimacy

The closest we have yet come to representing teacher knowledge adequately is through stories. I share the current enthusiasm for them, and I am glad to see them achieve at least a temporary authority in the discourse about teaching and learning in composition and in education generally. Recent issues of *Educational Researcher* have published papers on teacher knowing and "narrative inquiry." The *Harvard Educational Review* has, for several years, been running a regular section of autobiographical reflections called "On Teachers and Teaching." Richard Graves's third edition of *Rhetoric and Composition* has introduced a new group of essays entitled "Stories from the Writing Classroom." And in 1990 an award-winning article in *Teaching English in the Two-Year College* was Joseph Trimmer's "Telling Stories about Stories."

Stories are everywhere these days. Robert Coles argues for their profoundly educative influence in *The Call of Stories*. Carolyn Heilbrun goes further: we can only live, she says, "by the stories we have read or heard" (37). Barbara Hardy says that we cannot keep from telling stories, and Harold Rosen maintains, in *Stories and Meanings*, that stories "become a way in which the story-teller appraises his life-experience" (10). Diane Gillespie, among others, points to the value of narrative specifically for teachers, arguing that stories let us reclaim ourselves as persons in an increasingly bureaucratized profession.

Polanyi's conception of personal knowing helps explain the power of stories in expressing teacher knowledge. In the complex moments of practice, teachers perform intricate acts of knowing, bringing to bear a whole host of ideas, plans, beliefs, expectations, and hopes. They coordinate all they know and believe for a particular purpose in a specific context. But while this coordination remains largely tacit and their knowing largely inexpressible, stories permit them to articulate at least obliquely what they know. Stories give teachers indirect access to the personal acts of interpretation, integration, and insight in which their knowledge of teaching is embedded.

Keith Odell, an instructor at Radford University, told a group of his colleagues about teaching by telling them about flying. In one glorious, improbable afternoon, he had realized the dream of his youth. "Absolute freedom," he called it—piloting an airplane by himself—an adventure as sweet as he had ever imagined it could be. His eyes grew large as he recounted its pleasure aloud: all the hours he had spent at the local airport, cleaning out the hangars, volunteering for the ground crew of the civil air patrol— just to be near the planes; the gift of instructional time his coworkers had given him because they knew he could not afford lessons; his merciless instructor, sitting next to him in the cockpit during training flights, shouting in his ear. And then, at last, he made the flight, an hour in the air alone, without the instructor, the plane quick and light. It was exquisite. Keith could do anything he wanted—dip the wings, roll his turns, climb like Icarus into the sun.

But when he tried to describe his flight in writing, he explained, he experienced the same frustration his students had voiced about their own efforts. His words could not express the full depth of his feeling or convey how important that hour of freedom had been to him. The memory still made him weep and sing with delight (as he flew, he told us, he boomed out at the top of his lungs the only song he knew, "Amazing Grace"). But, unlike his voice and eyes, his writing was flat. The consummate moment of his experience kept coming out sounding like a cliché.

It was a story of frustration and illumination. It marked for him as a teacher a new understanding of his students' writing. He had been asking them to write about personal experiences that were deeply important to them, but when he read what they wrote it was often inert. "I tried to describe what I felt," they would say to him, "but I don't think I've got it yet." Keith's own frustrated writing permitted him to understand that one reason for such failure may be precisely the depth of the feeling. Instead of ending in triumph, then, or in song, his story ended in silence. Yet that silence resonated for those who heard the story, and it filled the room with other stories unspoken.

Another of my colleagues, Jill Kazmierczak, wrote a story about teaching and learning that began with a young man named Chris, a student in her freshman English class. Jill and Chris met in conference to discuss a draft of Chris's paper about his dying aunt's irrepressible spirit. Jill made some suggestions, and Chris went away and came back with an excellent revision. Although Jill congratulated him on his success, she admitted that she secretly chalked it up to the power of conferences and her helpfulness as a writing teacher. "I was taking the bows," she wrote, "thinking—there are the images I suggested he develop; there is the voice of his aunt I suggested he bring in."

Jill's story is really two stories—one about this student, the other about her work with her son at home. They come together in a way all teachers recognize: knowledge is not compartmentalized; homes and classrooms coalesce. Jill is both a writing teacher and a mother; her knowing at school is inseparable from her knowing at home.

One evening she was helping her Laotian foster son prepare for an English spelling test. When they came laboriously to the word *curtain*, Phaythoune made several unsuccessful attempts to spell the last syllable: t-a-n; t-u-n. Jill prompted him with clues. She tried to think of a rule for the difficult diphthong but could not come up with one. Then suddenly, unexpectedly,

Phaythoune looked out the window across the Floyd valley to the mountains in the distance and said, "Mom, 'curtain' similar 'mountain': c-u-r-T-A-I-N."

It was a startling moment for her. It made her laugh, and it made her think—not just about Phaythoune and spelling tests but about Chris and his favorite aunt, about how much credit Jill herself should take for that marvelous revision he had written. Maybe Chris's talk with her in conference, she thought, had had nothing to do with it after all. Maybe Chris had looked out the window like Phaythoune and, in a flash of mysterious insight, seen what he needed. That is what it felt like to Jill. "He'd reached beyond," she wrote. "He'd mentally journeyed to some place I couldn't go. . . . I was no teacher. The learning occurred in his looking through that window."

Jill's narrative about her student and her son glosses Polanyi's account of personal knowledge. Learning how to spell is like looking across the valley to a mountain. Stories about teaching are like windows on a mystery. When Jill concluded that Phaythoune reached beyond, she might just as well have said that he reached *in*. His entering into the patterns of those words was just the sort of imaginative investment of self Polanyi calls indwelling. Chris's insight into the spirit of his aunt, Jill's memory of her work with Phaythoune and Chris, our imaginative participation in her story and Keith's—all these intimate acts of knowing are acts of love.

It was this idea about knowledge that was missing from the manuscript I took to England to write. I had many pages and a working title I wanted to keep, even though I was not sure what it meant—*The Calculus of Intimacy*. As I looked out the window of the flat over the village square, I thought about teaching and read Polanyi and remembered. I had only just begun when the phone message came from California: "Your father," the woman said.

I stood in the rain in the village phone booth, making plane reservations and arranging for a car. It was still night when I drove out of Leeds onto the M-60, passing strange road signs under yellow lamps, on my way to Manchester, London, and then San Francisco for the funeral of my father, his son a writing teacher.

Radford University

Argumentation and Critique: College Composition and Enlightenment Ideals

George Dillon

IN CELEBRATION of the six hundredth birthday of the University of Heidelberg in 1986, Jürgen Habermas gave a lecture, entitled "The Idea of the University: Learning Processes," that asked the question, What holds the various activities currently housed within universities together? What, in other words, is distinctive about university culture and practice? It is a philosophical and, one might say, a Germanic question, Anglo-Saxons being less inclined to assume that communities or institutions are necessarily held together by "Ideen." Not surprising to those familiar with Habermas's thought, his answer was "the communicative forms of scientific and scholarly argumentation" (124). Habermas believes that the heritage of Enlightenment ideals is not exhausted and that the disinterested, cooperative pursuit of truth and the general good, long claimed to guide academic discourse, still has normative force. In particular, he maintains that academic expert discourses are not simply some form of ideological state apparatus functioning essentially to legitimate institutions and train functionaries; rather, these discourses remain able to promote critical reflection on both social system and cultural "lifeworld" and, hence, to foster the "learning processes" (both individual and collective) that make possible greater autonomy and justice. Although Habermas stops short of claiming that academic discourse is the paragon of communicative rationality, it does, he says, "share emphatically" in that rationality, certainly more so than does society as a whole ("Idea" 125). To some, this idea may seem resoundingly self-evident; to others, it may sound preposterously self-congratulatory and complacent. This range of opinion is apparent in current reflections about the goals of college composition courses: some at this margin of academe outrightly despise academic writing, and even proponents rarely claim as much for it as Habermas seems to do.[1] But since Habermas is generally quite critical of the institutions, practices, and developmental dynamic of late capitalism, and he is certainly not their apologist, his theories should stir the earth around some of our most rooted assumptions, and that is a cultivation worth having.

It is not at all clear whether Habermas and the opponents of academic writing are talking about the same thing, but they are surely not focusing on the same aspects. The opponents tend to think of it as a product and to inveigh against impersonality and (pseudo)objectivity as models either of expository style or of the knowing subject's true position. Habermas's approach is social from the outset, and it focuses on the processes of dialectic and debate. He views academic culture not as a repository of received public knowledge but as a speech or discourse community embodying and inculcating certain values and practices, among them the reflection on values and the critique of practices. Hence, for him, what goes on in the classroom is a more immediate and concrete instance of what goes on "in the journals." Those who take such a social view thus prefer the term *academic discourse* to *academic writing*: *discourse* includes spoken and written media and does not foreground documents or suggest the apparently solitary act of producing them.

Habermas has frequently been accused of being "intellectualist" and "professorial" for his description of the ideal speech situation, which, he argues, is present as an ideal, implicit norm whenever people undertake to resolve a matter by reasoned argument (Dreyfus and Rabinow 119, 120). Among the salient aspects of this speech situation are the following: both (or all) participants have an equal right to speak; they suspend the limitations and urgencies of the immediate circumstances and argue without fear or favor, agreeing to accede to the force of the best argument. Hence, they avoid intimidation, name-calling, personal attack, and other techniques that are essentially coercive rather than respectful of the other parties' reasonableness. Habermas's recent discussions of practical discourse (i.e., deliberation with regard to action) have emphasized the reciprocity of perspectives and decentering so that each party can understand the other's position in its own terms (Habermas, *Moral Consciousness*). Habermas thus gives "reason" a distinctly social and ethical basis. It is not merely or solely a matter of logic, that is, of whether the definitions, evidence, and consecutiveness of what is said are sound. Nor is it a stylistic ideal. He celebrates, for example, not cool, clear, dispassionate discourse as the epitome of reason but the binding and bonding force of reaching an understanding. The "good" of a good argument is finally ethical, not technical, and it arises from a commitment or orientation shared by participants, not a decorum governing their discourse.

Habermas and his defenders readily concede that while arguments conducted under ideal conditions are rare in anyone's experience, such arguments still constitute the norm of fair and candid dealing that can produce consensus and reasoned assent while maximally honoring the integrity and freedom of individuals. Measured against this standard, most public and persuasive discourse, and even the personal and private, seems distorted to various degrees—deceitful, manipulative, obfuscating, or intimidating—but the ideal provides a basis for critique of existing discursive practices.

Resistance to this notion has been articulated in many ways, but it probably

springs from a sense of distance between the norm and our actual experiences:
What is the point of any norm that is impossibly remote from the realities?
In particular, academics and intellectuals, who pride themselves on being
self-critical, may resist the admittedly comfortable idea that the discourse of
their colleagues shares emphatically in communicative rationality. But colleges and universities have traditionally upheld a norm of discourse not unlike
that of the ideal speech situation (which descends, Habermas acknowledges,
from Enlightenment liberalism). A form of it is implicit in traditional composition teaching, and the composition classroom provides a natural testing
ground for the norm in relation to "real" practice. The classroom also provides
one place where the values of communicative rationality can be inculcated
with the hope of affecting practice, though in an obviously long-term and
limited way. Thus Habermas's abstract, Germanic, social-philosophical reflections can trigger some review of our own version of education as enlightenment, though we derive our enlightenment from Newton and Locke and
Mill, not Lessing and Herder and Kant, and hence most likely think of
emancipation in intellectual rather than political terms. Instead of beginning
so far back, however, I will just touch a few points.

Despite the gusts and swirling winds of change, American colleges and
universities still operate under the ideals of Enlightenment liberalism, among
which three come instantly to mind: (1) Classrooms should be forums for
impartial discussion of issues and evaluation of arguments; credit should be
given on the quality of the arguments and evidence—the force of best reasons
should prevail; intimidation, polemic, deviousness, and appeals to fear and
prejudice should be reprehended. (2) Teachers should identify and foster
trenchancy, choiceness of expression, the use of wide and discerning reading,
and other signs of love for language as a cultural institution. (3) Students
should learn to identify and resist mass culture and media programming,
prevailing myths, stereotypes, and propaganda. In short, the ideals promote
values of argument, language, and thought, or truth, beauty, and justice.

These triads seem almost embarrassingly quaint, but in some sense they
have withstood the buffeting of theorizing about foundations and elitism and
sexism. Though stripped of their self-evidence and innocence, they still
provide the vocabulary of praise and especially dispraise that can get people
into trouble, for example on student evaluation forms. They remain suited to
a traditional pedagogy that judges papers on their qualities as objects (faulty
reasoning, cumbersome wording, clichéd expression, and so on)—the practice
that avoids attacking the students' attitudes and values or exposing those of
the teacher or peer reader. According to the code, we all probably have
prejudices, tastes, and issues we feel strongly about, but we value open-
mindedness and try to evaluate the way an audience of reasonable, educated
people would respond: we try to constitute ourselves as members of an ideal
discourse community in something like Habermas's sense of the term, even

though commentary on papers is fairly one-sided, abbreviated, and selective. As long as the writer avoids a partisan or polemical stance, we can extend this careful generosity without much difficulty. (By *we* I mean instructors and students—the kind of "we" that emerges in class discussion of passages: negotiated, consensual, with the instructor to various degrees primus inter pares.) The code usually works smoothly with canonical reflective essays such as "Shooting an Elephant," "Once More to the Lake," and "The Death of a Moth," which themselves inscribe a fair-minded, impartial, reasonable reader, but it begins to develop serious instabilities when faced with controversial pieces.

Such pieces can be brought in for discussion either by the teacher (assigned readings) or by the student (the practice I enlarge on below). When the teacher chooses the pieces, an academically naive student may assume that the teacher endorses them and wants to proselytize for their views by assigning them. That is, introducing such works may compromise the teacher's stance as a model of impartiality, and students with opposing views may feel that the teacher has stacked the deck against them as the power to assign grades leaps to the fore and obliterates the model of an ideal community of inquiry. Some may accuse the teacher of having an agenda or of dragging politics into the classroom, as some students do on the evaluation forms Dale Bauer discusses. Bauer maintains that "the teacher is responsible for clarifying the agenda of the classroom, the student for challenging that agenda" (388), but a freshman is likely to find such challenging much riskier and more conflict-laden than a graduate student would. Freshmen have had much less experience exercising their rights and responsibilities as equal members of a discourse community, and they have less reason to be confident that this teacher will honor those rights and insist on those responsibilities. I do not intend to imply that teachers of freshman composition should avoid raising controversial issues or issues about which they possess strong moral convictions. In fact, one can draw the opposite conclusion—namely, that the conventions of fair, free, and mutually respecting argument only prove their strength and worth when they must be invoked to contain and focus discussion of difficult issues. The charge of "politics in the classroom" muddies the current argument since politics is commonly regarded as the process through which partial and irreconcilable interests are negotiated and accommodated. That is, politics appears as a zero-sum game, and advancing some interests inevitably diminishes others. But emancipation is not zero-sum, and when a teacher holds a vision of the common good, it is certainly proper to put it up for consideration and discussion in the classroom.

If the teacher decides to let the students set the reading for the class—which, incidentally, makes it possible for teachers to learn from and about the students—controversial pieces may again make their appearance, some of which may conflict not only with the teacher's convictions but with the very norms of fair, careful, reasoned argument the course upholds. Argumentation has its own analogue of Gresham's law—bad argument drives out good—and one almost suspects that some students delight in overturning the delicately balanced apple cart, challenging the agenda of fair, reasoned argument and consensus mutually arrived at. Recently, I have been asking students in my advanced expository writing course to bring in pieces they think are strong; some of their selections flout the code, foregrounding the issue of reasonableness that is then socially negotiated in classroom interactions. I turn now to this process of testing and extending the code into the area of popular deliberation.

I ask my students to choose a passage of moderate length, a copy of which they place in a packet that becomes the anthology of prose for the class. Students present brief class reports on the passages they have chosen and then write final analyses that include the responses of the class to the passage. I caution them that the passage should be strong in the way it is written rather than in what it says and that they may want to choose one that persuasively advocates a position with which they do not agree. The students still bring in the chestnuts, but recently they have also been selecting pieces from the *National Review* and its counterparts in the liberal press, as well as articles dealing with racial prejudice, pop culture, and a number of other hot topics. I'm not sure how political my students are, but they certainly are fascinated by the power of political rhetorics and interested in the problem of discussing them critically. Sometimes several of the passages selected pair with others, so that the need for a fairly neutral vocabulary and uniform criteria for evaluation becomes evident: students want to appear to be judicious and independent thinkers—not just written-upon young mouthers of slogans— and they want to appeal to other students whose values and perspectives may be quite different from their own.

One such pairing occurred with an article and a response to it. A student contributed a piece from the *National Review*, "That Old Devil Music," by Stuart Goldman, which attacks the current scene in rock and roll. Tim, a second student, who was a reader of *Rolling Stone*, knew that Goldman had been answered in that magazine by Kurt Loder; he offered to present the Loder piece and strove "to mediate the bickering" between the pieces in his final paper. (*Bicker*, I might note, was a very strong word in Seattle student slang of the late 1980s.) Loder's piece begins:

> Few things in the realm of public foofaraw can guarantee such unalloyed amusement as the spectacle of iron-lipped conservative ideologues mounting yet another assault upon the battered fastness of rock culture—and inevitably tumbling assholes over elbows back down the slippery incline of their own vast incomprehension of the subject.

It was in anticipation of this evergreen pleasure that I opened the February 24th issue of *National Review*, the conservative fortnightly—a magazine edited by gentleman-polemicist William F. Buckley, Jr., for the smug delectation of what I had always assumed to be the ascots-and-yachting element of the Republican party.   (57)

Loder's article only answers Goldman's in kind, Tim shows, and it in fact employs many of the same techniques of vituperation, contempt, sneering parentheticals, and general abuse that Goldman introduced. Loder, Tim notes, enjoys the position of "he started it, but I'll have the last word." Tim's choice of *mediator* to describe his role is slightly off, but it does reflect a decision to be "in the middle" and to be impartial, and it leads him to develop an assessment that Loder "wins" because of superior factual accuracy:

Loder's essay is composed of two methods—debate and insult. It certainly would be more objective without the severe insults, but by using the conservatives' own "point-scoring" methods, Loder can convince most of his readers and link Goldman's faux pas—at least indirectly—with serious insufficiencies in the entire argument for conservatism. There is no doubt that Loder won this debate and that his facts are straight, but by preaching only to those already converted (the liberal following of rock culture) he loses something vital to the universal believability of his essay. It is good that Loder took the time to look out for "cranks" (and actually found one), but when he brings out his facts, changes them into insults, and begins to make victims of his accusers, he is feeding the fire of needless controversy.

Chaim Perelman and Lucie Olbrechts-Tyteca could not have said it better. Tim's analysis suggests that, if Goldman's and Loder's pieces do have a persuasive aim, it is to confirm and heighten the adherence of the faithful and to recruit only by displaying "how much fun we have in our church." Perhaps Loder most subtly undermines Goldman's attack by treating it from the outset as a familiar, almost ritual, rhetorical exercise rather than any sort of serious or novel argument. Tim's final point is interesting as well: he objects to "insult" in argument because it tends to keep the fight going. Controversy of that type is "needless" since it does not clarify issues or serve the purpose of coming to an understanding.

The project of analyzing political opinion pieces in a college class may play into liberal values and assumptions; certainly, students at the University of Washington with conservative views sometimes feel defensive and defiant, in spite of the teacher's attempts to ensure that all views, if clearly argued and defended, have a fair hearing. Those attempts are "liberal," at least in the free-market sense. In a class I recently taught, however, a piece by George Will from *Newsweek*, "The Journey up from Guilt," paired rather nicely with one by Lewis Lapham, "A Political Opiate," from *Harper's Magazine*. The pieces used similar devices of exaggeration, outrage, derision, and sarcastic quotation and featured dark, sweeping views of contemporary history, along with erudite vocabularies and some of the apparatus of scholarship. The two students who presented the essays were articulate and canny, and both responded in their final papers to the comments made by the class. Here, for example, is Lapham's antepenultimate paragraph, which one class member described as a "paroxysm of liberal paranoia":

> Even so, and not withstanding its habitual incompetence and greed, the govern-
> ment doesn't lightly relinquish the spoils of power seized under the pretexts of
> apocalypse. What the government grasps, the government seeks to keep and
> hold. The militarization of the rhetoric supporting the war on drugs rots the
> public debate with a corrosive silence. The political weather turns gray and
> pinched. People who become accustomed to the arbitrary intrusions of the
> police also learn to speak more softly in the presence of political authority, to
> bow and smile and fill out the printed forms with the cowed obsequiousness
> of musicians playing waltzes at a Mafia wedding.   (48)

The student, Beth, agreed with Lapham's resistance to drug-war hysteria, but she was embarrassed by his fighting fire with fire. Her conclusion begins in truly academic fashion:

> But in the final analysis, I'm not sure we actually arrive at the "Opiate Conclu-
> sion." The rallying tone and emotional arm-waving of Lapham's sweeping and
> grandiose generalizations and martial-law accusations seem to fall apart in the
> end. In a sense he falls victim to the very same theatrical devices that he
> condemns the politicians and journalists for employing.

Beth then enumerates the devices but concludes that the piece is well directed to its liberal audience and "quite effective" in sending "us" away with "an increased awareness of the issue and the undeniable sense that President Bush's trick with the bag of cocaine is shabby indeed." The academic qualifiers ("I'm not sure," "seem," "in a sense") come thick and fast here, but Beth makes effective use of them to reestablish a community of judicious *we*s—a moderate, middle-of-the-road community that is, above all, sanely striving to avoid hysteria. She chooses the role of Lapham's apologist, conceding a few excesses and toning down the "theatricality."

Linda, the student who presented the Will article, explained to the class members that she was a neutral, political naïf who had only recently started looking at some conservative writers who made interesting and thought-provoking points. This move did not disarm the liberals in the class, some of whom knew from her previous work that she expressed a conservative line on most of the issues that had come up in class. They fell on the piece with a fury, lambasting it for disingenuity, silly statistics, poor logic, and overwrought, cutesy phrase making. One of the older students called it "intellectually barren." After this unpleasant experience, how would Linda retrench? Here is her conclusion, which follows a list of Will's hyphenated name-calling adjectives ("guilt-mongering," "guilt-drenched," "elbow-throwing," "welfare-state"):

> Liberals screw up their faces, and conservatives cheer at these words. Middle roaders take the quotation marks off of "compassion" and "sensitivity," and slide across terms such as "egregious guilt factory," "codified compassion," "grievance industry" and "proliferating communities of victimhood." Then before he goes into his spiel about capital punishment, they try to maintain his primary point: the white middle class wants to be comfortable looking minorities in the eyes without feeling like they've personally caused them any suffering. The conservatives and the liberals are kept alive by George Will, and the in-betweens are kept exhausted.

Again, the student undertakes a rescue effort to save the primary point; Will's vehement support for capital punishment as affirming "the correctness of the doctrine of personal responsibility for behavior" was simply too much for the class to take, and Linda is willing to jettison it as a distracting "spiel." Her strategy for retrenchment is to objectify the responses, suggesting an identification with "middle roaders" and "in-betweens" but not even risking a *we* to describe that group. Her comment on exhaustion indicates that the polemical firefight has been costly, but not to Will's effectiveness so much as to the reader's ability to extract a usable point from the article—usable in conversation with your classmates, that is?

White middle-class guilt was a major theme in many of the selections this class made; it came up in relation to race in two other pieces chosen, both of which referred to the great popularity of Bill Cosby's family television show. One piece was a chapter ("Cosby Knows Best") from Mark Crispin Miller's *Boxed In: The Culture of TV.* Alternately distinguishing Cosby from the character he portrays (Cliff Huxtable) and merging the two, Miller attacks the show for ignoring the facts of racial antagonism and presenting an ideal, benign black who calms white fears. In discussing the selection, students commented that there were no blacks in the class, that Miller was not black, and that it smacked considerably of colonialism for the class to discourse on the reality of black experience or feelings. Miller, students observed, also assumes a position of great discursive privilege. By the end of the chapter, he has attained an omniscience that Lisa, the student offering the piece, found excessive and overdone. Miller writes:

> As a willing advertisement for the system that pays him well, Cliff Huxtable also represents a threat contained. Although dark-skinned and physically imposing, he ingratiates us with his childlike mien and enviable lifestyle, a

surrender that must offer some deep solace to a white public terrified that, one day, blacks might come with guns to steal the copperware, the juicer, the microwave, the VCR, even the TV itself.   (74)

Lisa responds:

> He has begun subtly shifting his target audience, making it even narrower by talking primarily to America's "whites," and by the final page of the article including himself in the group when describing how television attempts to calm the fears of the white viewers, making them believe that the "blacks won't hurt us." He speaks as though a spokesperson for the general subconscious of white people everywhere, discoursing on the fear that blacks will somehow invade and steal "the copperware, the juicer, the microwave."

Lisa describes Miller's voicing of these fears as "going too far." Like some of the other writers, she adopts the strategy of extracting the grain of truth. Indeed, most of my students give instant assent to diatribes against manipulative schlock on prime-time television in consumerist America. But, in her conclusion, Lisa makes the unusual move of extracting a grain that is at most only implicit in what Miller says and that is, rather, her own version of what ought to have been said. Miller's paragraph reads:

> Thus, Cliff is not just an image of the dark Other capitulating to the white establishment, but also the reflection of any constant viewer, who, whatever his/her race, must also feel like an outsider, lucky to be tolerated by the distant powers that be. There is no negativity allowed, not anywhere; and so Cliff serves both as our guide and as our double. His look of tense playfulness is more than just a sign that blacks won't hurt us; it is an expression that we too would each be wise to adopt, lest we betray some devastating sign of anger or dissatisfaction. If we stay cool and cheerful, white like him, and learn to get by with his sort of managerial acumen, we too, perhaps can be protected from the world by a barrier of new appliances, and learn to put down others as each of us has, somehow, been put down.   (75)

Of this, Lisa says:

> In the final paragraph of the essay Miller allows himself to go completely overboard, observing that all of society is beginning to feel that they should surround themselves in a "barrier of appliances" in order to protect themselves from the corporate powers in a consumerist world. While his phrasing is overblown and his examples overdone, Miller does bring up the valid point that t.v. has totally wiped out all signs of negativity, and this will likely have the effect of alienating the audience, whoever they may be, making the real people in the real world feel out of place, failures in the face of their t.v. counterparts.

This reading of the situation is considerably less paranoid than the one Miller on the whole purveys. Of course, Lisa might be misreading Miller by assuming that he has brought up not just the negativity matter but its likely result. She could have argued with him, explicitly contrasting what she thinks will result with what he seems to assume. But interpretation and critique do have wide scope in practice, and one can bend an authority to one's own ends if no one objects.

The objectionable practice in Miller's piece is not an unfair attack on the opposing position but the arrogance of moral and intellectual superiority. Miller goes beyond the code of academic argument in not acknowledging the limits of his position as knowing subject. Such acknowledgment, though not absolutely required in academic discourse, is implicit both in the traditional admonitions to qualify and take account of possible objections and in the Gricean maxim of quality (say no more than you have good grounds for believing to be true), which is one part of the cooperative principle said to govern conversation. Lisa's heavy use of qualifiers in her own prose is probably a response to their absence in the Miller piece.

By coincidence, another student contributed a piece on black rhetoric, "Black and White: Race and Blame," by a black English professor, Shelby Steele, which appeared in *Harper's Magazine*. Steele begins by describing a pleasant, genteel dinner party in mixed-racial company that suddenly freezes and dies when a black guest reminds the company of the effect of race in educational opportunity. Steele says that the incident reflects a failure in the guest's rhetoric—essentially the rhetoric of accusation and confrontation— and offers Cosby as a model of the "negotiator" stance, which Steele argues has proved constructive for blacks (since it is not based on victimhood) as well as whites. The class was uncomfortable with being told by a black person just what George Will says they want to hear and, moreover, with seeing it being offered to blacks by a black. One could still quarrel with Steele's decision to speak for and to blacks, and mutterings of "Tom" were heard, but the students realized they couldn't be the judge of Steele's qualifications.[2] Unfortunately, the student who chose the piece was delighted by it: she thought Steele told good, vivid stories, some of them pleasantly self-deprecating, though he did perhaps go on a bit long. Because the piece did not require her to examine her beliefs or to take any action, it confirmed her feeling that confrontational blacks aren't doing themselves or anyone else any good, and it did not seem to stimulate any resistance or questioning. The paper she submitted was serenely unruffled by critical comments offered by classmates. Of course, she was not troubled by Steele's prose either, since it was decorously academic and unpolemical. Argumentative misbehavior is easier to see and to analyze.

From these examples, we may conclude that the students did work out a rough vocabulary for criticizing the pieces they chose and that, above all, they invoked the venerably moderate, quintessentially academic notion of "going too far," which let them speak as a "reasonable center," a "we" that emerged from their listening to, and attempting to synthesize, the responses of the class. Paradoxically, their independent-mindedness arose in part from having to acknowledge and concede some ground to the critical comments of their classmates. Reasonableness in the practical sense was socially negotiated in the classroom. In working out ways to assess writing that transgressed academic codes of good argument, they extended the code beyond the ivory tower and came out a little better equipped to handle themselves reasonably in the hurly-burly of public, unacademic discourse.

Most of the code-challenging pieces we have looked at here fall under the heading of polemic. We may return to our starting point by asking in what way polemic disrupts argumentation oriented toward reaching understanding within an idealized speech situation and, hence, from the Habermasian point of view, deserves the term *misbehavior*. For one thing, it does not respect the reasonableness or good faith of the opposing position; rather, polemic exaggerates and parodies the opposition and threatens it with contempt. Thus, we have been inclined to say that these passages do not so much seek the assent of persons on the other side as revel in the power of "our side" to arouse sneers at our enemies. We might argue that polemic is a holiday from argumentation oriented toward reaching understanding. At the same time, however, my students showed that it could be translated into some propositions that were not exaggerated and maliciously parodic; students applied the commonsense procedure of "grain of truth" extraction, assuming that the writers of the pieces were striking negotiating positions that deliberately claimed more than any reader other than the most sympathetic would grant, thus supplying themselves (or their apologists) with plenty of ground to concede in the formation of a negotiated consensus. But academics are bound by the code to claim no more than that for which they have adequate grounds—a limitation that may also explain why academic salaries are so low. Such a principle certainly has much to recommend it by way of reducing the time spent separating the grains of truth from the posturing and, as Tim suggests, by way of reducing time spent on pointless, contentious wrangling. I think we do have some good reasons for valuing a mutually arrived at understanding as the basis for common action and some reasons for prizing one type of debate over another—in relation to which the techniques we have been examining can be judged neither very constructive nor very helpful— but I don't think we ought to be complacent or sniffy about it: reasonableness on most topics and occasions is an achievement, one we should analyze and prize and teach.

The attentive and perhaps skeptical reader may have noted that I have de-emphasized issues of power in the classroom, among which we might include the political and social views of the majority and the unequal role of the instructor as primary articulator, referee, and evaluator of the students' performance. That is, the move toward consensus could also be viewed as the result of the group's inducing conformity, and the instructor may be ruling as much by authority as by "good reasons." These practical questions of group dynamics return us to the problem of the ideal and the real arising in Habermas's ideal speech situation. Perhaps we can always give a nonideal account of interactions that claim to be guided by a normative ideal, and perhaps all classroom transactions fall short of the glory of the ideal speech situation. But when we seek adherence and the resolution of disputes, it makes a difference, I think, if we are oriented toward better reasons and arguments rather than toward vehemence, appeal to prejudice, vituperation, and the whole slew of other tactics traditionally (and rightly) called "bad." Habermas's contribution is to affirm that such an orientation is a profound social good, the benefit of which extends well beyond the halls and walls of academe.

University of Washington

NOTES

[1] Peter Elbow, for example, outlines the general intellectual-rhetorical stance of academic discourse in terms similar to those emphasized by Habermas. Although he calls it "admirable," he sounds as if he is rehearsing platitudes and does not say why he endorses it ("Reflections").

[2] At the 1991 conference Education for a Pluralistic Society at which Steele spoke, Don Williamson, a black editor of the *Seattle Times* and a respondent to the speech, called Steele a "pimp." Williamson defended his charge in a column in the *Seattle Times*, emending the epithet to "prostitute."

PART TWO

Postmodern Subjectivities

both involve the study of signifying practices, of language use in writing and speaking and language interpretation in reading and listening, with the focus on the relation of these practices to the disposition of power—economic, social, and political—at a particular historical moment. To paraphrase Eagleton, cultural studies might then be described as the examination of the ways discursive formations are related to power or, alternately, the study of language's uses in the service of power. Indeed, this is the very definition of rhetoric many of us in composition studies are now invoking.

In "Cultural Studies and Teaching Writing," John Trimbur has issued the first fully articulated account of the convergences to be discovered in the projects of cultural studies and contemporary composition studies. In this essay, I wish both to follow his lead and to answer the challenge he poses to workers in composition. I will, however, make my case somewhat differently. My first task will be to show briefly that composition studies since its inception in the modern college English department has contained voices that have attempted to define rhetoric as cultural studies in the sense just described. My second effort will be to outline the shape this undertaking is presently assuming. I cannot emphasize too strongly, however, that I will in no sense suggest that cultural studies is to be considered a deliverer come to save writing teachers from the errors of their ways. Instead, my argument is that the endeavors of cultural studies and the endeavors of composition studies are mutually enriching. While we in rhetoric can benefit from examining the workers in cultural studies, they in turn have much to gain from considering what we are about. Our problematics are finally similar and thoroughly compatible. Indeed, in this essay I wish to show Eagleton to be even more right than he realizes in asserting that in many important respects cultural studies is an attempt to recover the role rhetoric has historically played.

Before beginning the historical analysis of the relations of composition to cultural studies, I would like to consider a formulation of cultural studies developed at the Birmingham Department of Cultural Studies, a program that I would argue best demonstrates projects parallel to current work in composition studies. In "What Is Cultural Studies Anyway?" Richard Johnson, past head of the Birmingham department, has explained that cultural studies can best be considered in terms of its characteristic *objects* of study and in terms of its *methods*. Both objects and methods are organized around an examination of the formations of consciousness and subjectivity: "[C]ultural studies is about the historical forms of consciousness or subjectivity, or the subjective forms we live by, or, in a rather perilous compression, perhaps a reduction, the subjective side of social relations" (43). For Johnson, cultural studies is related to the projects of structuralism and poststructuralism: "[S]ubjectivities are produced, not given, and are therefore the objects of inquiry, not the premises or starting points" (44). Signifying practices then become crucial features of investigation, constituting "the structured character of the forms we inhabit subjectively: language, signs, ideologies, discourses, myths" (45). In other words, cultural studies concerns itself with the ways social formations and practices shape consciousness, and this shaping is mediated by language and situated in concrete historical conditions. The important addendum is that this relation between the social and the subjective is ideological, is imbricated in economic, social, and political considerations that are always historically specific. It is no coincidence that calls for cultural studies in the English department are coming most insistently from the left, from those most likely to see relations of power in all discursive practices. Thus cultural studies involves the ideological formation of subjects, of forms of consciousness, within historically specific signifying practices that are enmeshed in power. For Johnson, then, the objects of cultural studies are the production, distribution, and reception of signifying practices within the myriad social formations that are shaping subjectivities. These formations range from the family, the school, the workplace, and the peer group to the more familiar activities associated with the cultural sphere, such as the arts (high and low) and the media and their modes of production and consumption. In other words, wherever signifying practices are shaping consciousness in daily life, cultural studies has work to do.

Although Johnson considers the *methods* of cultural studies to be varied and interdisciplinary, his discussion of them is sometimes obscure. Vincent Leitch provides an effective summary: "The modes of inquiry employed in cultural studies included not only established survey techniques, field interviews, textual explications, and researches into sociohistorical backgrounds, but also especially institutional and ideological analysis." The interdisciplinary nature of these methods is unmistakable. More important, in all cases, the data gathered by these diverse means are situated within the institution—family, work, art—that sponsored the examined activities and are related to the ideological—the arena of language, idea, and value. In "What Is Cultural Studies," Johnson is especially concerned with elucidating the kinds of research cultural studies has encouraged, seeing these methods as appearing across them. The research activities fall into three general categories: production-based studies; text-based studies; and studies of culture as a lived activity. These categories, as we shall see, are particularly resonant within discussions of current research in composition studies.

Production-based studies deal with the "production and social organization of cultural forms" (Johnson 54). This includes a broad range of objects of study, from public relations, advertising, and the mass media to the production of race, class, and gender behavior within the schools. The methods are diverse, calling on the procedures of the social sciences as well as textual analysis. This group of approaches focuses on the conditions of cultural production and distribution—of the media, an artwork, or the schools—without regard to the negotiation and resistance involved at the point of consumption. For Johnson, this oversight is a serious flaw, especially in the tendency of certain mechanistic Marxisms to insist that the economic base determines consciousness.

A second group of studies involves text-based efforts derived from work with literary productions and their reception and interpretation. Johnson particularly has in mind the powerful methods of textual analysis developed by structuralist and poststructuralist literary theory and the ways these methods are able to address the relation of texts to subject formation. For example, one could study the relation of the kinds of literary texts read in school, and the means of interpreting them, to formations of class, race, and gender expectations among schoolchildren. The strategies discovered in textual interpretation are connected to students' lived experience. Johnson, however, takes pains to emphasize that reading is itself an act of production, not simply a passive act of receiving a determinate text. Once again, we must consider the readers' negotiation of, and resistance to, a text.

The third cluster of approaches focuses on "lived cultures" and attempts "to grasp the more *concrete* and more *private* moments of cultural circulation" (Johnson 69). Ethnography is the primary research method in the attempt to locate responses to cultural experience. Johnson points to studies of the ways adolescent girls and boys appropriate cultural forms for their own ends, ends that often subvert the producers' intentions—as, for example, in Dick Hebdige's study of adolescent culture in London. Since, at the point of lived culture, interpretive strategies of negotiation and resistance are involved, textual strategies again may become important.

The major flaw in all three approaches, Johnson explains, is that each tends to dwell on one moment of cultural performance—production or the cultural product or cultural negotiation—without regard for the entire process.

In describing the objects and methods of cultural studies, Johnson has endorsed Eagleton's contention that the project of cultural studies is closely related to the historical project of rhetorical studies. Johnson has also improved on Eagleton in emphasizing the complex relation between the production and reception of cultural artifacts and in placing consciousness formation at the center of cultural studies. Eagleton, however, usefully reminds us that rhetoric has historically studied the ways discourse—in both production and interpretation—shapes the experiences of individuals, and, particularly in its classical manifestation, discourse's role in power and the political process.

This brings me to the historical dimension of my presentation. Composition studies, since its formation in college English departments a hundred years ago, has in many of its manifestations attempted to become a variety of cultural studies. In other words, it has worked to form itself as an activity that studies the construction of subjects within social formations, focusing on the signifying practices of written and spoken texts and the implication of those practices in power and ideology. It has, furthermore, attempted to offer a critique of these practices and power formations. Of the three dominant paradigms of composition studies that have appeared during this time, two—the expressionistic and the social constructionist, unlike their strongest competitor, the current-traditional—have self-consciously criticized dominant power arrangements, thus attempting to provide students with the means for negotiation and resistance. Both, however, have failed as cultural studies, each in its unique way falling short of its promise to provide a comprehensive program that can critique the production and reception of discourse within the realm of power and politics. Nevertheless, this account demonstrates that the current move to cultural studies in English departments, as Eagleton has unintentionally underscored, is not without historical precedents and that we can locate one set of precedents in the devalorized "service" sector of the department. (Brantlinger has recently found others in Victorian studies and American studies.) Here we discover the important political and cultural work that composition has been asked to do, a task no less ambitious than distinguishing true from untrue discourse in disputations about power and privilege.

In considering these rhetorics, I analyze certain features of their ideological predispositions, calling on a method based on the work of Goran Therborn in *The Ideology of Power and the Power of Ideology*. (I discuss Therborn at greater length in "Rhetoric and Ideology in the Writing Class.") From this perspective, ideology interpellates subjects—that is, addresses and shapes them—through discourses that point out what exists, what is good, and what is possible. Significantly, ideology also includes a version of power formations governing the agent in relation to all these designations. Thus, as Therborn explains, directives about the existent deal with "who we are, what the world is, what nature, society, men, and women are like. In this way we acquire a sense of identity, becoming conscious of what is real and true." The good indicates what is "right, just, beautiful, attractive, enjoyable, and its opposites" (18). The good concerns the realms of politics and ethics and art. The possible tells us what can be accomplished given the existent and the good. It grants us "our sense of the mutability of our being-in-the-world, and the consequences of change are hereby patterned, and our hopes, ambitions, and fears given shape" (18). The last consideration is closely related to the question of power, its distribution, and its control. From this perspective, the subject is the point of intersection of various discourses—discourses about class, race, gender, ethnicity, age, religion, and the like—and it is influenced by these discourses. Equally important, the subject in turn affects these very discourses. The individual is the location of a variety of significations but is also an agent of change, not simply an unwitting product of external discursive and material forces. The subject negotiates and resists codes instead of simply accommodating them.

I now turn to the two English department rhetorics that have attempted to do the work of cultural studies, along with the reasons for their failures. Once again, I consider the effort these rhetorics make to examine signifying practices in the formation of subjectivities within concrete material, social, and political conditions. I am especially attentive to their conceptions of the existent, the good, and the possible and the larger relations of power within these elements.

The Rhetoric of Liberal Culture and Expressionism

As both David Russell and I have shown, the rhetoric of liberal culture was a strong reactionary force in the new university during the last century. While Harvard, Cornell, and the recently established state universities were working to create a new meritocracy of certified scientific experts, Yale, Princeton, and others were clinging to the notion of education as a perquisite of birth and breeding. Against the position that the new scientific discourse set the standard for writing and reading practices, liberal culturists argued that the only discourse worthy of consideration was the poetic. Endorsing a mandarin Romanticism, this rhetoric insisted that art is the product of genius and that genius is the product of class and cultivation. Thus, only men (not women) of genius should be encouraged to produce genuine discourse—that is, poetic texts—while the rest of humankind, which usually (but not always) included women, should work to interpret these texts. And just as the great male heroes in poetry were to instruct the inferior orders, only great heroes in economic, social, and political institutions should be entrusted with power. Art and public affairs mutually reinforced the authority and privilege of a small leadership class.

Liberal culture was the response of a declining Anglo-Protestant power elite in the face of serious threats to its status, threats posed by the new bourgeoisie in economic matters and the new urban immigrant working class in politics. The rhetoric of liberal culture finally experienced a dramatic transformation during the 1920s. The poetic text remained the highest manifestation of genuine discourse, but the ability to produce these texts was democratized. Inspired culturally by the child-study movement, a bowdlerized Freudianism, and aesthetic expressionism, proponents of these new ideas henceforth considered genius the birthright of all human beings. Expressionist rhetoric was thus self-consciously political, forwarding a democratic agenda of equality. It responded to the horrors of capitalism, particularly the dehumanizing mechanization of everyday urban experience and the oppression of the individual. The causes of economic, social, and political problems were accordingly attributed to institutional violations of the uniqueness of each human being. The responses to these violations, however, were seldom either economic or political. Instead, they were portrayed as private and personal.

Writing and reading practices were thus depicted as solitary acts providing the means to restore the subject to his or her true nature, or authentic self, putting the subject in touch with the inner voice that is each person's unique center and guide. The ideology of this rhetoric then located the existent in the individual, and the good and possible were to serve the individual and subvert the herd impulse of social arrangements. Text production emphasized looking within (sometimes even including meditation techniques) and personal writing (the journal, the letter, the lyric). Furthermore, metaphoric language was central since it was the only means writers had to suggest the subtleties of their private visions. In contrast, the language of direct statement represented the dehumanized discourse of science, which stood for the oppressiveness of urban capitalism. Thus, in this discourse system, scientific textual practices were placed in opposition to particular poetic practices, and all authentic writing aspired to the condition of poetry. Indeed, rhetoric attempted to reproduce the effects of poetry for both writer and reader since all genuine signifying practices were necessarily aesthetic.

In the 1960s and 1970s, many expressionists aligned themselves with the New Left. They still regarded writing and reading as personal, private, and creative acts of resistance. Indeed, they offered such acts to counter the socially imposed cruelties of dominant institutional discourses that enforced racism, inequitable economic arrangements, and an unjust war. The expressionists thought that institutional signifying practices, including those of the university, destroyed the unified, coherent, transcendent self, and they encouraged their students to resist these socially imposed directives and retreat to the personal and private.

Expressionist rhetoric is radically democratic, opposing dominant class, race, and gender divisions in the interests of equality. I show in "Rhetoric and Ideology in the Writing Class," however, that as a cultural studies this rhetoric lacks the devices to participate in effective critique, creating as it does a simple binary opposition between the personal and the social. It refuses the possibility that the self the individual discovers is finally a response to social and cultural formations, a script at least in part written by class, race, and gender codes. Thus, when students know in their hearts that a certain text—their own or someone else's—is true and authentic, they often are making a judgment based on a class-defined notion, not a personal and private criterion, the student having invoked a socially inscribed conception of the self in making the judgment. This is of course another way of saying that expressionism's uncritical acceptance of the unified, coherent, and originary self renders its critique suspect. Expressionist rhetoric, furthermore, argues for a privatized notion of power, seeing larger economic and political formations in narrowly personal terms. Institutions are simply individuals writ large, and all opposition to them is to be conducted in strictly personal terms. This formulation prevents a realistic examination of the ways power operates within social formations. Critique and resistance are ineffective in dealing with the institutional forces that are beyond the remedy of individuals acting alone—whether inside or outside the institution. Expressionist reading and writing practices often result in quietism and the acceptance of defeat, self-help therapeutic ministrations in response to a world gone wrong (see Faigley, "Judging").

Social Constructionist Rhetoric

As I demonstrate in *Rhetoric and Reality*, social constructionist rhetoric appeared at the turn of the century, primarily in the Midwest but also at a number of eastern colleges, especially women's schools. Growing out of progressive politics—itself a response to the cruelties of urban capitalism—and democratic populism, this position acknowledged the influence of social forces in the formation of the individual. Because each person is first and foremost a member of a community, any claim to individuality can only be articulated within a social context. The existent, the good, and the possible are determined by consulting the welfare of the populace as a whole. All citizens must learn reading and writing in order to take part in the dialogue of democracy. These activities, moreover, call on a social hermeneutic, measuring the value of a text in relation to its importance to the larger society. Thus, the expertise of the new meritocratic class must be employed in the service of the community, and the community, not the experts themselves, must finally decide on solutions to economic, social, and political problems. In the schools, John Dewey's pragmatism obviously had a strong influence on this rhetoric, which placed reading and writing practices at the center of communal decision making. It was the counterpart of a literary criticism that regarded poetic texts in relation to their social and cultural context, for example, in the work of Fred Newton Scott, Gertrude Buck, Vida Dutton Scudder, Moses Coit Tyler, and Frederick Lewis Pattee.

During the 1920s, this rhetoric spawned the "ideas approach," an attempt to regard the writing course as training in political discourse. Students read contradictory points of view on contemporary social problems and wrote essays stating their own positions. During the Depression, socially oriented approaches took a leftist turn. For example, Warren Taylor of Wisconsin voiced the hope that school and college rhetoric courses would help students learn to examine their cultural experience—"advertisement, editorial, newsreel, radio speech, article, or book" (853)—for threats to the democratic process at a time of national crisis. Fearful that an elite might prevail against the claims of the community, this rhetoric saw the critical examination of the subtle effects of signifying practices as a key to egalitarian decision making. A similar effort was taken up after World War II when the communications course—a course combining writing, reading, speaking, and listening—was forwarded as a safeguard for democracy, particularly against the threats of propaganda. General semantics was especially prominent, arguing for a scientific notion of signifying practices that enabled discrimination between true and deceptive political discourse. Of course, during the 1960s and 1970s, responses to racial injustice, poverty, and the Vietnam conflict once again encouraged a rhetoric of public discourse that demanded communal participation in decision making—for example, in the work of Harold Martin, the early Richard Ohmann, and Kenneth Bruffee.

Despite the considerable attractions of this social rhetoric, its flaws cannot be denied. While it emphasizes the communal and social constitution of subjectivity, it never abandons the notion of the individual as finally a sovereign free agent, capable of transcending mere material and social conditions. Although it does look to democratic political institutions as the solution to social problems, it lacks a critique of economic arrangements, arguing that the political is primary and, finally, determinative. The critique of capitalism occasionally found during the 1930s was thus abandoned after the war. This rhetoric also displays an innocence about power, lacking the means for the critique of it beyond a faith in the possibility of open public discourse and the ballot box. It cannot, for example, problematize the obvious inequities in access to public discourse or the failures of the elective process when candidates do not offer genuine alternatives. And while this rhetoric sees the manipulative power of discourse, it continues to believe that a universal, ahistorical, rational discourse is possible. As a result, it regards itself as a disinterested and objective arbiter of competing ideological claims, occupying a neutral space above the fray of conflict. In other words, it is incapable of examining its own ideological commitments, which it mistakes for accurate reflections of eternal truths. It accepts its signifying practices as indisputably representative of things as they really are.

Social Epistemic Rhetoric

Social epistemic rhetoric has attempted to take into account the challenge to discourse study posed by recent Marxist, structuralist, and poststructuralist theory—in short, an attempt that has led rhetoric and composition studies to mirror developments in the cultural studies forwarded by Eagleton and the Birmingham group. Trimbur has effectively described the historical conditions that have encouraged this rhetoric, locating them in a return to the participatory political impulse of the 1960s, a response to the exploitation of composition teachers in English departments, the crisis in the literary canon, and, of course, the reaction to poststructuralism, particularly the decentering of the self ("Cultural Studies"). I would add to this the politicizing of education begun by Richard Nixon in 1968 and carried to its farthest reaches in the Reagan administration. After William Bennett, E. D. Hirsch, Jr., and Allan Bloom, it is difficult for English teachers to argue that any texts, literary or otherwise, occupy a position above the fray of political contention.

Social epistemic rhetoric has two corresponding but separate historical trajectories in English and communication departments, both independent of European influences, at least until recently (see Berlin, "Rhetoric Programs"). This rhetoric is instead functioning within the framework of earlier social rhetorics. Most important, social epistemic rhetoric has maintained its commitment to preparing students for citizenship in a democratic society. Public discourse openly and freely pursued remains a central objective. Departures from its predecessors, however, are more significant. This newly formulated rhetoric is self-reflexive, acknowledging its own rhetoricity, its own discursive constitution and limitations. It does not deny its inescapable ideological predispositions, its condition of always already being committed politically. It does not claim to be above ideology, a transcendent discourse that objectively adjudicates competing ideological judgments. It knows that it is ideologically situated, an intervention in the political process, as are all rhetorics. At the same time, it is aware of its historical contingency, of its limitation and incompleteness, and it remains open to change and revision.

Social epistemic rhetoric argues that the writing subject is a discursive construction, the subject serving as a point of conjuncture for a plethora of discourses—a rich variety of texts inscribed in the persona of the individual. The subject is thus a construction of the play of discourses that a culture provides. These discourses interpellate or address us, providing each of us with directions about our behavior, scripts that have to do with such categories as race, class, and gender. These discursive formations, or cultural codes, exist prior to us, being inscribed in the institutional and social practices that constitute our historical moment. Equally important, they not only form the subject, they also indicate the subject's very conception of the material, social, and political. In other words, the subject's possible responses to experience are all textually situated, are all the result of the interaction of discursive structures, cultural codes revealing the possible relations that can exist in and among these elements. The individual never responds to things in themselves but to discursive formations of things in themselves. Concrete material conditions do of course finally shape and limit behavior, but they are always mediated by discourse.

This formulation does not preclude the possibility of individuality and agency. As Trimbur, following Mikhail Bakhtin, has shown, each individual represents a unique combination of discourses, of voices, because each individual occupies a unique position in the network of discourses encountered ("Essayist Literacy"). One may act in and through these discourses, working to change them and the material conditions they mediate in one's experience.

This project is not, however, undertaken in a domain of complete freedom. The individual is always forced to act within material conditions and signifying practices not of his or her own making.

This conception of the subject, material reality, and signifying practices clearly calls for a revised model of writing and reading. Both composing and interpreting texts become acts of discourse analysis and negotiation. Indeed, writing and reading are themselves verbally coded acts, discursive procedures that guide the production and interpretation of meanings, making a certain range more likely to appear and others more improbable. This exclusionary coding is apparent, for example, in reflections on the directives for text production and reception provided in the expressionist and the social rhetorics considered earlier: for expressionist rhetoric, only personal and metaphorical accounts can be regarded as meaningful; for social rhetoric, only accounts that are communal and rational. In addition, writing and reading become acts of discourse analysis as individuals attempt to understand the semiotic codes operating in their discursive situations. Composing and reception are thus interactive since both are performances of production, requiring the active construction of meaning according to one or another coded procedure. The opposition between the active writer and the passive reader is displaced: both writing and reading are regarded as constructive. The work of rhetoric is to develop a lexicon that articulates the complex coding activity involved in writing and reading.

Composition Studies and Cultural Studies

Composition studies is undertaking projects in both pedagogy and research that parallel those in cultural studies. Some of these efforts signal the emergence of a social epistemic rhetoric, a rhetoric that considers signifying practices in relation to the ideological formation of the self within a context of economics, politics, and power. Two recent essay collections indicate that composition studies has arrived at a conception of itself that refuses to apologize for rhetoric's historical commitment to the classroom. Furthermore, their appearance represents an effort to bring together the work of theory, politics, and classroom practice to produce a rich new form of dialogue in English studies, a dialogue that characterizes the projects of cultural studies at every turn.

Reclaiming Pedagogy: The Rhetoric of the Classroom, edited by Patricia Donahue and Ellen Quandahl, examines the relation between the composition class and critical theory. The volume argues not that theory and practice will simply correct or justify each other but that together they will enable a new discourse including and transcending both. This position recovers the space Aristotle designated the jurisdiction of rhetoric, the historically contingent domain of the productive arts lying between theory and practice (Atwill). The result is a poststructuralist and political rhetoric and pedagogy.

Having called for a refigured discourse for rhetoric and the classroom, Donahue and Quandahl set forth the premises of the collection, and here their self-conscious alignment with the projects of cultural studies is everywhere apparent. The participants pointedly deny the unified, coherent, transcendent self of liberal humanism, arguing "that there is no such thing as creating words out of yourself, since subjectivity, one's self, is a social order, preexisting the individual. . . . One enters rather than generates a textual history" (13). Once again, however, the social and the subject interact:

> Put simply, the symbolic order of culture is its collective set of signifying systems, one of which is language, and language is a system that preexists the individual. The individual enters that system at a particular stage of develop-ment, uses it to produce meaning, and is produced by it.   (12)

These essays thus take textuality as their center, the pedagogy offered being "textual, text-oriented," an assertion that involves a number of consequences. Language is seen "as a system of power and . . . the reader as a constituent of that system." Students are encouraged to engage in "resistant readings," readings that "resist the monologic voice that depends for its meaning upon readers thoroughly sharing the assumptions of writers." The point is to allow "variously circulating interpretive codes to come into play . . . not to awaken the ideologically complacent, but to teach ways in which discursive authority functions" (3). Thus, signifying practices are regarded not only as diverse and conflictual but as immersed in ideology. Language is further identified "as the site of struggle to determine 'truth' and to control its production" (4). All positions are considered always already ideological so that teacher and student must acknowledge their own political situatedness. But the classroom cannot simply reproduce the shaping process of culture and ideology. Instead, the attention must be directed to "the cultural inscriptions in any text, including the pedagogical scene" (9). The detection of cultural codes is essential, as is cultivation of the student's ability to resist texts. Students are "to assert power, to own rules, and to shape a new content" (11). In short, they are to engage in interpretive practices that enable critique, a critique that is always ideologically situated. Donahue and Quandahl, however, are not altogether sanguine that it is possible to create a resistant subject capable of recognizing concealed conflicts and examining the reasons for that conceal-ment. They recognize the constraints of their situation: "[I]n spite of the strong rhetoric of subversion in many of the theorists cited in this volume, we know that there is even stronger institutional pressure to align new theory with the known" (15). Yet this "rhetoric of subversion" is in remarkably short supply in the collection as a whole, with the attention to theory continually superseding the commitment to a radical politics.

The premise of *Composition and Resistance*, edited by C. Mark Hurlbert and Michael Blitz, is closely related to that of *Reclaiming Pedagogy*. One significant difference is the strong insistence that the rhetorical and pedagogical practices offered are contestatory. This time the theory-practice association is at every turn related to the ideological and political nature of discourse. Indeed, *Composition and Resistance* is self-consciously committed to change outside as well as within the classroom, since the essays foreground an agenda of social transformation that would promote democratic practices at all levels and phases of society.

The social constructionist text regards the subject as the product of inter-secting and conflicting discourses, all part of power formations. The role of the writing class then becomes to intervene in this process of construction, locating the conflicts in order to make them the center of writing. Thus, the editors explain: "Composition teachers must work with students to examine and intervene in the 'construction' which produces people as subjects and by which people subject other people to inequitable, abusive, intolerable conditions" (25). Since language is at the center of the formation of the subject, serving as the mediator between material conditions and the individ-ual, writing—text production—is a manifestation of the central process of self and social formation. Echoing both poststructuralist and Marxist catego-ries, the editors argue that, as language rewrites the subject and society, the subject can rewrite language in reshaping the self and social arrangements. Writing is therefore both social and personal, providing students with the means "to make learning a personal act toward taking greater control" of their lives, and it must situate this process "in and with social order" (4).

Text production and reception then become essential acts of human agency in a democratic society, a society that promises a space for open and free critique and yet denies it at every turn. The impulse is to take the promise of democracy seriously, to take "literally the kinds of rights and freedoms that people in positions of political/social/economic power *profess* to guarantee" (22). There is no question that the "required" form of academic discourse discourages these freedoms, enforcing instead a conformity of thought and expression, demanding "codes of silence" (4). The alternative is not to abandon academic discourse altogether—the volume is not without it—but to test its limits by examining its excluded other, the discourse of students themselves, by "supporting students' efforts to move back and forth (one meaning of interpretation) between dialects and styles" (23). The classroom encourages new ways of writing and reading without neglecting the contrasting ways of the old; students consider "Plato *and* Navaho folk tales, Shakespeare *and* Jacqueline Susann, rap *as well as* papers of/on literary criticism, or better, critical papers infused with the power of rap—the power to speak for change by speaking in a new way and in and for a new place—by self-consciously calling for participation and action" (24). This participation and action, furthermore, is once again self-consciously social: it asks for collaboration not only among student writers but also among teachers—a call for enacting as well as endorsing a social rhetoric.

The participants in *Composition and Resistance*, like their counterparts in *Reclaiming Pedagogy*, do not underestimate the obstacles to their objectives. Indeed, the essays in the collection record the difficulties in this undertaking. Asking a group of students to interrogate the conventions of the privileged social class they are working hard to enter—the class to which the teachers already comfortably belong—is not an easy task, and the process may involve discomfort for teachers and students alike. To refuse to engage the ideological dimensions of "ordinary discourse," however, is to acquiesce to injustices that underwrite class, race, gender, age, and other invidious distinctions. This collection, then, offers no easy answers or solutions, but it does "attempt to introduce incoherence—a loss of composure—into 'the entrenched order of things,' " not for the sake of anarchy or deconstructionist free play, but in the interests of bringing about a better social and personal order. Despite all their doubts, confusions, and failures, the participants in this collection remain committed to writing as a political act of transformation and betterment.

These two remarkable volumes firmly establish the parallel trajectories of certain projects in composition studies and cultural studies. Other book-length projects take up some of their major themes, most notably Susan Miller's *Rescuing the Subject*, David Bleich's *The Double Perspective*, and Marilyn Cooper and Michael Holzman's *Writing as Social Action*. In addition, a number of other research efforts under way in composition studies—efforts sometimes deliberately centered on the classroom and sometimes not—share the problematic and inquiry agendas of cultural studies. Johnson's description of the three major kinds of cultural studies projects so far attempted—productive, textual, and lived experience—provides a useful organizing device for considering a few of these efforts. I hasten to add that this research is not the only kind of project I recommend for composition studies. Janice Lauer and Andrea Lunsford's quite different description of the three major emphases of rhetoric and composition graduate programs—history, theory, and empirical studies—is a better scheme for conceptualizing the field as a whole. I am instead interested in research that cuts across these useful divisions without replacing them. In other words, these endeavors expand without replacing present work in rhetoric and composition.

Johnson's tripartite division of cultural studies into productive, textual, and lived experience categories is related to a specific model of cultural dissemination. This model corresponds generally with the rhetorical model of communication described by figures as diverse as Aristotle, Kenneth Burke, and Andrea Lunsford. In short, cultural artifacts are produced, the production assumes some textual form (print, film, television, conversation), the text is consumed by an audience in the form of negotiated interpretations, and the interpretations are part of the lived cultures or social relations of the interpreters. As I said earlier, Johnson criticizes the examples of cultural studies he presents because they tend to focus on one moment of the process instead of considering the process as a whole.

One conspicuous strength of recent work in rhetoric and composition studies is its attempt to focus on the process of text production. While the dominant paradigms in literary studies have been restricted to text interpretation and, then, apart from any influencing context, labeling production an inaccessible function of genius, composition has attempted to study and describe the concrete activities of text production. This approach, of course, is in keeping with rhetoric's historical emphasis on teaching strategies for generating texts, primarily heuristic procedures for invention, patterns of arrangement, and principles of syntax and style.

More recently, the concern for production has been seen in empirical studies of the composing process, from the case studies of Janet Emig to the protocol analysis of Linda Flower and John R. Hayes and others. As some observers have pointed out, these studies often suffer from a conception of composing as an exclusively private, psychologically determined act, a stance that distorts because it neglects the larger social contexts of composing. Addressing this inadequacy in considering text production is the turn in composition research to ethnographic study or, in the terms favored by the Birmingham group, the study of culture as lived activity. The pioneer in this effort in English studies in the United States has been Shirley Brice Heath, who has related patterns of learning in language to subject formation within structures of class, race, and gender. Two recent volumes have shown the effects of this work: *Reclaiming the Classroom*, edited by Dixie Goswami and Peter R. Stillman; and *The Writing Teacher as Researcher*, edited by Donald A. Daiker and Max Morenberg. The teacher-as-researcher impulse is an attempt to make all teachers ethnographic researchers of the concrete economic and social conditions of their students, situating instruction in text production and interpretation within the lived cultures of students, within class, race, gender, and ethnic determinations. Both volumes, furthermore, have begun the work of considering the ideological as well as the narrowly institutional settings of learning, and both examine student signifying practices within the conflicts of concrete economic, social, and political conditions. Although these studies have so far been somewhat tentative in stating that their investigations are political, at their best they examine signifying practices within the entire context of production, texts, readings, and lived cultures. (I return to the uses of ethnography later.)

Other studies dealing with text production have been organized around a consideration of collaborative learning and writing, a subject treated historically in Anne Gere's engaging monograph. Current work in this area is extensive, but Kenneth Bruffee is the person whose name is most often associated with this project. A number of critiques of his work—critiques not necessarily unfriendly—have recently attempted to figure collaboration in relation to the place of signifying practices in forming subjectivities within concrete social and material conditions. Lisa Ede and Andrea Lunsford, for example, have invoked the theories of Roland Barthes and Michel Foucault on authorship and the actual practices of writers outside the classroom to argue that collaborative writing constitutes the norm for composing and that writing is necessarily communal. Trimbur has also called on ideological critique in treating the strengths and weaknesses of collaborative practices, attempting to refigure them in the light of a social conception of subject formation that allows for struggle and resistance at the site of group efforts ("Consensus"). In short, discussions of text production within the context of collaborative learning have begun to interrogate the insistence on writing as an exclusively private and personal act of a docile and quiescent subject.

The many methods of textual critique that rely on structuralist and post-structuralist language theory generally fall into two groups. The first of these seeks to analyze the discourse of various disciplinary formations in order to locate their part in shaping subjectivities within historical conditions. Mina Shaughnessy undertook this form of analysis when she identified the use of medical language to discuss basic writers and the disadvantaged social groups from which they often emerge. For Shaughnessy, as Trimbur points out,

> cultural studies of writing might begin in at least one important respect as an effort of writing teachers to resist the dominant representations of subordinate groups and to contest the social construction of otherness as pathological problems for the professional intervention of educators, social workers, urban planners, and policy-makers.   ("Cultural Studies" 15)

Shaughnessy has in turn encouraged a host of resistant readings of institutional constructions of teachers and students, most notably in the work of Linda Brodkey, David Bartholomae, Patricia Bizzell, and Greg Myers. The use of textual as well as ethnographic analysis along distinctly feminist lines in examining signifying practices and self-formations in writing is also seen in the recent work of Elizabeth Flynn.

Others in this first category have tried to locate the workings of discursive practices in the formation of scientific disciplines, exploring the structure of disciplinary formations and the subjectivities that inhabit them as a function of signifying practices. Carolyn Miller, Greg Myers, and Charles Bazerman have been especially prominent in this undertaking. Some researchers have attempted the textual analysis of signifying practices in various nonacademic settings. For example, Barbara Hamilton has combined an ethnographic method with textual analysis in examining written presentence recommendations in criminal offenses in a Detroit court. Myrna Harrienger has considered the signifying practices of ill, elderly women in nursing homes and the ways in which medical discourse silences them. Gary Heba, emulating Hebdige's work on youth subcultures, has examined the relation of youth movies to adolescents' resistance to hegemonic discourse practices.

The second group of textual studies focuses on developing lexicons for locating and examining the imbrications of textual practices and power, considering the methods of textuality in forming subjectivity. Much work along these lines has been conducted in communication departments as a part of media studies—for example, the projects of Arthur Asa Berger, Stewart Ewen, and John Fiske. Much less has appeared in English departments, but the work has begun. George Dillon, for example, discusses the cultural codes inscribed within popular advice books, calling on the language of structuralist and poststructuralist categories. W. Ross Winterowd's recent *The Rhetoric of the "Other" Literature* attempts to provide a critical language for nonliterary texts, invoking the work of Aristotle, Burke, and poststructuralism. Both authors regard reading and writing practices as interchangeable in that they are constructive rather than simply reflective of experience, although the two works also share a timidity about discussing the politics of signifying practices. Still these projects represent a start in the right direction. Workers in composition studies must now devise lexicons to enable the discussion of the structures and ideological strategies of written texts that take into account recent Marxist and poststructuralist developments; terminologies and methods are needed to act as counterparts, for example, to the rich work of Fiske in television studies. If students are to evaluate the role of signifying practices in forming consciousness through their own writing and reading, teachers must provide a language for identifying these practices and their operations.

I have already discussed the study of lived cultures through ethnographic means as recommended by the teacher-as-researcher development. As Janice Lauer and J. William Asher have indicated, ethnographic study of lived cultures has been undertaken in settings outside the school, more specifically, in writing in the workplace. Until recently, however, these studies have not challenged the practices considered, taking them as objects of analysis, not of critique. Jennie Dautermann has shown new possibilities by examining the discourses of female nurses in a hospital setting as they collaboratively compose a manual for nursing procedures. Her study reveals the conflicts in power formations and the way subordinate groups negotiate them in a setting in which male doctors give orders and female nurses carry them out. In "Interpersonal Conflict in Collaborative Writing," Mary M. Lay is also concerned with gender codes and their relation to power in collaborative writing in business settings. In "Ideology and Collaboration in the Classroom and in the Corporation," James E. Porter attempts to apply an ideological critique to the teaching of collaborative writing in the business writing classroom as well as in the business writing setting itself. All these studies focus on the conflicts generated as signifying practices form discursive subject locations within an institutional setting, conflicts that reproduce the class, race, and gender struggles of the larger society.

The composition studies described in this essay is finally consistent with the historical role rhetoric has performed in most Western societies, but it is also a salutary departure from that role. Ruling classes after all have always made certain that their members are adept at the signifying practices that ensure the continuance of their power. Rhetorics as diverse as those of Plato, Cicero, Augustine, Hugh Blair, and I. A. Richards have been forwarded in the name of a "true" discourse, a discourse, however, that actually best served the interests of a particular ruling group. The important difference in the rhetoric outlined here is the commitment to democratic practices, that is, practices that work for the equitable distribution of the power to speak and write among all groups in a society. In addition, this rhetoric includes the commitment to make available to these groups the rhetorical competence to present their positions effectively, including the means to resist and subvert dominant discourse practices. Both its research program and its pedagogical practices are accordingly dedicated to establishing the social conditions for genuinely democratic discourse communities. For some, sad to say, this effort will be considered inappropriate and misguided or even dangerously close to "indoctrination," as Maxine Hairston has recently charged in a burst of anti-intellectual conservatism. For its adherents, though, it seems the only possible hope for a society that too often prefers the exchange of violence to the exchange of language in addressing conflicts. Rhetoric, after all, was invented to resolve disputes peacefully, as an alternative to armed conflict, and it remains the best option in a perilous time.

Purdue University

COMPOSITION STUDIES:
POSTMODERN OR POPULAR

John Trimbur

COMPOSITION studies has emerged over the last two decades as an intellectual project to constitute the study and teaching of writing as a field of knowledge. I use the term *field* here instead of *discipline* because much of the work carried out in composition studies has situated itself at the margins of the established academic disciplines. Instead of staking out sharp boundaries, the founding of composition studies has produced an open field that has resisted the codified methods and governing research programs that define the terrain of the traditional disciplines. Its openness to external influence, however, places composition studies in a problematic relation to the sources it draws on, to disciplines such as cognitive psychology, ethnography, philosophy, literary studies, and linguistics and to intellectual currents in rhetoric, critical theory, and, more recently, cultural studies.

This relation is problematic in part because composition studies has drawn on these sources largely on its own, for its own purposes, without the participation or even the knowledge of members of other fields. The invention of composition studies, in this respect, results from poaching, from appropriating what is available. We have learned, as it were, to live off the land, hunting and gathering in a nomadic existence without a sedentary center. Composition studies has composed itself not by systematic engineering but by a kind of piecemeal bricolage, cutting and splicing elements from the intellectual landscape that seem useful. The result is that composition studies looks more like a collage—a postmodern pastiche of juxtaposed parts—than a unified field.

But there is also a second reason that the relation between composition studies and the established disciplines is problematic: the founding of composition studies as a mobile and heterogeneous set of interests has been influenced by dedisciplinary impulses in contemporary intellectual work. At just the moment composition studies has attempted to constitute itself as an interdisciplinary field, the traditional disciplines themselves seem to be collapsing under the weight of a radical critique. As Louise Wetherbee Phelps puts it:

> Across the disciplines all the old realities are in doubt, placed under radical
> critiques—critiques that challenge reason, consciousness, knowledge, mean-
> ing, communication, freedom, and other values asserted by the Enlightenment
> and developed in the modern sciences, humanities, and public life.
>
> (*Composition* 5)

The postmodern world composition studies has been born into is a far remove
from the positivist certainties that founded the modern academic disciplines.
We apparently must now live—and maneuver the study and teaching of
writing—in a postmodern free-for-all that has blurred the lines between fields
of study, that has fragmented and undermined the disciplinary projects of
normal academic work.

Because of this predicament, the invention of composition studies cannot
be a matter of academic business as usual. Instead, at least by a postmodernist
account, it must be a mobile project of borrowing and quoting, of resisting
codified methods, of radical disbelief. At first glance, the choices seem clear:
we can curse the margins we occupy or we can go with the postmodern flow.
In the chair's address "Composing Ourselves," delivered to the 1989 CCCC
meeting, Andrea Lunsford recommends the latter course. Lunsford describes
composition studies as a "postmodern discipline" characterized by blurred
genres of writing and scholarship, heteroglossic and dialogic modes of discourse, and nonhierarchical and collaborative relations of work.

I find Lunsford's vision of composition studies an appealing one. At the
same time, however, I suggest that we should not embrace postmodernism
hastily. The purpose of this essay is to offer a cautionary tale—to argue that
despite (or perhaps because of) its seductive appeal, we should resist falling
for postmodernism wholesale. We need to step back for a moment, to examine
the pressures and limits of postmodernism, what it makes possible and what
it constrains. Like its description of the world, postmodernism is neither a
stable nor a unified cultural formation. Postmodernism differs from its avant-
gardist predecessors, such as dadaism, futurism, and surrealism, that announced their eruption onto the cultural scene through manifestos for revolutionary change. Postmodernism is not so much a doctrine or a movement as
an attitude and mood in the air that has crept up on us, a structure of feeling
that suffuses the contemporary, traversing practices and forms of expression
that range from Jean Baudrillard's "hyperreality" to *In Living Color*.

While postmodernism is often treated within composition studies as a
theoretical breakthrough, I picture postmodernism not just as a radical critique but also as a symptom of the current historical conjuncture. To do this,
I locate postmodernism in relation to the great modernist projects for human
emancipation and a civil society separate from state power and the market
economy. The very subversions of postmodernism—its disbelief in metanarratives, its resistance to totalizing schemata, its historicizing and localizing

critical energies, its attention to dissensus and the incommensurability of discourses—simultaneously run the risk, whether inadvertently or otherwise, of contributing to the decline of public discourse and utopian aspirations to create popular spheres of influence within civil society.[1]

I do not suggest that we can or should go back to Enlightenment notions of a universal consensus of reason or an undifferentiated public of autonomous, freely constituted citizen-subjects as the guarantee of open exchange and unconstrained discourse. The apparently radical politics of postmodernism, however, can exert privatizing and depoliticizing effects. While self-consciously rhetorical, the overriding sense of contingency in postmodernism can dissolve the rhetor into a function instead of the agent of discourse, locked in what Fredric Jameson calls a "prison house of language" that offers no escape, no strategy to increase popular participation in public life. In this sense, postmodernism presents itself as a contradictory phenomenon: it is both a powerfully destabilizing intellectual strategy and a mark of cultural exhaustion in the history of the contemporary.

Modernism and Postmodernism: Figuring Metropolitan Experience

There are a number of ways to describe the relation between modernism and postmodernism, ranging from aesthetics to epistemology to political theory. I follow the suggestion made by Raymond Williams, Marshall Berman, David Harvey, and others that the emergence of the modern city in the nineteenth century is central to the modernist vision of human emancipation and the enrichment of everyday life. The image and fact of the modern city—or, perhaps better put, what Williams calls "metropolitan perception"—capture the creative destruction of modernity (37–48). By overturning the bounded world of traditional society, the revolutionary energies of modernity created a civil society within the interstices of the old order, a new domain of freedom where science, reason, and art could liberate humanity from material scarcity, arbitrary power, and the irrationality of superstition, myth, and religion.

The modernism of Baudelaire, Balzac, Hugo, Manet, Dickens, Dostoevsky, and other nineteenth-century writers and artists represents an effort to come to grips with the modernity of the city—Paris, London, Saint Petersburg—and the emergence of modern class society with its convulsive energies and contradictions. The modernists of the nineteenth century pictured the city as a maelstrom of perpetual change and utopian possibilities. Metropolitan perception, as Williams notes, registers not only the alienation and social atomization of the "crowd of strangers" thrown together on the urban streets but also "new possibilities of unity" in the "vitality, the variety, the liberatory diversity and mobility of the city" (41–43). The modern city, as Baudelaire was perhaps the first to discover, offers the strolling flaneur— "an 'I' with an insatiable appetite for the 'non-I' "—rich and dissociating encounters with otherness (9). At the same time, metropolitan experience also represents the promise of what Berman calls a "paradoxical unity, a unity of disunity" (15).

This tension between unity and otherness, utopian renewal and social disintegration is a strategic source of creative energy for the modernists of metropolitan experience. In a seminal essay on modernism, "The Painter of Modern Life," Baudelaire says, "Modernity is the transient, the fleeting, the contingent; it is the one half of art, the other being the eternal and immutable." For Baudelaire, the modernity of metropolitan experience is concentrated in the "passing moment and all the suggestions of eternity that it contains" (13). Caught up in the movement and multiplicity of urban life, Baudelaire's quintessential figure of modernity, the flaneur, reveals the "eternal" in the radiant surfaces and fugitive beauty of the city. For the flaneur, the city is an artificial paradise of impenetrable mysteries and inexhaustible differences.

Like Marx, Baudelaire recognized that modernity was marked decisively by the appearance of the masses as historical subjects. In Baudelaire's Paris, the streets belonged to the people, a legacy of 1789 kept alive by what Baudelaire calls the "popular movements, republican clubs, and pageantry of 1848" (24). For Baudelaire, the popular sovereignty of life in the streets opened up a new cultural space and new aesthetic possibilities for the artist and writer in revolt against the official academicism of the day. The task of the modern artist, therefore, is to "set up his house in the heart of the multitude, amid the ebb and flow of motion, in the fugitive and the infinite." According to Baudelaire, the practice of modernity drives the modern artist out of the academy and into the streets, into the "moving chaos" of urban life, to "enter the crowd as though it were an immense reservoir of electrical energy." A "kaleidoscope gifted with consciousness," the modern artist captures the fragmented unity of metropolitan experience (9).

Baudelaire's injunction to merge the modernist sensibility into the metropolitan rhythms of the crowd discloses one of the essential dialectics of modernism: the interplay of spontaneity and consciousness. For Baudelaire, as well as for Marx, modernity registers the creative tension between the revolutionary energies of the masses in the street and the utopian visions of avant-gardist art and vanguard politics. Artists and revolutionists alike pictured the nineteenth-century city as the site of spontaneous upheavals from below and of social engineering from above. Across Europe in 1848, in the Paris Commune of 1870 and the soviets of 1905 and 1917, in Barcelona in 1936, in Budapest in 1956, and in Paris in 1968, the urban masses sought to turn the city into an arena of popular justice and participatory politics. But if the city figures as the scene of self-determining mass action, it has also become the subject of social planning by urbanists and revolutionary theorists. From Otto Wagner's plan to transform fin de siècle Vienna and Ebenezer Howard's "green cities" to Le Corbusier's *City of Tomorrow*, Frank Lloyd Wright's Broadacre project of 1935, and the urban renewal projects of the 1950s and 1960s in American cities, the city figures as a utopian machine for living. The city itself has become the agent of social change.

As Harvey argues, the emergence of postmodernism signals a break with the creative tensions between spontaneity and consciousness, between the chaotic energies of the popular will and the utopian visions of the vanguard in art and politics. According to Harvey, postmodernism amounts to an antimodernist reaction that rejects social planning as totalizing and opposes delusive self-confidence and utopian revolutionary theory as potentially repressive disciplinary practices. This rejection of the utopian impulses that form one half of modernism, moreover, has led to what Harvey sees as the "most startling fact about postmodernism: its total acceptance of the ephemerality, fragmentation, discontinuity, and the chaotic" in metropolitan experience. Instead of engaging the tension between the chaotic and the utopian, postmodernism, he says, "swims, even wallows in the fragmentary and the chaotic currents of change as if that is all there is" (44). Harvey's characterization of postmodernism requires some qualification, but its very starkness can be useful in sorting out the way postmodernism has sought to disengage itself from the tensions and projects of modernism in order to refigure metropolitan experience. The postmodern metropolis, as Jonathan Raban has dubbed it, is a "soft city." No longer the "machinery and the hero of modernity" (de Certeau 95), the city has been re-presented as a semiotic theater relentlessly disseminating images and signs, new fashions, styles, cultural codes, and personal identities, dissolving the social subject in its intertextual maze. If Ludwig Wittgenstein drew on the metaphor of the city to figure the actuality of language as a life form we inhabit, postmodernism has reversed this procedure to figure the city as a system of language that speaks us.

Postmodernism: Resistance and Reaction

Postmodernism emerged specifically from a crisis within modernism in the late 1950s and early 1960s. This crisis occurred, ironically enough, not because modernism had failed but rather because it had "won." In the postwar period, modernism became the official culture. The oppositional energies and scandalous productions of dadaism, futurism, expressionism, and surrealism were absorbed (and funded) by the museums, the "legitimate" theater, the university curriculum, the foundations and national endowments as the new canon. At the same time, modernist styles and modes of expression were incorporated into the vernacular of the mass media, Hollywood, and the advertising industry. Modernism's revolt against tradition had in fact become the traditional repertoire, a negation of its own creative tensions and trans-formative projects. Modernism, as Jürgen Habermas puts it, is now "domi-nant but dead" ("Modernity" 6), as likely to turn up on Madison Avenue as in art history textbooks.

The problem of postmodernism begins, then, with its own belatedness, with its modernist predecessors having already written the cultural landscape to the saturation point. If the injunction of modernism, in Ezra Pound's famous dictum, was to "make it new," how could postmodernism start over to revolutionize the present? How, the art critic Hal Foster asks, "can we exceed the modern? How can we break with a program that makes a value of crisis (modernism), or progress beyond an era of Progress (modernity), or transgress the ideology of the transgressive (avantgardism)?" (*Anti-aesthetic* ix).

The questions Foster poses can help us understand why postmodernism, as Harvey forcefully argues, privileges its own ephemerality and contingency: postmodernism cannot extricate itself from the empty triumph of modernism to find its own ground to stand on, without returning to the very foundations of modernism as a utopian project to remake culture and society. Postmodern-ism, in this sense, remains wedded to the language of modernism as its point of departure and necessary other. From this perspective, postmodernism's fascination with the sign and the cultural code results not just from the "linguistic turn" in the human sciences at the theoretical level but also from the perception at the practical level that all the stories have been told, retold, and circulated by mass communications; all the images painted and reproduced by the museums, the media, and advertising.

But if a commodified and institutionalized modernism defines the postwar cultural landscape, there are significant differences, Foster suggests, between the types of responses postmodernists have made to the crisis in modernism. According to Foster, a "basic opposition" exists between a "postmodernism of resistance" and a "postmodernism of reaction" (*Recodings* 121). Influenced by poststructuralist theory, the postmodernism of resistance begins with a radical critique of representation and historical narrativity. By contrast, the postmodernism of reaction depends on a stylistic revivification of representa-tion, a return to narrative, to the figure, to decorative effects, to history.

Cindy Sherman's photographs illustrate how postmodernist strategies of resistance have sought to deconstruct the expressive realism of modernism and to disclose the techniques by which representation naturalizes the image, in particular the female image as the object of the male gaze. In an untitled series of black-and-white photos that initially appear to be film stills, Sherman costumed herself as the heroine of grade-B Hollywood films from the 1950s and photographed herself in poses that imply an imminent danger just beyond the frame. But the stability of the image of the heroine in distress is precisely what Sherman's series of film stills seeks to deny. If her photos are self-portraits, they are portraits not of a self that can be represented simply or expressed directly but of a postmodern subject that has been subjected, a subject as object, a replication of a model, a copy of an original that causes the apparent opposition between original and copy to collapse altogether, problematizing representation itself.[2]

Sherman's writing over of "original" film stills, fashion photos, magazine centerfolds, fairy tales, and art masterpieces, always with herself as the subject-object at the unstable center of the frame, is a characteristic postmodernist gesture that not only calls into question the authenticity of artistic expression but also confounds the clichéd responses of the spectator. In this sense, Sherman's photographs represent a critical interrogation of the contingency of both artist and viewer, producer and consumer, by foregrounding their mutual implication in the textuality of contemporary life. As Foster notes, the recycling of worn images and narratives employed by artists like Sherman "entails a shift in position: the artist becomes a manipulator of signs more than a producer of art objects, and the viewer an active reader of messages rather than a passive contemplator of the aesthetic or consumer of the spectacular" (*Recodings* 100). Art becomes a "situational aesthetic" in which the public space of galleries, museums, billboards, or sides of buildings turns into a site of cultural demystification and a critique of the art object as a commodity and a tool in the technology of power. Postmodernist art of resistance, we might say, has rejected the ideology of creative expression in order to investigate the rhetoric of art.

The postmodernism of reaction, too, has based its practices on the rhetoricity of art, on recycling and writing over, but to significantly different effect. The postmodern architecture of Robert Venturi and Philip Johnson, for example, begins by rejecting the modernist program to "make it new." Their postmodernist buildings signal a break both with the self-confidence and optimism of the sleek, simplified, forward-looking lines of the international style and with the totalizing, utopian impulses of Le Corbusier and Wright. The postmodernism of reaction has replaced the sweeping futuristic energies of modernist architectural practice and city planning with localized strategies of pastiche and historical eclecticism, a return to older styles, decoration, ornamentation, and period detail. If Sherman and other postmodernists of resistance have ransacked the archive of images and narratives to produce radical critiques of representation, the postmodernists of reaction have returned to the past—to history and the architect as *auteur*—not to interrogate a fragmented and contingent present but to fashion a campy pop-classical facade for the contemporary edifice.

Johnson's AT&T building in New York offers a good example of the eclectic recombination of existing and heterogeneous elements that characterizes the postmodernism of reaction. The AT&T building resembles the skyscrapers of the international style that seem to rise effortlessly out of the urban canyons of American cities. It is capped, however, by an incongruous Chippendale top. If Johnson has appropriated a vernacular style, the impulse here is not a revivalist one that pays homage to the past or glorifies a preindustrial utopia (as did, say, the Gothic revivalism of the Victorian age). Johnson's strategy of composition and design quotes from the past but not to redeem a demoted history. Instead, Johnson presents history reduced to a matter of style, a set of codes to mix and match—a historicism that makes history into an incoherent repertoire of styles at the same time that it (quite literally) disguises the present reality of the contemporary multinational corporation behind the nostalgia of period detail.

This return to history, to tradition, to representation that figures prominently in the postmodernism of reaction amounts to an effort to be affirmative, to break with modernism's adversarial culture. In contrast to the elitist "difficulties" in the works of high modernism (Joyce, Eliot, Gertrude Stein, Picasso, and others), the postmodernists of reaction style their work as populist and accessible. This rapprochement with the public (and the market) is evident in nostalgia films that recycle film noir and Saturday afternoon serials, in Julian Schnabel's smirking and kitschy oil-on-velvet paintings, in *Big Chill* commemorations of the style (but not the content) of the 1960s, in Venturi's celebration of strip architecture and the decorated shed in his influential manifesto for postmodernist architecture *Learning from Las Vegas*. The *retro-nuevo* impulses of the postmodernism of reaction offer a history that amounts to a grab bag of stylistic elements, a historicism that amounts to the evacuation of historical meaning, a return to the past that reproduces without interrogating the fragmentation of the present and mystifies the public space of the museum, the gallery, the city as a spectacle of nostalgic, campy consumption.

Venturi poses the problem of the postmodernism of reaction when he says that "Americans don't need piazzas—they should be home watching TV" (qtd. in Foster, *Recodings* 122). If postmodernists of resistance have sought to deconstruct the spectacle of mass culture by problematizing the nature and function of representation and narrativity, the postmodernists of reaction have embraced mass culture and the collapse of the public sphere under the weight of privatized experience. What the postmodernists of reaction seem to have intuited, as Foster remarks, is that "the consensual guarantee of traditional culture is no longer so crucial to social order, for today we are socialized less through an indoctrination into tradition than through a *consumption* of the cultural" (*Recodings* 159).

If this consumption occurs willy-nilly for the individual, through a startling variety of media and artifacts, it has been systematized by a postmodernist architecture of reaction in the form of Boston's Faneuil Hall, New York's South Street Seaport, Baltimore's Harbor Place, San Francisco's Fisherman's Wharf, and other urban redevelopment projects. Designed to occupy historic sites in the old city, these projects are not just glorified shopping malls and entertainment centers. They are signs of the absence of productive labor in the contemporary deindustrialized landscape, spectacular fictions to replace the historical functions of urban life. As Fredric Jameson might say, these projects do not so much renew metropolitan experience as create a "hyper-space" that replaces the urban trajectories of the older promenade, providing "narrative strolls . . . we are no longer allowed to conduct on our own" ("Postmodernism" 83).

Cultural Studies and the Popular

What I have suggested so far is that postmodernists of reaction have reduced the public space of metropolitan experience to an arena of private consumption, a spectacle of images and narratives. The postmodernists of resistance, however, have sought, often with powerful results, to demystify the social processes by which individuals produce and consume images and narratives. While the works of Cindy Sherman, Barbara Kruger, Jenny Holzer, and other postmodernists are important critiques of representation, I return now to David Harvey's characterization of postmodernism, to worry whether the postmodern deconstruction of representation does not, despite its subversive intentions, serve to reproduce a logic of domination. Sherman's photographic demonstration that the self is socially constructed and spectacularly consumed may initially appear to be liberatory, but it can harden, as a postmodern convention, into a concession to our own contingency—a critical recognition, on the one hand, of cultural imprisonment but, on the other, a sense of powerlessness in the face of subjectification.

This, at any rate, is what I see as the current dilemma of postmodernism, a dilemma from which a number of questions might arise: Is there a way out of postmodernism's sense of contingency? Is the subject no more than "the transient, the fleeting, the contingent" product of the discursive apparatus of contemporary metropolitan experience? Does contemporary cultural experience amount to the relentless dissemination of signifiers and the private consumption of commodified images and narratives? Is it possible, short of asserting a new and no doubt preposterous metanarrative of the "eternal and immutable," to locate a critical perspective that revives the social hopes and utopian aspirations of modernism?

I do not pretend to answer these questions to my own or the reader's satisfaction. My point, however, is that we ought to be asking ourselves these questions when we consider the claim that composition studies is (or should be) a postmodern field. I suggest two strategies to address the dilemma of postmodernism.

The first strategy, which I treat only briefly, is to think of postmodernism

not only as a theoretical breakthrough—one that has deconstructed the subject, subverted the universality of metanarratives, disclosed the knowledge-
power equation, and revealed the textuality of everyday life—but also as a
symptom of contemporary metropolitan experience. Postmodernism, as I
indicated earlier, needs to be located in its historical moment. In this regard,
Jameson's notion of postmodernism as the cultural logic of late capitalism
offers an important historicizing lead. According to Jameson, postmodernism
represents the spatiotemporal order of the multinational corporation, a "new
decentered global network . . . of power and control" that is "difficult for
our minds and imaginations to grasp" ("Postmodernism" 80), that in fact we
experience schizophrenically as an inapprehensible and fragmented reality.
This description of the contemporary cultural landscape is powerful, but I am
skeptical about Jameson's claim that postmodernism and the late capitalism
it embodies actually constitute a new historical stage.

A new historical stage, at least in the Marxist tradition, is predicated
on a systematic expansion of the means of production that transcends the
contradictions of the previous socioeconomic formation. For example, the
transition from entrepreneurial to monopoly capitalism—from the first to the
second stage of capital—in the late nineteenth and early twentieth centuries
resolved, at least temporarily, the crises of overproduction that resulted from
intense and anarchic intercapitalist competition by consolidating vertically
integrated corporations and world markets for capitalist products. The late
capitalism Jameson presents as the third stage of capital may result, however,
not so much from the productive vitality of a new historical stage of economic
development as from the inability of revolutionary movements in the West
to replace capitalist social relations with a new order. Late capitalism, that
is, may not be the result of new objective conditions brought about by an
economic expansion of capital worldwide that has granted the ruling classes
a new lease on life. Instead, it may result from the persistence of monopoly
capitalism—what Lenin called imperialism, the highest stage of capitalism—
brought about by the subjective failure of mass working-class parties to take
power. Moreover, if late capitalism actually embodies the advanced senility
of monopoly capitalism, and not Jameson's third stage of capital, then postmodernism as its cultural logic can best be seen as an expression of cultural
exhaustion and political defeat, not of a new historical era.

By this account, the structure of feeling that pervades postmodernism is
inflected decisively by the inability of the French worker-student alliance to
overthrow Gaullism in 1968. By the same token, the hiatus of popular social
movements in the United States, combined with what Ira Shor calls the
"conservative restoration" of Reaganism in the 1980s, has weighed heavily
on the postmodern sensibility, producing a kind of psychic Thermidor that
makes it difficult to imagine the social subject as something more than the
effect of endless cycles of consumption and private experience. To speak of

the historical agency of the subject or the possibility of a reconstructive public discourse sounds naive in a postmodern world where the adversarial energies of modernism have been depleted and co-opted and then repudiated altogether by a postmodernism of reaction that offers the privatized pleasures of mass consumer culture. It sounds equally naive to talk about popular aspirations for justice in a political landscape where the New Right of Reaganism and Thatcherism has appropriated the rhetorical grounds to speak for the people or when the supposedly subversive recognition of racial, sexual, class, and ethnic difference has, in the current discourse and practice of everyday life, polarized society and threatened the civility of metropolitan experience.

But it is precisely for these reasons that I suggest a second strategy to address the dilemma of postmodernism. This strategy figures metropolitan experience by taking into account the necessarily social construction of subjectivity but without the fatalistic and overpowering sense of contingency that suffuses the structure of feeling in much of postmodernism. What I have in mind is the political-intellectual project of cultural studies.

The tradition of cultural studies ranges from Richard Hoggart's detailed and loving evocation of British working-class life in *The Uses of Literacy* through the writings of Raymond Williams and Stuart Hall to Paul Willis's critical ethnography of British working-class students, Dick Hebdige's study of punk and Rasta subcultures, Lawrence Grossberg's work on rock 'n' roll fans, and Janice Radway's study of romance readers. What holds this line of inquiry together is a sustained effort to balance the semiosis of contemporary life against the lived and living experience of individuals and groups. Cultural studies, that is, portrays spectators and consumers not only as subject positions created by the discursive apparatus of the state, the media, and the culture industry but also as active interpreters of their own experience who use the cultural practices and productions they encounter differentially and for their own purposes. In other words, cultural studies has raised a question that apparently has not occurred within the discourse of postmodernism. How do people in the course of their everyday lives incorporate the images and narratives of metropolitan experience, and how do people make popular the codes of mass-mediated culture and the practices of a regulated social order?

To pose the question of metropolitan experience this way—as a matter not just of socially constructed subject positions but of the popular practices individuals and groups have devised to negotiate the discursive maze of urban life—seems helpful for a number of reasons. For one thing, the notion of the popular revises the severe textualism of postmodernism. Instead of assuming, as postmodernists often do, that the effective meanings of social texts can be deciphered from the constitutive surfaces of popular entertainment and mass-mediated culture by acts of critical reading, cultural studies has sought to shift the focus from the history of the text (and its interrogation by the expert critic) to the history of readers (and accounts of ordinary experience).

This shift involves a significant complication of received models of communication. On the one hand, cultural studies disrupts the conventional view of communication as imparting a single meaning from receiver to sender and rejects traditional forms of content analysis that see the social text as a transparent bearer of messages. But cultural studies has also distanced itself, on the other hand, from more recent poststructuralist theories that see social texts not as expressing meanings or reflecting reality but as producing representations of the "real" by placing the viewer in ideologically situated subject positions. For cultural studies, as Dave Morley notes, "the meaning produced by the encounter of text and subject cannot be read off straight from its 'textual characteristics' or discursive strategies." Rather, the viewer as a social subject will always *exceed* the subject implied by the text, mobilizing a specific and historically concrete repertoire of reading strategies that are determined not only by "the performance of the subject by the text" but also by other texts, competing discourses, and extra discursive social relations and experiences (170).

In blunt terms, what you (or the expert critic) see is not necessarily what you get (at the level of the reading subject in history). For cultural studies, the reception of social texts is not the result of an inexhaustible play of signifiers or an indeterminate plurality of (mis)readings. Reading the world remains bound by the pressures and limits of structured and overdetermined discursive spaces—but not in a simple way. "The meaning(s) of a text," Morley says, "will . . . be constructed differently depending on the discourses (knowledges, prejudices, resistances) *brought to bear on the text by the reader*" (171).

This bringing of discourses to bear on the text is how individuals and groups make an apparently monolithic mass culture popular, how they insert themselves and their experience into the fissures in the dominant cultural order. These activities are what Michel de Certeau calls the "practice of everyday life," the ruses, trickeries, evasions, and deceptions ordinary people employ to foil the constraints and compulsions of a bureaucratic commercial order by turning public places and social texts into their own cultural spaces. Secretaries who steal time on the job to read or write letters, workers who "borrow" the boss's tools to make their own furniture, teenagers who use malls to hang out, students who insert popular magazines into their textbooks in school are all making do, manipulating the official system of social control by using its own resources to create popular practices that evade the surveillance of the supervisor and the disciplines of power.

By this account, the popular refers not so much to particular genres or cultural products but to practices, to the ways in which ordinary people make the act of consumption—whether of texts, entertainments, or public places—into productions of cultural meaning. The popular operates, that is, at the micropolitical level of everyday life. "It is concerned," John Fiske says, "with the day-to-day negotiation of unequal power relations in such structures as the family, the immediate work environment, and the classroom." The popular is not radical in the sense of imagining systematic change, but it is progressive because, as Fiske notes, it "is concerned with redistributing power within these structures toward the disempowered" (*Understanding* 56). Popular practices carve out cultural spaces for self-determined activity within a managed social order. In this sense, if the popular is prepolitical, it is also implicitly utopian in its desire to redeem the lived experience of ordinary men and women.

A second reason the notion of the popular seems helpful follows from the emphasis in cultural studies on the strategies and tactics of everyday life. The popular as it has been developed by cultural studies avoids the pessimism of the Frankfurt school's account of mass culture as a colonization of private life worlds by the media and the culture industry. At the same time, it avoids the essentialized class identities ascribed to the working class and other subordinate groups by traditional Marxism. The sphere of the popular, as Hall suggests, cannot be understood as an authentic, autonomous enclave—whether of working-class struggle, women's domestic space, African American traditions, or youth subcultures—outside of and by definition oppositional to cultural power. Instead, the popular points to the intersection of the private and the public, the personal and the political, the subaltern and the dominant in metropolitan experience. The notion of the popular refers to the practices by which individuals and groups negotiate meanings and social identities in the course of everyday life, articulating their own histories but only within a web of shifting and unstable relations, interests, and powers. Such negotiations, moreover, cannot be predicted in advance but, rather, are enacted in bounded ways at given times and places from multiple available possibilities.

There can be little question, as Stuart Hall has commented about Great Britain and Richard Ohmann has said about the United States, that the period from 1880 to 1920 brought about a profound transformation of metropolitan experience. The rise of mass communications—newspapers, magazines, advertising, the radio—and the increasing commodification of popular entertainments such as sports, dancing, musical performance, and other types of recreation and public ritual decisively changed the very textures of urban life. If the metropolitan experience of the late eighteenth and nineteenth century was marked by the creation of public spheres of opinion and influence within civil society, the rise of mass communications radically altered the relations between civil society and the state, the mass media, the culture industry. The chautauquas, mechanics institutes, salons, coffeehouses, dance halls, working-class clubs, and mutual aid societies were gradually incorporated by a mass culture of compulsory education, commodified pleasures, and corporate structures.

The notion of the popular can reinsert a sense of agency that will not be unproblematically incorporated into an increasingly regulated social order. For cultural studies, the hegemonic discourses and practices of metropolitan experience are indeed ideologically charged, but they are "leaky" sites of struggle and ongoing negotiation where no outcomes can be guaranteed in advance. The pleasures of the popular, as Grossberg argues, are constantly overspilling the semiotic bounds of the social text, making the determination of effective meaning a matter of how individuals and groups articulate their own experiences to the given social order. And in this sense the notion of the popular refers to a kind of nomadic subjectivity that attempts, interdiscursively and episodically, to make a social world cohere from the fractured totality of contemporary life—to produce a self held together in what Louis Althusser calls "teeth-gritting harmony" (150). Cultural studies has sought to fill in the gap left vacant by the postmodern death of the subject with a nonessentialized self that allows for agency and utopian aspirations.

Implications for Composition Studies

It is difficult to say exactly what the implications of this notion of the popular are for composition studies. To look for direct applications only reproduces and reinforces the sense of intellectual dependence that often haunts composition studies. I want to be careful, therefore, not to suggest that cultural studies represents the "next thing," the new paradigm we have been waiting for. Rather, cultural studies and the notion of the popular it has developed offer useful perspectives to sort out the current infatuation with postmodernism. If postmodernism should be seen not just as a radical critique but also as a sign of the cultural exhaustion that has infiltrated the current historical conjuncture, then we cannot simply replace postmodernism with a new theory. We need to work our way through the present moment, to reorient ourselves within the history of the contemporary.

The shift cultural studies has taken from the history of the text to the histories of readers can aid in such a reorientation because, as I have noted, it offers an alternative to the severe textualism of postmodernism. It shows that we need to connect rhetoric both to sign systems and to lived experience in order to understand what Richard Johnson calls the "logic of combination" by which individuals splice together a sense of self from the textual shards of the most mass-mediated culture in human history (69). We need, that is, to counter—but not to reject—the sense of contingency that pervades postmodernism with a sense of historical agency, to see how individuals and groups engage in self-formation not as an autonomous activity but as a practice of everyday life, of poaching on the dominant culture to create popular spaces of resistance, evasion, and making do.

Such a perspective, for example, might offer a way to recast the current impasse in composition studies that has polarized personal voice and authentic selves on the one side and academic discourse and textual selves on the other. We might regard this impasse not just as a matter of competing theories and pedagogies but also as a symptom of the historical polarization of the public and the private, a polarization that individuals and groups have sought to sidestep by the inventive strategies of the popular. From the perspective of the popular, we might look at the study and teaching of writing as neither an affirmation of an essential subject nor an initiation into the language of power but rather as a topoi where the everyday life and personal experience of students intersect with schooled knowledge and the discourse of experts. We might then think of the study and teaching of writing as a way to explore how students internalize, resist, and evade the relations of power in schooling as they learn to separate work from play, academic life from social life, reading for comprehension from reading for pleasure.

The notion of the popular, moreover, might lead us to an expanded sense of what is involved in students' emergence into literacy. As Jerome C. Harste, Virginia Woodward, and Carolyn R. Burke have suggested, early literacy is a sociosemiotic activity by which small children learn how language makes meaning as they "read"—before they are able to read—the environmental print that surrounds them, on signs, logos, television screens, cereal boxes, and so on. From this perspective, the study and teaching of writing necessarily entails attention to mass communications and the textuality of everyday life. When speech communication faculty members left the Modern Language Association and then the National Council of Teachers of English in the early part of the century to set up their own departments, they not only relocated rhetoric outside English studies but also laid the groundwork for the unfortunate separation of composition studies and communication theory. Although the founders of the Conference on College Composition and Communication hoped to bridge this gap, the evolution of the study and teaching of writing has taken place by and large in isolation from the study of the mass media, popular culture, and communication theory.

Finally, we need to reconsider the relation between modernism and postmodernism. I worry that postmodernism has based its authority on a kind of intellectual blackmail that makes it difficult to argue against the current climate of radical disbelief without sounding hopelessly naive, unfashionable, and incipiently totalitarian. While we cannot go back to self-evident belief in the great modernist metanarratives of rationality and human emancipation, we need nonetheless to acknowledge the price of postmodernism's radical critique and the limits of its strategies of subversion and demystification. The notion of the popular is potentially useful as a way to refigure the creative tension modernism found in metropolitan experience, to link the contingent to utopian aspirations through the practice of everyday life.

Worcester Polytechnic Institute

NOTES

[1] I borrow freely in this section and throughout the essay from Jürgen Habermas's problematic notion of the "public sphere," developed most fully in *The Structural Transformation of the Public Sphere*. Critics argue that Habermas's account idealizes the liberal public sphere by failing to analyze its exclusion of women, children, workers, and people of color, thereby reinforcing ideological divisions between public and private life worlds. I cannot do justice here to the problem of Habermas's public sphere, its limitations and utopian aspirations, or to the usefulness of thinking in terms of multiple publics or what Nancy Fraser calls "subaltern counterpublics" in her "Rethinking the Public Sphere."

[2] In the late 1980s, Sherman briefly abandoned her strategy of writing over to produce a series of photographs that perhaps can best be described as derepresentations—images of oozing, protoplasmic organic forms that appear to signify the breakdown of representation altogether. In her most recent gallery show, Sherman returned to the art masterpiece as the site of writing over. Her photographs can be seen in *History Portraits: Cindy Sherman*.

Subjectivity and Its Role in "Constructed" Knowledge: Composition, Feminist Theory, and Psychoanalysis

Irene Papoulis

> It was in graduate school, one woman said—a recent graduate student—that she learned the meaning of "the disciplines." In graduate school she had to put aside her questions about political science (her chosen field) and learn what were the right questions or the questions she should ask if she wanted to become a good political scientist. . . .
>
> —Carol Gilligan

AS A university writing teacher, I am dismayed by the infectiousness of the notion that to think well in a discipline one must put aside one's subjective reactions to academic material. Every college student, of course, must assimilate disciplinary conventions, but unless students learn to articulate their subjective responses to the thoughts they encounter, they will be crippled when it comes time to generate their own ideas. Original thought, by definition, resists established systems; the argument that one must even temporarily abandon one's own responses in order to build a framework from which one can eventually think creatively does not make sense, particularly for students who come to college with a hesitant attitude about their own ideas.

Because our courses emphasize methods rather than specific subject matter, college composition teachers are in a unique position to help students gain access to their own perspectives. Furthermore, as we examine the negotiation that takes place in the writing process between the subjective self and the external world, composition theorists can both learn from and influence other disciplines. My interest here is in a conversation we can have with two fields— feminist theory and psychoanalysis—about the subjective self.

I turn first to feminist theory. In *Women's Ways of Knowing*, Mary Field Belenky et al. present a series of steps, or levels of intellectual development, that women move through on their way to becoming sophisticated, independent thinkers: silence, the fear of expressing any idea; received knowledge, primarily valuing the ideas of external authorities; subjective knowledge, being immersed in one's own responses; procedural knowledge, being concerned with methods; and constructed knowledge, synthesizing subjective ideas with the "reality" of the world at large.

As a composition teacher, I use this scheme to help me understand the intellectual development of female writing students. For my purposes here, however, I want to adapt the scheme, viewing it instead as a description of stances in the writing process of both sexes. Writers of a single essay might move along a line from silence, the inability to express anything, to received knowledge, an appeal to outside ideas: what they think they should write. After that, if allowed to, they may become immersed in a subjective sense of their topic, from which they might emerge with a desire to explore external methods of organizing their thoughts. If they finally manage to write an effective essay, they will have synthesized their subjective realities with a clear, other-oriented means of expression, and thus they will be functioning as "constructed" writers.

Having established a conversation of sorts between the stages in *Women's Ways of Knowing* and the writing process, I must question the impulse Belenky et al. have to view the stages as linear. As a writing teacher, I see students move from one phase to the next in an unpredictable order. Some writers, for example, begin with a subjective stance before considering any other perspective. Others concern themselves naturally with procedures before they have any inkling of their own ideas. Even the final constructed stage—which Belenky et al. regard as the most desirable because it synthesizes inner and outer—could be followed by an intensification of a writer's self-examination and thus a move back into a subjective, or even a silent, orientation.

Because writing and experience are fluid, then, I reject the model of stages—steps on a ladder whose goal is the final stage, at which the other stages are no longer necessary—and replace it with stances, various positions that writers and thinkers take, each of which is valuable and none of which is necessarily better or higher on the scale than another. Different stances are appropriate for different writing tasks; some genres call for a primarily subjective orientation, while others depend on procedural methods.

Though I apply the scheme of Belenky et al. to the writing process of both men and women, I do not ignore the authors' feminist perspective. A significant difference between their scheme, the result of studies of women, and male-oriented taxonomies like William Perry's model is their positing of subjectivity as a pivotal moment. The association of subjectivity with women in particular is very important to feminist theory: women have historically been associated with the personal realm of feelings, and that realm has traditionally been considered less rigorous than the world of abstract ideas. With their exploration of the subjective stage as a critical part of intellectual development, Belenky et al. call attention to the limitations of an emphasis solely on the impersonal.

That emphasis is ingrained in our notions of academic discourse. The graduate student in my epigraph, for example, probably read her instructors in the field of political science correctly when she assumed they would not immediately welcome her questions. Many academics hold fast to the belief that disciplinary knowledge is something necessarily imposed from outside: students should absorb the voices and conventions of a discipline without referring to their own subjective views. One insight of feminist theory is that our hierarchical culture tends to discourage everyone from exploring and attempting to articulate personal and idiosyncratic intuitions. Composition can help remedy this situation by encouraging other disciplines to incorporate subjective responses more explicitly into their discourse; our knowledge about the interaction between intuitive insights and theoretical ideas can help us find ways to allow subjectivity to become part of the academic writing of both women and men. First, though, we have to resist our own indoctrination about the transcendent power of impersonal, abstract ideas, and we have much to learn from feminist theory about how to do so (see Papoulis).

To understand the personal more fully, I turn to what Belenky et al. call the subjective stage. By viewing it instead as a stance, I can apply it to the writing process:

> [F]or subjectivists, the self is nascent and amorphous; the inner voice is a new experience. They must ignore other voices so that they can nurture the seeds of the self. They often dismiss or deny other people and other realities.
>
> (Belenky et al. 136)

Writers who take a subjective stance need the freedom to pay close attention to their own perceptions and questions, without considering the perspectives of others. A concern with audience is counterproductive, because even an imagined other could, by judging, intimidate writers into abandoning their most personal ideas. Writing teachers are often aware of students' need to take a subjective stance. Our so-called prewriting exercises—for example, free writing, focused free writing, and various journal writing methods— engage students at the subjective level by enabling them to "ignore other voices" and explore their individual ideas, even when their overall topic is abstract and not directly related to their own experience. Among many other commonly used exercises, Peter Elbow's loop writing (see *Writing with Power*) is an excellent device for helping students tap their unique fund of subjective insights. Students might free-write their first thoughts and assumptions, compose spontaneous dialogues, address unusual audiences, or imagine still photographs that illustrate abstract topics.

Belenky et al. point out that the subjective stance in itself is limited, because it precludes interaction with others. Subjectivists, they say, eventually need to find ways to move outward into a more constructed stance that takes the external world into account. I resist the notion that a move to constructed knowledge is final; the subjective stance can be an important position for the most constructed knower to retreat into. At the same time, an overall movement toward a constructed essay is necessary in the writing process, even if that movement occurs not in a linear way but by moving back and forth between inner and outer stances. Subjective material alone is not enough if one wants to write an essay for others to understand.

When we teachers want to help students make a link between the subjective material generated by informal writing exercises and a more constructed argument, however, we often get stuck. All we can think to do, sometimes, is simply tell students to go home and turn it into an essay. Yes, the students respond, but how? Without clear guidance, the process of transforming unstructured notes into a formal paper frequently involves abandoning all subjectivity and starting over with a more procedural stance—begun, perhaps, with an outline—that corresponds only to writers' often misguided sense of what they should be thinking and noticing. The result can be an unimaginative piece of writing in which students completely ignore the subjective material they arrived at earlier. Furthermore, if students believe—as many of them seem to—that "real" academic essays are "objective" and voiceless, they understandably come to view subjective prewriting as a waste of time.

To make better use of the subjective stance as an integral part of the process of creating an academic essay, teachers should think of such an essay as simultaneously retaining the subjective material and achieving an effective negotiation between inner and outer realities. To understand how that process might occur, we can interact with another field—psychoanalysis. Freud's "Constructions in Analysis" is the essay I use to represent psychoanalysis; of course, it is a tiny fragment of the field as a whole. In spite of Freud's notoriety for ignoring or misunderstanding female experience, his exploration of subjective reality is extremely helpful to feminists, and his understanding of the mechanisms of the exploration of self can be quite useful, as well, to composition theorists. While the difference between our field and Freud's is obvious—psychoanalysts work primarily with the patient's emotions in a private setting, and we focus on students' intellectual lives in a more public forum—composition teachers can establish a useful dialogue with Freud.

Freud's overall aim in "Constructions in Analysis" is to discuss his process of uncovering what is buried in a patient's repressed unconscious. That unconscious is a locus of ideas, sensations, and experiences, but at the beginning of the analytic process it is often no clearer to the patient than it is to the analyst, a stranger. I see a direct parallel between the patient's unconscious and the fund of intuitive opinions, responses, and ideas about academic topics that all students, whether they realize it or not, bring to the composition classroom.

Freud comments that the analyst's work is similar to an archaeologist's, since both must discover something long buried. The analyst's job is easier, he says, because the subject being investigated is still alive, but both kinds of scientists must work with fragments (of buildings for the archaeologist and of memories for the analyst) and build a clear whole, which for the analyst is an understanding of the patient's unconscious (259). The teacher or peer who is responding to writing in process does some work that involves the same principles as those of both the archaeologist and the analyst. Patients in analysis and students who have no idea what to write with their pages of unorganized scribbles have something in common: they need someone to help them unearth the latent meaning in their seemingly irrational subjectivity. Freud tells us that through the faith that unconscious truths can be brought to light, the analyst can guide patients toward a clear view of their own unconscious. This guidance takes the form of a verbal construction by the analyst, a studied reflection of the patient's words. The analyst must retain faith in the process, Freud says; otherwise, the analysis will not yield the desired results.

Composition teachers, too, work best when they have a similar faith that students do have insights—buried, perhaps, but waiting to emerge. Even with such faith, though, a responder to writing could easily be at a loss when faced with a student's subjective material—for example, free writing and fragments of drafts—since there is no obvious way to help unearth a constructed essay from chaotic intuitions. A responder might be inclined to usurp a writer's work by stating an opinion of it or by making an outline from it. Yet, at the same time, the responder might sense that such responses do nothing to help the writer's own unconscious structures and ideas come forth. Out of frustration, the responder might dismiss the work by declaring it nonsensical and insisting that the writer start over by thinking more logically about the topic.

We writing teachers can learn how to avoid either usurping or dismissing students' raw material if we enter Freud's discussion about the process of responding to an analysand. We can also use our insight into hermeneutics to challenge and question Freud. As the ground for this conversation, I examine two of Freud's basic arguments in "Constructions in Analysis": first, the danger of interpreting as opposed to constructing what the patient, or analysand, says; second, the various meanings of the patient's possible responses to the analyst's construction, examined in the light of the idea of resistance.

Freud, in describing why he advocates construction and not interpretation as the method an analyst should use, says:

. . . I think that "construction" is by far the more appropriate description. "Interpretation" applies to something that one does to some single element of the material, such as an association or a parapraxis. But it is a "construction" when one lays before the subject of the analysis a piece of his early history that he has forgotten, in some such way as this: "Up to your nth year you regarded yourself as the sole and unlimited possessor of your mother; then came another baby and brought you grave disillusionment. Your mother left you for some time and even after her reappearance she was never again devoted to you exclusively. Your feelings toward your mother became ambivalent . . ." and so on.   (261)

In this construction, Freud feeds back the very information the patient has given him, but in a way that, unlike the patient's seemingly haphazard speech, sounds linear and systematic. Instead of giving an analyst's interpretation, which would manipulate and transform the raw data of the patient's unconscious, Freud acts as an agent who selflessly enables the patient to hear what he or she unwittingly has been saying all along. In analysis, Freud theorizes, a patient is at a moment of heightened subjectivity. Lying on the couch and speaking, the patient works to enter the subjective stance as deeply as possible. The analyst's job is to help construct a picture of the unconscious that will be discernible to the patient's conscious mind. The analyst attempts not to change the raw material the patient has revealed but to repeat it clearly, acting as a mirror of what has been said. Thus the analyst serves as a representative of the logical order of the external world, an order to which the patient, submerged in subjectivity, has no access.

Although both Freud and Belenky et al. use the term *construction*, the two uses are quite different, at least on the surface. When Belenky et al. describe "the basic insights of constructivist thought," they tell us that "[a]ll knowledge is constructed, and the knower is an intimate part of the known" (137). They cite Adele, a "constructed knower, who says her sort of knowledge: 'You let the inside out and the outside in' " (135). In other words, they are rejecting the traditional model of knowledge as something static that the knower simply absorbs. To Belenky et al., the sophisticated knower should actively interact with—that is, *construct*—the outside world. The knower's own consciousness affects and changes what he or she knows, with the end result that "knowledge" is never monolithic—it consists of an inevitable and constant interplay between the internal being of the knower-constructor and the external being of the thing to be known.

Construction in Freud's framework seems at first to resist such interplay. When he advocates that the analyst construct instead of interpret, his aim is to avoid injecting his own subjectivity into the patient's framework. His *construction*, then, seems to result in less action for the constructor, who tries to become static in the face of the patient's fluidity.

The two forms of construction, however, have more in common than they seem to at first. Both honor the subjective stance, and both point to the need for an interaction between internal and external realities. In the scheme of Belenky et al., the construction occurs *within* the knowers—they use their own subjectivity to construct the external world. In Freud, the construction occurs as a result of an interaction between the patient and the analyst. Because patients are not yet conscious of their subjective knowledge, the analyst's job is to make a construction that enables them to view their latent ideas in the light of day and thereby begin to construct their own ideas. By interacting with a constructing analyst, then, Freud's patients become the same kind of knowers that Belenky et al. discuss; the analyst simply acts as a temporary assistant. As I explain in a moment, responders to writing at all levels can act as interim constructors as well, helping writers eventually learn to make their own constructions.

Before I go on, though, I want to further composition's dialogue with psychoanalysis by putting forth a challenge to Freud. In his insistence that analysts resist their own interpretations and act as mirrors, Freud fails to see interpretation as an inevitable component of any act that claims to be objective. By merely telling himself to refrain from interpreting, or from putting forth his own sense of the patient's issues, he believes that he can act as an unambiguous reflector of the patient's words. Writing teachers, however, know that every act of reconstructing verbal material necessarily involves interpretation. We could point out, for example, that no two analysts would produce the same construction of a given patient's words, even if both analysts felt that they were objectively avoiding interpretation. By believing that his construction is unbiased, Freud could unwittingly impose much more of an interpretation on patients than he is willing to admit, and his professed objectivity could confuse them, especially if they feel that their own sense of their words differs from Freud's. Composition, then, could help Freud give analysts a more effective direction: "constructors" should not only keep a constant vigil against their own biases but also accept that those biases inevitably exist. The more responsibility constructors take for their hidden prejudices, the more able they will be to listen to others' ideas.

By questioning the validity of Freud's belief in his own credentials as an unbiased vehicle for patients' ideas, however, we in composition can learn something useful from the underlying motivation for that belief. We can benefit from Freud's finding that raw, subjective material is often invisible to the patient's conscious mind, even when fragments of it are spoken aloud, and from his exploration of the negotiation with the external world that must occur if that material is to become conscious. Like Freud's analyst, we responders to writing can reflect students' subjectivity in a way that nudges latent material and allows it to emerge, even as, unlike Freud, we take responsibility for the inevitable interpretations behind our constructions.

For example, consider Peter Elbow and Pat Belanoff's concept of "sayback," in which "the author reads and the listener 'says back' what she hears: what she hears the writer is 'getting at' " (*Sharing* 13). This exchange evokes Freud's method: the responder, by repeating the writer's ideas, gives the writer a chance to view those ideas differently. Like Freud's constructions, sayback might seem at first to be an ineffectual activity. Surely, one might argue, the writer or analysand knows what he or she has said, and thus hearing it repeated by an external voice is unnecessary. To answer that comment, I appeal to the point of connection between psychoanalysis, with its examination of unconscious material, and composition, with its work on students' latent ideas. Both fields recognize the need for intuited material to become conscious, and both observe that when people are too deeply submerged in their latent material, they cannot view it in a way that enables them to communicate with anyone else. They are trapped, however temporarily, within the subjective stage that Belenky et al. describe. Oddly enough, sometimes all it takes for a person to get out of that stage is for another person—a representative of the external world—to act as a kind of mirror of the writer's or analysand's unconscious, or at least not consciously perceivable, ideas.

We acknowledge that every time Freud attempted to act as a mirror, he was in fact interpreting and thus not reflecting exactly what the patient said. His method of construction, however, was much more effective than overt interpretation because it allowed the patient to come to terms with material previously too subterranean for the patient to understand consciously. In a similar way, sayback helps students appreciate the richness that is latent in their own seemingly chaotic thinking.

Sayback is useful in working with drafts of essays, but it is also effective as a response to focused free writing, in which a student does not plan what to say beforehand but writes nonstop, often disjointedly, about a topic. Sayback to a piece of focused free writing in response to a novel might take the following form:

> First you tell us about your irritation with this character Joe, then you move to a discussion of your father's anger, and then you move back to the character and his relationship to his daughter. . . .

The most obvious purpose of this kind of sayback is to get writers to see their ideas from an external perspective. While sayback tries to be objective, it inevitably contains elements of the responder's bias. What the above responder saw as irritation, for example, someone else could have described as, say, impatience or hatred. Another responder, focusing not on the writer's thinking but on feelings, might have said, "You seemed upset about the way your father got so mad." Each attempted construction then, is a function of the constructor's worldview. Nevertheless, hearing the sequence of one's ideas laid out in a way that aims to capture the progress of one's own meandering thinking can allow a writer's heretofore inarticulated subjective intuitions to begin their negotiation with the external world. "You mean I said that? It doesn't sound so crazy after all" is a common response to sayback. The author of the free-written passage about Joe might well have been unaware as she wrote that her response to the novel could "go anywhere," and, oddly enough, even if she silently read her free writing before getting a response, she might simply have pronounced it worthless chaos, as many students do with their own free writing. She could make such a pronouncement because, like a stuck analysand, she was unable, for whatever reason, to move far enough outside the subjective stance to be able to see it clearly.

Like Freud's interpretation, the traditional mode of response to drafts prevents a student's latent subjective insights from emerging. For example, a responder who says "You clearly want to discuss how your father and Joe are similar" takes over the writer's work, transforms it, injects it with a new subjectivity—in short, explains the writer's meaning to the writer. The responder might also shape the material into an outline that fits his or her sense of the topic, thereby ignoring the writer's own subjective direction. That kind of usurping, even with the intention of helping the student finish the paper, can be quite destructive, especially to writers who lack confidence in their ideas. Those writers could easily decide that the responder's interpretation is definitive and abandon their own insights. Freud's caution about the danger of interpretation points to the perils of such a process; interpretation, with its focus on the responder, moves too far away from the subjectivity of the patient or writer and consequently can squelch original insights. It is only when responders resist their own subjectivity and respectfully enter the writer's mental scheme—however quirky—that they can help propel the writer into a deeper understanding of his or her subjectivity. For this progress to occur, responders must be self-aware, empathetic, and willing to play what Elbow terms the "believing game" (*Writing without Teachers* 162–66).

That game, which involves putting aside one's own perspective in an effort to appreciate someone else's, is also useful in understanding another of Freud's discussions in "Constructions in Analysis": his examination of the possible responses that patients give to the analyst's constructions. A patient, he says, will most likely have one of three responses: yes, no, or no comment. Each can be useful to the analyst, but not necessarily in the way the patient intends. The response of no comment, or at least none with any energy or enthusiasm, in which "the patient remains as though he were untouched by what has been said" (261), is valuable in its indication that the analyst's construction does not resonate at all with the patient. In a similar way, writing teachers' attempted constructions—"So you are saying that the character Joe is exactly like your father?"—that elicit no genuine response are probably moving in the wrong direction. They most likely indicate the teacher's interest much more than the student's. It is tempting, of course, when I read a student's essay, to exert my own will over it. I might do so by offering an interpretation that takes my own interests into account and pushes the student in a direction I myself would pursue if I were writing the essay. I might say, for example, that both the character Joe and the student's father seem to represent a certain kind of dominant male and that perhaps the writer's underlying point is to show how a certain kind of male power is deeply destructive to the spirits of the women who come in contact with it. This view could grow out of my own interests, and it might appear quite forceful and even "objective" to the student if she sees me as explaining her ideas to her. However, she may have her own, different direction in mind, either consciously or unconsciously, as I should acknowledge if she shows little or no immediate enthusiasm for my construction. She might want to explore the *differences* between her father and Joe, for example. She might wonder what makes their two kinds of angers generate dissimilar responses, both in others and, ultimately, in themselves. By taking responsibility for my biases, I should be able to put aside my ego and dismiss my remarks easily when faced with her lack of interest in my attempted sayback, and I should take the time to trust her to develop her own idea. Sometimes this activity takes great patience on a teacher's part, but that patience is often rewarded by a flowering of the student's original point of view.

A writer or analysand's show of enthusiasm in response to a construction also has various meanings. Freud tells us that a "plain 'Yes' from a patient is by no means unambiguous. . . . The 'Yes' has no value unless it is followed by indirect confirmations, unless the patient . . . produces new memories which complete and extend the construction" (262). Mere agreement with the analyst or responder is not enough; it may mask the unwillingness of patients or writers to confront their own subjectivity. It is often easier for writers to agree with what a responder says than to figure out exactly where they disagree. Their assent may be an attempt to placate the responder, to move the scrutiny away from the deeper reality of what they genuinely have to say. Moreover, when the responder is a teacher or other authority figure, students, in a desire to get a good grade or simply to please, may dismiss their own ideas. Responders must be wary, then, of ready assents; some comments—"Yes, sure, I *do* want to write about patriarchal dominance. That must be what I had in mind all along!"—might well mask an inner, inarticulated dissent.

If the yes is genuine, however, it can serve as a useful prompt for new information from the writer. Often writers will say more than yes, adding more information about what they are trying to get across. For example, the remark "Yes, I know they are both dominant men, but actually I think they both act very differently" would be a way for a student to "complete and extend the construction." An illustration of the power of the yes occurs in Elbow and Belanoff's instructions for sayback, when the responder repeats the writer's words in a slightly open, questioning fashion in order to invite the reader to restate what she means. In effect the listener is saying, "Do you mean . . . ?" so that the writer can say, "No, not quite. What I mean is . . ." or even—and this is pay dirt—"yes, I was saying that, but now I want to say . . ." . . . In short, sayback is an invitation to the writer to . . . move in her thinking.

(*Sharing* 13)

Often, an individual alone will not be able to "move in her thinking" without this sort of outside feedback. When writers cannot move, it is because their ideas are trapped in the unvoiced subjective stance, from which they are unable alone to establish a negotiation with the external world. Both psychoanalysis and composition recognize the danger of such a trap, and both acknowledge that sometimes it is only through an interaction with an outside person that writers or patients can learn to "construct" their own unconscious material for themselves.

Freud says more about this process in his analysis of the no from the patient:

As a rule [the patient] will not give his assent until he has learnt the whole truth—which often covers a very great deal of ground. So that the only safe interpretation of his 'No' is that it points to incompleteness; there can be no doubt that the construction has not told him everything.   (263)

The no here—"No, there is no parallel at all between Joe and my father"— is not definitive at first. It may end up being definitive, but it almost always can work instead as a stimulus to more thought. Thus, when faced with a no, responders can give writers time to articulate their disagreement. A writer's own, often slow, analysis might point toward new realizations that the responder could not otherwise have had access to. For example, the writer might say, "No, there is no real similarity, though they do both get angry. I think they have different *kinds* of anger. Maybe I want to say something about those two kinds."

One of Freud's fundamental insights—the theory of resistance—can assist the responder whose aim is to help writers articulate their subjective views in a more constructed way. Resistance to one's own deepest truths, of course, takes many forms. In "Constructions in Analysis," Freud discusses the analysand's resistance when it is manifested as a preoccupation with minor details of the memory under consideration. For example, Freud's patients sometimes cannot recollect the major event that their analysis is pursuing. Instead, they will remember "with abnormal sharpness the faces of . . . people . . . or the rooms in which something . . . might have happened," though the memories might not have to do with the actual event that the patient needs to recall. This behavior is the result of resistance against the significant memory: patients unconsciously prevent themselves from becoming aware of painful truths. To Freud, it is a "vain effort" for the analyst to try to convince the patient that such a "delusion" is a "contradiction of reality. On the contrary," he continues, "the recognition of its kernel of truth would afford common ground upon which the therapeutic work could develop" (266–68).

A writer's resistance is similar to that of the psychoanalytic patient in a crucial way—it is the result of fear. The two resistances, however, are not identical. The psychoanalytic patient fears some deeply repressed memory of an event and resists facing the truth about the experience because that truth, for whatever reason, is too painful. Writers fear their own ideas and their own worldview, which they may deem unacceptable because it seems inappropriate, though not necessarily painful. Even the most outwardly confident writers can experience this difficulty; they might be able to write strong, coherent essays on "acceptable" topics, but when it comes to their own truths, they may lapse into ambiguity and awkwardness. These writers are afraid of being taught—by teachers, parents, peers, television, whatever—that their most honest views are not interesting or valuable. Such a concern is rarely conscious; if it were, it would be easier to locate and overcome. Instead, the mechanism of resistance prevents people from being aware of the degree to which they repress important facts about themselves and their worldviews. A student writer's fear might manifest itself consciously as a desire to avoid the risk of appearing ridiculous, as a belief that one's true thoughts are irrelevant, or as an assumption that school is a place where one learns only what one is supposed to think. In any case, this fear has the effect of forcing students, sometimes unconsciously, to censor their own insights as those insights arise, and that censoring has a deadly effect on intellectual development. Belenky et al. notwithstanding, even writers who have learned not to censor their ideas on certain topics—say, their personal lives—might have a deep resistance when it comes to other topics, such as political science.

By resisting their own points, writers make their essays far less interesting and far less challenging than those documents could otherwise be. On an unconscious level, students may express their latent and self-denying desire to move away from their own truths by ignoring the bulk of their subjective ideas and dwelling instead on minor insights. The insignificant details of an argument, for example, parallel the furnishings in the rooms of Freud's patients in that they divert attention from more sensitive and important matters. When pressed, students often come right out and say things like "I didn't want to offend anyone" or "I wasn't sure if that's what you wanted"; their attempt to substitute other voices for their own pushes them toward flatter, duller writing. They tend to welcome and expect a responder who will steer them away from their quirks and into the realm of the safe, usually by presenting them with explicit directions about what they should say. Such a responder, though, can do great damage to students' ability to generate creative theoretical insights. As Belenky et al. tell us, the desire to comply with the teacher's perspective causes students to retreat behind "acceptable lies" that arrest growth and change (218).

In commenting that some of the ideas in a vague and subjective free-writing piece are not interesting or useful, or in explaining how to "fix" an essay, perhaps by acknowledging other voices and moving into received or procedural knowledge, a responder may prevent students from saying what they want to say. They will say instead what they believe the responder wants them to say, and thus both parties will collaborate with the students' resistance. In contrast, the responder who knows that a writer's words contain a "kernel of truth" can attempt to shift attention toward that kernel. Elbow's idea of a "center of gravity," which invites the responder to locate sources of energy in the writing, can help overcome resistance when writers are willing to allow key parts of their raw material to act as doors into a deeper understanding of what they have to say (*Sharing* 16). By resisting the impulse to make writers complete their essays prematurely and by honoring and focusing on their subjective knowledge, the responder can help writers prepare the ground for constructed knowledge. Otherwise, they may abandon the traces of their deepest insights for a more superficial analysis and thus miss discovering their most original points.

While students must understand academic frameworks—for example, the rules and conventions of the study of political science—they can only become creative thinkers in their own right if they find a way to ask and begin to answer their own questions. Gilligan's political science student exemplifies the confusion many students feel when they are confronted with the unfamiliar world of the university: they need a bridge between their inner, unformulated reactions and the external, structured world of academic discourse. Composition, particularly in its function as an integral part of a freshman's introduction to academic life, can damage students when it encourages them to abandon their own questions in the name of, say, "thinking like a historian." Instead, composition can influence students' burgeoning academic understanding by teaching them both to respect their subjective insights and to find ways to construct those insights in relation to the external world.

The more we allow our students to gain further access to their subjectivity, the more likely they will be to grow intellectually. Such growth is scary, both for students and, Freud's professed objectivity notwithstanding, for their teachers and other guides. It may result in emotional upheaval, since subjective responses even to the most abstract academic subjects are intertwined with a thinker's emotions. The authors of *Women's Ways of Knowing* acknowledge this relation, and they posit a "connected" or "midwife" teaching, whose concern is to "preserve students' fragile newborn thoughts" and to allow those ideas to grow and change:

> The connected class recognizes the core of truth in the subjectivist view that each of us has a unique perspective that is in some sense irrefutably "right" by virtue of its existence. But the connected class transforms these private truths into "objects," publicly available to the members of the class who, through

"stretching and sharing," add to themselves as knowers by absorbing in their
own fashion their classmates' ideas.   (Belenky et al. 222–23)

Embracing one's own ideas does not result in a solipsistic alienation from
others; in fact, it is what allows the negotiation to begin with the outside
world, with the result that both inner and outer worlds are altered.

My overall point, then, is that only by entering the realm of their own
subjectivity can writers begin to articulate what is most vibrant in their ideas.
Psychoanalysis, feminist theory, and composition all recommend an informed
give-and-take in interactions with the subjective voice, which is virtually
always fragile at its moment of encounter with the external world, and needs
to be allowed some autonomy before it is challenged and changed. Some
composition theorists deeply misunderstand this position when they worry
that it invites a self-absorbed exploration of one's own psyche, without the
important intellectual rigor that "genuine"—impersonal?—academic discourse requires. *Subjective* does not necessarily mean self-absorbed or even
personal in the sense of exploring one's own life experience. The subjective
stance is a door to one's intellectual originality, and unless thinkers embrace
that originality they will be constricted, however comfortably, by the ideas
of others.

Composition scholars often get trapped in the received or procedural stance
by conforming too readily to what we imagine other fields expect of us. We
are afraid that if students concentrate on their own ideas they will be unable
to write in the language of the university. Such a fear is justified, however,
only if we view subjective response as alien to an academic context. In fact,
the most respected academics are those who have a deep trust in their own
subjective ideas. Composition theorists can benefit from having more conversations about subjectivity with scholars in other fields. We can learn from
other perspectives, and, drawing on our understanding of hermeneutics and
the fluidity of the composing process, we have much to teach.

Western New England College

CREATIVITY AND INSIGHT:
TOWARD A POETICS OF COMPOSITION

Rosemary Gates

WHEN composition began to take its contemporary shape twenty years ago, theorists and researchers attempted to define the field as a place of language study focused on writing processes and forms. Pressed severely by the need for better ways to teach composition to more students than ever before, many of them less well-prepared students than their predecessors, the discipline developed a primarily pedagogical emphasis, with theory drawn from whatever discipline seemed useful to the tasks at hand. This practical exigency has driven a varied and lively research program. But unlike other fields, composition's basis in praxis has required that it remain eclectic, that it compose from diverse materials and processes its own form and substance.

A perhaps more accurate reading of the current situation is that the field has composed, or is composing, its own forms and substances and that, with these, it is developing its own processes. For despite being a practical art, the teaching of writing has become a discipline that is already better described as a poetics. In a few short years from the late 1960s on, our theoretical origins were assembled from varied interdisciplinary materials and shaped with reference to real writers and real texts. Important foundational works were James Britton's *Language and Learning* and *The Development of Writing Abilities*, James Moffett's *Teaching the Universe of Discourse* and *A Student-Centered Language Arts Curriculum*, Janet Emig's *The Composing Processes of Twelfth Graders*, and James Kinneavy's "tentative paradigm," *A Theory of Discourse*. Since then we have had a burgeoning of theories, methods, and practices, communicated in over three dozen journals and thousands of books and cataloged in several large bibliographies. Since then we have lamented, been angered by, and sometimes rejoiced in our lack of clear identity and status within the academy. What is the field of composition? Is it a discipline? Does it have an identifying central paradigm? Must it have a paradigm? Must its importance in English departments depend on the service of teaching a set of skills—or even an "art"? Is there a core metaphysics, with a stemma theory generating an expanding research program? Is there, or should there be, "content" in composition courses? Is a scientific study of writing processes and products possible? We have let these questions divide us, let theoretical beliefs and classroom practices divide us. We have no core paradigm, but perhaps we have several. We must find a way to identify ourselves and to do so on our own terms, not the terms of other disciplines.

I think that what identifies composition studies is composing itself—a putting together, a taking and making of whatever helps us to gain insight. We study our own writing, student writing, our writing lives and environments, all kinds of writing, all manners in which it is produced and makes meaning. In our study, we follow the path of written discursive practices: we are creating the field as we create our writing about writing.

In composition, there is a signal willingness to be open to the new, to create moments for trying out, to combine diverse materials and methods from diverse disciplines, to test insights with real writers in real situations, to consider the individual, to search the intuitive. Our approaches to the study of writing problems are eclectic in a way that is unconventional for other disciplines. And our eclectic openness and intuitiveness constitute the strength of our field.

As the essays in this volume argue, we may best characterize the field as a zone of interaction of creative theories and practices that produces new ideas about writing. The insights we gain about writing may in turn influence the development of knowledge in or about the disciplines that enter the zone, as writing becomes a focus for the making of knowledge in general and in specific instances involving written language. The zone of interaction has a rich potential for insights about the making of written verbal structure and for an interplay of theory and method, research and teaching; both theory and method are imbued with the same processes that writing entails—a making of knowledge through creative insight that develops from teaching practice and feeds directly back into teaching.

Theory, method, and practice are inseparably enmeshed in ways and to a degree not characteristic of any other field. Our focus is the composing of written verbal structures. We study the complex problems and interplay of thought, writing, and learning that are the territory of a poetics. Our discipline has already developed in such a way that a poetics rather than a theoretical paradigm best defines it.

Creativity and Insight: The Making of Meaning in Verbal Structures

In "Kubla Khan," Coleridge offers an extended image of the creative process: violence and darkness are transformed into calm and light, clashing rocks into the rhythm of the dance, hail and flail into harvested grain. The poet introduces the piece "rather as a psychological curiosity, than on the ground of any supposed *poetic* merits" (474). A study of inner life, the poem inscribes in external form felt emotion and thought; it transforms and makes present an outward something that was latent and inward. Written in an opium "sleep," in which the mind is more creatively open to intense visual images than is usual, "Kubla Khan" stands as an example of the creative process: it features the rich matching of patterns—a texturizing of expression of feeling and meaning in a text structure of language and verse arrangement. In this instance of creation during a drug-induced state, the processes of the unconscious are made more visible. The poem becomes a sign of meaning made during a sudden, sustained moment of insight, whose creative moment is still visible in the verbal structure.

Creativity is largely an unconscious process that is little understood, but it has to do with generating structure. Summarizing research on and major theories of creativity, Silvano Arieti finds them to be variations on Graham Wallas's model of the creation of new knowledge, which is characterized by four stages: preparation, incubation, illumination, and verification (Arieti 14–36). Of these, illumination—or the moment of insight—is the most important to creative thought. But the crucial processes leading to it happen in the unconscious and cannot be seen directly. Basic cognitive processes must therefore be theorized, but theorists agree that convergent and divergent thinking are key. These two types involve the ability to bring diverse and unusual materials together in unconventional ways; that is, restructuring or recomposing. Recomposition carries with it various types of meaning— imagistic or emotional, lexical, propositional, and so on. Insight is thus a *seeing* (*theorein* in Greek), a making of new knowledge that is a representation in a metaphoric, abstract way of that which is seen. It has structure, and a making of new knowledge is a making of new structures. Reviewing the history of the term *insight*, Patricia E. Connors writes that the word has varied from referring to logical thought to sudden inspiration to direct infusion of knowledge from God. In cognitive psychology, it is a sudden arising into consciousness of new knowledge. Cognitive studies define insight as "an ability to detect patterns with relatively little information." The ability is closely related to "noticing"—that is, to the ability to "see"—and it requires a large and diverse information base (Connors 76–77). The mind needs exemplary patterns (*paradeigma*) to apply in its search for order—for convergence—amid divergent materials.

Thought may take two (re)presentations in the mind: image or word. Two ways of being conscious, two ways of knowing, two ways of structuring, two ways of composing: our stories about how we know include these two ways. Albert Einstein described his insight process as a grasping of knowledge before language: "For me it is not dubious that our thinking goes on for the most part without the use of signs (words) and beyond that to a considerable degree unconsciously" (Schilpp 9). E. M. Forster reported that his insight arrived through language; his seeing happened when the writing was before him: "How can I tell what I think till I see what I say?" (152). Image knowing can be transformed into language knowing, but in transformation a new form of knowledge is still created. It is not a translation, but it requires a new kind of seeing, of grasping. The modes of thought share the process of detecting patterns (insight), since both organize materials through detecting or creating patterns as structural forms. The kind of knowledge writing makes is different from image knowing. Writing limits, draws boundaries, forms linearly. Poetic aspects of writing preserve some of the visual, field, and iconic dimensions by working against language's linearity on the page and its rule-boundedness. Writing in which connections are made partakes of the poetic function of language by fusing separated elements into new meanings. In this way, even scientific writing may be rich with connections to culture, as M. A. K. Halliday has demonstrated for Darwin's writing, for instance. It is creative; it is poetic. It is knowing that is only partially articulatable in propositional content. Some of the meaning remains transformed in the style—in the lexicosyntactic structure of text.

The formation of image and word are poetic processes as well as processes of creating knowledge. Knowledge making inevitably has poetic moments, as Richard Rorty has argued, and it is inescapably and inevitably story making, as Jean-François Lyotard has exposed. In composition studies, such making is self-consciously poetic. The stories in which we compose our experience in researching and teaching and seeing (theorizing) what happens in our encounters with writing and learning are poetic versions of some other story, and they participate in one ideological narrative or another.

But these poststructuralist versions of thought and language rely on structuralist and prestructuralist versions. Sigmund Freud wrote of the image representation of thought, which he called the primary process, and the narrativizing of image into word, which he called the secondary process (see "Dreams"). Both processes are present in ordinary thought, with the primary process prominent in dream (and daydream) and the secondary process prominent in logical, linguistic, rational thought, such as dream interpretation. Both processes employ two major tropes: metaphor and metonymy. Roman Jakobson theorized about the same research on aphasics as Freud did, and he saw metaphor and metonym as the central tropic processes of language formation (Jakobson and Halle 76–82). Each of these processes requires elaboration within a view of creating knowledge.

Martin A. Greenman's model of insight incorporates Freud's work on dream processes and dream analysis, and it is based on Wallas's four-stage model of creating new thought. Writing about philosophical understanding, Greenman says that the preparatory stage involves

> everything that "feeds" the unconscious dimensions of the intuitive process. Everything is grist for the philosophical mill. The preparatory stage provides intuition its base, i.e., the "material" it has to work with. The "richness" of that material determines, in part, the limits of insight.   (125)

In the incubation stage that follows, the mental activities of absorbing preparatory material and searching for patterns to organize the material are largely unconscious. Greenman likens the relation between the preparatory material and incubation to the relation "between the latent and manifest content of the dream [that] is concealed within the process that forms the dream" (126). The original thought (latent content) and the processes remain hidden, while the manifest content is the image or word that is the transformation by unconscious processes (metonymic and metaphoric) of the latent content. The processes hold the key to the relation between the manifest (conscious) and latent (unconscious) material because it is the processes that usher insight forward into consciousness. It follows, then, that the *process* of writing should hold the key to the formation of new thought that proceeds from the writing process itself. (For a more detailed account of Greenman's model, see Gates.)

The process of writing is analogous to the process of dream interpretation, just as the formation of the representation of thought is analogous to the formation of the dream image. Greenman sees these processes as *ways of encountering*. They are also structured, learned ways of meeting, interacting with, and perceiving the material in the preparatory base. Psychoanalysis, myth, methodologies—all are ways of encountering material. As structures for encountering, they have content; a structured process is, in other words, a kind of knowledge. These ways of encountering must be in mind before some kinds of knowledge, which require certain ways of encountering in order to be structured, are able to be formed—that is, learned. Dream images are formed by similarity, substitution, and combination—the processes of metaphor and metonymy. Dream analysis, however, is to a greater extent a conscious process of learned approaches, though it is by no means entirely conscious. Nevertheless, the primary process that forms the images—metaphor and metonymy—also forms the language in which the analysis takes place, and these are innate, rather than learned, processes. Parts of arrangement, style, and invention are unconscious, and they hold in their shape meanings that are analogous to dream images—nondiscursive meaning shapes that are symbolic, presymbolic, and powerful.

Jakobson saw that these two distinct processes structure our language, though thought may take place in both modes separately, as can be seen in aphasia. Metaphor is the process of finding similarity in dissimilar objects and of selecting a representation that most closely resembles the object to be represented. The representations selected are combined to form the syntax of more than one item of representation. The seeing of similarity, selection from similarity and dissimilarity, and combination into sequence is the poetic function. Jakobson maintained that poetics "treats the poetic function in its relationship to the other functions of language" (305). The poetic function occurs in and affects all utterances. When the poetic function becomes dominant in an utterance, language calls attention to itself, so that language as language is highlighted. Other functions (emotive, referential, etc.) are thrust into the background. Prominence is achieved by projecting the principle of equivalence that operates cognitively in the metaphor-selectional process—similarity in difference—onto the actual metonymic-combinatorial process of concatenating words. The pattern-making process is brought into conscious view in the surface text (manifest content) but is displaced from the metaphoric process to the syntactic process, creating a syntax of likeness that makes the text cohere in virtue of patterns of language as well as patterns of thought. Jakobson's example in the famous essay "Linguistics and Poetics" in which he presents this theory is *I like Ike*. Because the utterance disports the principle of equivalence, it is therefore poetic, despite its use as rhetoric. Its appeal is precisely its patterning. Poststructuralist views of language and knowledge adopted Jakobson's insight into the forming act of language as poetic in such claims as the presence of "poetic moments" in all thought making (Rorty). Not only are the academic disciplines rhetorical, they are also poetic at certain instances of knowledge formation. This sense of constructedness into patterns—the madeness of knowledge—runs through postmodern thought. In this sense that the mind seeks equivalences among disparities, knowledge making is poetic. A figuration—as visible configuration—is sought by the mind to represent thought in a nonlinguistic, but equally specific, way.

The making of images is the primary process that forms thoughts into patterns, which Freud saw as a reproduction of new content based on latent patterns. The desire to reproduce stored energy patterns was the basis for dream as well as behavioral or personality patterns. Until processed in the secondary mode—his "talk therapy"—the pattern would continue to spin reproductions of itself. Talk narrativized the material and released the stored energy, transforming the image or figuration content into language. The holistic, timeless, repeating image or figuration pattern is let go and replaced by a time-bound, discursive or figural account.

Piaget thought of this dissatisfaction as a felt dissonance and viewed the subject as continuing to configure until a felt consonance replaced the felt dissonance. A consciously felt resolution during the act of composing signals satisfaction of desire, the cessation of the need to continue to compose. The awareness of composure is present, but the reasons for knowing one is finished remain unconscious. In formal systems and in disciplines, this knowing when one is finished is guided by logics and methods. It constitutes the processes of validation and verification. In writing, the boundaries between the moment of illumination and verification (or validation) may blur. But the sense of having finished may remain intuitive: felt, but not understood in discursive terms. The type of knowledge and the domain to which it is applied determine the point at which the knowledge-making processes end—whether more validation than felt sense is required.

One must know the problems of verbal structure to know when a written form is adequate to task and context. In practice, where language is implicated in knowledge making, distinct boundaries are impossible to draw. One must know writing, know the discipline, know how the two involve each other. Knowing a field requires knowing the processes of verification and validation. As Greenman points out, these processes are either pragmatic and existential or discursive and coherential. To work in a field may require knowledge of writing. To communicate knowledge almost always does. Some writing for validation will produce further insights, at which point the validation stage is collapsed into the preparatory stage in which new incubation and insight are sought to confirm or disprove the insight.

The writing itself becomes the instrument, vehicle, and material for the production of knowledge. Writing *creates* the view of the world at the same time that it attempts to conform to the world with representation. As communication, as rhetoric, language enacts a representation that has the force of declaring something to be true in the world because language has the function of constructing something new in the world. As Mary Louise Pratt has argued, all language use has the illocutionary force John Searle reserved for institutional actions such as marrying, judging, and refereeing, which he classed as declarative-representatives. The utterance attempts to make a world-to-word fit (to match the word to what is true in the world), but because the occasion is institutional the utterance also makes a word-to-world fit; the word uttered makes what it said true in the world, thereby creating a new state of affairs, whether or not the world-to-word fit is accurate. Thus, judging (in a court of law), refereeing, and marrying create new states of affairs when uttered by the appropriate persons. Pratt argues that a new state of affairs is created in all language utterances because language creates a state of representation—that is, the view of the world—that was not present before and is present only because it is constituted in language. These views, or ideologies, create new states of affairs, and these constructions are poetically created. Lyotard's totalizing narratives, for example, do have force in the world because they are acted on. Our lives are lived by their patterns of thought and behavior.

Toward a Poetics of Composition

Jakobson defines poetics as a branch of linguistics that studies problems of verbal structure (296). While this definition is not adequate for our purposes, it is an appropriate beginning, as shall become clear. I have examined composing as the bringing together of patterns in language, the making of *verbal* structure. I have argued that the poetic process of language is essential to the process of forming knowledge and that structuring by selecting and combining elements of similarity and difference involves noticing patterns and producing meaning. I turn now to the question of why composition should be identified as a field guided by a poetics rather than a paradigm.

Grammars retain a figural structure that coexists with the discursive structure of language instances. Grammars, like images, impose an order on materials and on what is represented. So do logics and rhetorics. In the making of knowledge in language, the orders of grammars, logics, and rhetorics impose orders of meaning on what is being represented. Preparation and incubation are not distinct, because the materials and content to be processed into manifest view and form are drawn within the parameters of understanding according to the individual learner's capacities. The processing of incubation begins with the influx of information. It is already changed and reorganized as it enters mind.

What we have here is another version of the style and content debate—monism versus dualism. Are style and content separable? The debate strikes at the heart of the Einstein and Forster examples. The problem is that the selection of certain stylistic features indicates a contextual set of meanings and latent content that may render a meaning—whether of the setting or semantics—that would not result with another choice. But since no absolute norm exists that the selection varies from, the discussion of change in meaning cannot proceed from a scientific basis. Stylistic practice generates a theory of a text's style: the poetics of making utterly imbues the creation of text. Language is always parole. Without exception it exists as instances, and it is never abstract; theory and method, general and specific can only be artificially separated. We are left with an interplay of language forms and actions, not in which substance simply fills form but, rather, in which form envisions the substance drawn in it and in which substance draws in forms. It is not reciprocal but suffused.

But against this view of verbal structure we may bring another vision, one in which words are selected and then combined, in which all perception and thought do not depend on language, in which we can see palpably through our signs to physical reality and psychic imaginal reality, in which image and the felt sense are brought to bear in linguistic naming. Here, we must acknowledge an interplay of questioning and answering, an area where we are studying problems of verbal structure and allowing our study to consider open theorizing and reviewing. We have a field in which we practice the art of composing—a bringing together of diverse materials into new orders, in which we recognize the made, the partial, the fluctuating, the inclusive. The orders are not permanent and immutable. This open systemic poetics is the one Linda Hutcheon proposes in *A Poetics of Postmodernism*. Hutcheon sees that postmodernism is too diverse to be defined by a theory, a single definition or answer. Rather, there is a problematic of the relations between art and culture that only a poetics can satisfy. A poetics of postmodernism is "a flexible conceptual structure which could at once constitute and contain postmodern culture and our discourses both about it and adjacent to it" (Hutcheon ix). Delete *postmodern* and substitute *composition* and understand *culture* to mean humans, their beings and doings, and we have a view of what a poetics of composition would entail. Understand *constitute* as "create" or as material cause, and a poetics of composition becomes the field in the same way that a paradigm is the structural basis making up and extending to the edges of a discipline. Link *contain* and *container*, and we see a poetics of composition taking into its territory, its space, whatever writing has overlapping problematics with other fields, wherever that overlapping occurs. Solutions are not paradigm-driven but constituted within the poetics of discursive structures and practices. Creativity is key, and insight is the key moment of the poetic making. Insight brings orders of meaning and knowing. These orders and patterns, plural, grown from diverse fields and in diverse directions, are not derived from a single pattern, or stem or paradigm. And why should they be? Theory in a field should derive from the subject of study, and flexibility and openness of seeing and teaching are superior strengths. Shaping and reshaping, writing and teaching—all are arts of language. What do we need with a paradigm? Why contain our study so narrowly? What other field considers its own processes so self-reflexively? What other field reaches to contain such a vast and diverse space-scape? What other field places so many practical demands with so many human variables and individual variations?

We have moved beyond a structuralist notion of poetics to a poststructuralist field of poetics. We have in modern composition studies precisely the sort of theorizing about selves and culture and aesthetics with which postmodernism identifies itself. Concerned with contexts instead of an assumed totalizing ideology, composition studies attempts to see differences, cases, situations, cultures, languages, diversity. It is the academic discipline among the humanities and social sciences that has the surest identity because it is postmodernly inclusive and expansive. Reaching out into other disciplines to claim priority over the very means of making knowledge, composition threatens older disciplines developed under models of coherence and self-sufficient isolationist thinking in two ways: it insists that rhetoric and writing affect thought, procedure, knowledge, and contingency; and it is powerfully interdisciplinary because it reaches and takes hold and inserts itself everywhere there is writing.

And there *is* writing everywhere in modern culture, in all manner of forms and fragments and diversities and relations. The dominant character of the modern is the presence and influence of print and print's discursive practices. The postmodern is self-reflexive about writing, aware of the pure power of impression and structure as image. Jakobson's poetic principle is brought everywhere to the foreground, making us aware that messages are language, focusing away from communicating and toward aestheticizing. Surface threatens meaning. Schemes preempt tropes. Reproduction and placement in self-reflexive cultural contexts aestheticize. We become aware of the manufacture of language; we become aware of the manufacture of culture; we become aware of the manufacture of ourselves as we are because of language and culture. We become aware of language as image displacing the discursive, the communicative.

Writing, studying writing, and teaching writing become complicated and complex. But composition teachers and theorists have not adopted a single theoretical line of approach; rather, we have permitted and encouraged but sometimes fought diverse views and practices. What we have is an open field of theorizing about discourse and discoursing and teaching discourse. We do all this with contexts and situations—culture and rhetoric—in view. We think about what we might have missed; we think about the individual. We think about areas of likenesses—groups and subgroups. We love the instance, the case, the intuitive, the unexplainable, the mystery. We embrace all this, we study it, we struggle with it, and we love it. We try to include; we try not to exclude. We try to see connections. We put titles on our books and essays and conferences that identify us as seeking connections while allowing diversity. We like to make patterns, we embrace structures, and we let them go when a new and more interesting or useful pattern configures. We are poets at heart, in love with writing, with bringing order and meaning to our existence through writing.

But we are committed more to language than to whatever the language is speaking of. And that is as it should be, for the object of our study is the structuring of written language. It is our strength and our danger. It is what makes our discipline defined closer to a poetics than to a paradigm.

Hutcheon offers more than a dozen arguments in support of a poetics of postmodernism. I draw from them, expand on them, and add to them to offer arguments for a poetics of composition.

1. The *subject matter* of the field is the problem of written verbal structure, processes, and products. Processes are ways of encountering, they are unseen and structured, and they are knowledge. We must carry on flexible theorizing about these processes.

2. A poetics considers the relations of image as pattern, syntax as pattern, rhythm as pattern, and so on. It considers connections, coherences, cohesions.

3. Composing means bringing together in structured ways. It means placing together, and it means bringing to rest in a place. It means taking apart by rethinking and putting back together another way. Composing seeks harmony and coherence. It seeks harmony and wholeness by allowing the process of seeing and reseeing, creation and decreation. It is a holding of tentative balance, tentative answers, answers for a time and place, not timeless absolutes. When we work with human beings and languages and many cultures and many situations, all of which change over time and from place to place, the best we can do—and I mean we *do* our very best and think our very best—is to allow a flexible conceptual structure as container.

4. Many theories are required for us to answer many problems from many perspectives, to be interdisciplinary. No core paradigm is possible. Researchers must resist seeing any theory or pedagogic model as absolute. Theory may guide but not dominate. Researchers and practitioners must be willing to forgo theory to solve and resolve problems. A poetics seeks, rather, to articulate cultural processes and ways of writing. It is difficult to imagine that this articulation will cease as culture and language both undergo ongoing change.

5. A poetics is concerned with problems relevant to more than one area— teaching and writing, writing and cognition, writing and biography, writing and history, writing and law, and so on. It moves outside disciplinary and material boundaries, and it is concerned with structuring something new in language that speaks as pattern as well as discursively. W. K. Wimsatt, Jr., had already moved in this direction in equating style with meaning. Richard Ohmann went further by equating style with a writer's individual epistemology.

6. Writing is not a theory, method, science, or skill. It is a complex act of taking language and images and verbal scraps and patterns and remaking and reproducing.

7. A poetics recognizes the power and meaningfulness of nondiscursive structures—such as patterns of style, grammars, rhetorics, images, gestures, and timing. Latent psychobiographical and encultured material may be manifest in the *ways* of the writing, for these are the ways of encountering and knowing the world.

8. In a poetics, the approaches for validating insights are created out of the materials, forms, and situations. Externally imposed evaluative means must be used only when an external situation and its restrictions are relevant to the occasion and purpose of the writing task.

9. A poetics permits suspension of binary oppositions; it allows coexistence and mutuality of opposites, or it looks at the problems and text from a perspective in which the apparent oppositions no longer appear as opposites. Disunity is permitted.

10. A poetics admits that its knowledge is representation, partial, "fictional." There is a willingness to sustain paradox, to believe and disbelieve theories and results.

11. In a poetics, change is built in: rethink, resee, revise, retheorize, add, subtract, multiply, divide, omit, rearrange.

12. As in poems, several levels of meanings may be fused. The power and willingness to critique the layering of our own language, our own writing about writing, are self-theorizing, a fuller looking at our ways of encountering as they appear in the layers of language and arrangement we use. Writing is a means for validating and checking the means of validation of knowledge in the field.

13. A poetics implies a rhythmics: a dynamism creating a harmony of voices and materials, collaboration, dialogue, encounter, separation, movement. The rhythmic has structure and meanings. Meaning and importance exist in the abstract, nonlexical shape and movement.

14. A poetics does not displace rhetoric or a philosophy of composition. Rather, a poetics focuses composition studies on the problems of written verbal creation, structure, and meaning. Instrumental and teleological provinces of the verbal structures are areas of overlapping concern with writing.

A poetics of composition will take us further in the many directions in which we have already moved and in new directions. The field that identifies itself as based on a poetics has space to envision studying anything that involves writing and to draw in whatever it needs for its study. Students can be encouraged and guided in shaping their own identities and culture through the making potential of writing. They will have a conceptual model for practicing expansion and diversity, for developing a tolerant openness and critical mind. Other disciplines, already fragmenting under the pressure of postmodern thought, may discover in composition's identity as a poetics a revivifying disciplinary model.

Catholic University of America

COMPOSITION AS THE VOICING
OF MULTIPLE FICTIONS

Derek Owens

> I doubt that a person normally develops a coherent sense of iden-
> tity, and to the extent that he does, he may experience severe
> emotional stress. . . . [I]f playing a role does in fact lead to real
> changes in one's self-concept, we should learn to play more roles,
> to adopt any role that seems enjoyable [until] a storehouse of
> novel self-images emerges. The mask may be not the symbol of
> superficiality that we have thought it was, but the means of
> realizing our potential.
>
> —Campbell Tathem

> I tried to understand the mystery of names by staring into the
> mirror and repeating mine over and over. Or the word "me." As
> if one could come into language as into a room. Lost in the blank,
> my obsessive detachment spiraled out into the unusable space of
> infinity, indifferent nakedness. I sat down in it. No balcony for
> clearer view, but I could focus on the silvered lack of substance
> or the syllables that correspond to it because all resonance grows
> from consent to emptiness. But maybe, in my craving for hinges,
> I confused identity with someone else.
>
> —Rosmarie Waldrop

I CHOOSE to define composition within parameters so expansive as to render
the field inherently encyclopedic and far-reaching. To enter into the study of
composition can be akin to confronting umpteen different spheres of scholarly
inquiry, so tentacular is this discipline. To be concerned with matters of how
and why one writes leads to issues of how and why different tribes (including
those academic and professional) communicate: not only what rhetorics are
created, appropriated, subverted, and censored by different communities but
also what these people and institutions find important to say—to *compose*—
before one another. This attention to composition—the social need to hatch
out ideas through the sculptural medium of language—is exciting precisely
because it highlights creative discovery along multiple paths. From out of
the same alphabet come texts as disparate as *Finnegans Wake* and the *Wall*

Street Journal, dry dissertations and dada manifestos. Nor is composition concerned solely with the written: sermons, speeches, and impromptu dialogue are all compositions, as is any musical, performative, or artistic concoction. Feasibly, taken in this broadest sense, composition studies is a crossroads discipline, a catalytic zone where a motley assemblage of discourse communities and arenas for intellectual exploration converge, metamorphose, and regenerate. At the same time, we cannot study multiple disciplines without being brought back somehow to the art of composing: musically, syntactically, lexically, orally, dialogically, socially, politically, poetically.

What fascinates me is devising ways of teaching writing that reflect the incredible variety manifest in this field. At present, several goals and agendas seem essential if we are serious about implementing such a pedagogy. First, we have to emphasize teaching multiple rhetorics within the writing classroom—a pedagogy toward total inclusion, a pluralistic embracing of multiple genres and styles of discourse. This approach makes sense not only in composition classes but in many other courses where students are expected to write, since so many disciplines are themselves sites for numerous and conflicting rhetorical possibilities.

Second, we have to lay bare the drawbacks of advocating potentially static concepts of personal voice and intrinsic style in favor of reconsidering any writerly "voice" as only one fictive guise in an immense spread of other (also fictive) voices. Throughout this essay I invoke the work of the contemporary psychologist James Hillman, since many of his ideas complement those presented here. For example, Hillman's therapeutic technique of exposing, interpreting, and remaking the infinite range of personas that make up any one personality has rich implications for composition theory if we interpose "therapy" with our students' search for and explication of ways to define themselves through writing.

Third, since we can envision all rhetorical styles as relative fictions or "masks" across an (ideally) nonhierarchic scale, it follows that the boundaries between creative writing and critical expository prose can now dissolve, thus permitting the merging of serious scholarly analysis and poiesis. Finally, we are put to the task of translating these views into realistic practice, which means nothing less than restructuring the manner by which most English departments teach writing: specifically, how to transform selective and preclusive ideologies into relativistic pedagogies.

An inescapable condition of any college classroom where students are required to write, and then receive some sort of grade for their efforts, is that the instructor—no matter how conscientious or "objective"—cannot help but exert some formidable influence on the shape of the student texts. All student writing emanating from my classroom is in some way influenced by the powerful filter of my own predominant rhetoric; the moment I comment on a piece of student writing, or introduce supplementary reading, is the moment I have forced myself, in some sense, into the student's text.

Now, this situation in itself would not be so bad if students enjoyed the luxury of coming into contact with a wide range of faculty members, each of whom offered students a unique lens through which they could discover alternative means of writing. But such diversity rarely occurs. The scope of rhetorical styles students learn and interact with continues to reflect the academy at large—rhetorics influenced, for the most part, by the Eurocentric and patrifocal histories and ideologies on which colleges are built. These conditions persist whether the composition instructor embodies classical, current-traditional ideologies or more liberal, expressionist pedagogies. For example, students are apt to learn the art of composing Aristotelian arguments, not to encounter modes of discourse indigenous to Native American cultures. They might be encouraged to articulate in their journals personal statements inspired by "feminist" writers, but seldom are they encouraged to write in forms similar to those advocated by a burgeoning number of women creating their own versions of an exploratory "feminine" rhetoric. Students write academic essays on the poetry, novels, and plays written by others, not vice versa. In sum, it would appear that many of us never teach our students composition in any broad sense at all but, rather, indoctrinate them into those particularized genres that most closely mirror our own rhetorical predilections, while multiple alternatives are kept at bay.

I emphasize these discrepancies because lately I have come to recognize the biases inherent in my own pedagogy. As a white male trained in a fundamentally Eurocentric, middle-class environment, I run into problems if I try to guide students from vastly different ethnic, sexual, and class backgrounds to discover what I interpret to be their own voices. Who am I to determine how a woman's voice is supposed to sound if, as recent theorists like Rachel Blau DuPlessis, Susan Howe, Madeline Gins, and Monique Wittig argue, a more authentic woman's discourse might have to be characterized primarily by its resistance toward traditional male paradigms accepted as normative within the academy? Or, in the light of theorists like Molefi Kete Asante, Haki Madhubuti, and Henry Louis Gates, Jr., who have begun to articulate the foundations of an African American rhetoric, how can I consider myself a judge of what constitutes normalcy for students of other cultures? The issue becomes even more complex with students whose proclivities might, given the chance, take them in more contemporary directions, approaches toward composition influenced by the diverse and complex twentieth-century explorations into experimentalist, avant-garde, and postmodern means of shaping language.

And yet, although the condition of being a teacher forces one to adopt an inescapably persuasive, tutorial position, writing instructors can use this manipulative ground to the student's advantage. If we were to begin familiarizing ourselves with the infinitely broad world of voices, rhetorics, and discourses prevalent within and outside academic communities, providing environments where students can experiment with these forms, we would be moving several steps closer to instituting a culturally diverse, cross-gender, multidisciplinary academic milieu, in which composition would play a vital role. A major flaw with all the current professional hype about cultural diversity and "opening" the canon is that the conversations continue to revolve around the inclusion of specific literary texts; absent is an equivalent attention to introducing culturally diverse discourses and rhetorics into the academic classroom. Given this need, we have a great excuse for embracing as many variegated, contradictory forms and styles as we can in the unique atmosphere of the college writing course. The teaching of writing becomes an endless smorgasbord of styles and genres: classical academic essays as well as Afrocentric rhetoric; lab reports and *l'écriture féminine*; personal diaries and postmodern experiments in language; and on and on.

Understanding a gamut of rhetorical forms and philosophies of discourse brings us closer to understanding, appreciating, and interacting with the multifaceted communities circulating within and outside the academy—the final aim of the multiculturalist argument. Beyond this goal, though, a pluralistic philosophy of composition provides a means of grappling with troublesome concepts, like how to articulate a personal voice or rhetorical style—how the self is to be conveyed through language. If a major component of composition studies involves serving as a site within which writers can explore, devise, and articulate their own personalities and individualities, as much current liberal ideology would have us believe, then the type of inclusive pedagogy outlined here would be ideal toward such ends.

To help understand this reasoning, we might briefly investigate Hillman's work in contemporary psychology. By no means the most conventional of psychologists, Hillman suggests versions of psychology that are more likely to deal with matters of the "soul" within the psyche, of gods active within (and outside) the human imagination. In fact, his interpretations of therapy through psychological healing often read more like mythology, poetry, perhaps even alchemy—terms that in some ways are curiously apt descriptions of his critical method. In this sense his approach is not unlike that of Freud, who considered himself first and foremost a poet. These are Freud's words, recorded during an interview:

A man of letters by instinct, though a doctor by necessity, I conceived the idea of changing over a branch of medicine—psychiatry—into literature. Though

I have the appearance of a scientist I was and am a poet and novelist. Psychoanalysis is no more than an interpretation of a literary vocation in terms of psychology and pathology.   (qtd. in Hillman, *Re-visioning* 19)

This braiding of science and literature evolved because Freud, claims Hillman, "was engaged in both at once: fiction and case history; and ever since then in the history of our field, they are inseparable; our case histories are a way of writing fiction" (*Healing* 5). In addition, Hillman characterizes psychoanalysis as "a comprehensive fiction of the human soul, of its genealogy, its prehistoric cataclysms, its transpersonal realms and the powers that govern its fate. It succeeds not as a science but as a cosmological fiction" (*Re-visioning* 18).

An eclectic rethinking of Freudian, Jungian, and Adlerian psychologies, Hillman's work reinterprets the psyche by focusing entirely on the active imagination. Rather than attempt to dissect dreams and personal lives in order to discover motivations and archetypes of the lowest common denominator—searching, that is, for a point where we can translate our fantasies into what they "really mean" and explain away cognitive riddles into the clinical stasis of "fact"—Hillman posits that our realities are all no more, and no less, than intensely procedural, cumulative fictions, layered one on top of the other in an unending spiral display. Inherent in such a hermeneutics is the belief that it is the process, not the product, of the construction of these fictions wherein lies the definition of who we are—a definition that is constantly in flux, perpetually being redefined. The idea that our job is to "solve" these fictions is misguided, because any final solving is impossible. The impetus to continually reexamine (and thus reshape) the self never stops. We cannot exhaust the desire to contemplate who, what, why, and how we are. We are marked by an imperishable need to fashion and reinvent our histories. Although we desire self-realization, a chance to historicize ourselves and our actions into some finite context, our lives are arguably nothing more tangible than an ever-shifting current of fictions. And this relentless pursuit to understand the soul or mind or psyche is precisely the drive that characterizes us as quintessentially human. In many ways, this pursuit is rendered excitingly palpable through the dialogic artistry of writing and oral communication, made accessible through the active imagination.

It is important for us to understand how Hillman defines "active imagination." It is not, for example, a spiritual discipline, for there are no rules where the imagination is concerned; one works with what arises. Nor is the active imagination necessarily a preoccupation with aesthetic matters; it need not manifest itself as poems or paintings or other works of art. We may invest our creations with as much aesthetic form as we wish (a process Hillman encourages, in fact), but throughout the endeavor the primary aims are self-confrontation and reinterpretation, not necessarily the creation of an artistic artifact. This is an important clarification on Hillman's part, for it refutes the claim that only gifted artists have access to highly active imaginations. Hillman's philosophy thus recalls that of artists like Marcel Duchamp and Andy Warhol, who rebuked the image of the artist as the talented visionary rising above the masses. Everyone, as Walt Whitman and Mallarmé proclaimed, must be a poet.

The active imagination is not a mystical vision, either; to consider it such would impose spiritual intention on a psychological activity—that is, another unrecognized mask. Nor is it intended to lead one toward a state of transcendental contemplation; it is not a yogic or Buddhist activity. Dialogue, rather, and the communal retelling of stories are the goals, important considerations in that composition would then include not just a student's experiences with writing but the oral construction of texts in the classroom as well. The interaction of Hillman's psychology with composition studies makes conversation and collaborative interchange essential components for any writing class.

Particularly intriguing is Hillman's rereading of Jung's constant reiteration of the Platonic maxim "know thyself." By divorcing the phrase from the hackneyed contexts in which it often appears, we can understand just how radical this challenge is as Hillman points out the fallacy of introspection, a misconstruction that simply returns us to the relativism of subjectivity. In other words, the avoided question in matters of introspection is always, Who is doing the introspecting? And how does one introspect the introspector? Or, when we are thinking, who, precisely, is performing that activity—who thinks about the thinker? The concept of introspection risks lulling us into positing a Cartesian duality between the stationary, personal "I" of our psyches and all else residing within (or beyond) the exterior. Hillman believes that no such thing as a single, autonomous unifying entity exists but, rather, that splintered psyches do—shifting collective arrays of personas multiplying like so many rabbits of the mind, all of which we awkwardly attempt to encapsulate within one composite personality. Moreover, these crowded interior selves are in constant states of metamorphosis, in that our frames of reference, inescapably by-products of an unremittingly temporal dynamics, are forever in modulation. Consequently, we can't ever grasp "ourselves"—that is, contact, define, or pinpoint our "true" voices with any finality.

In essence, Hillman argues, we are deluding ourselves if we believe that cognitive activity is the result of a single, introspective I, and so we paint an unclear picture whenever we refer to ourselves as possessing an unvarying voice. When I was an undergraduate student studying art, my teachers encouraged me to seek out my own style, pushing me to unearth what made me unique from all other artists. Shortly thereafter, I was understandably confused when stumbling across an interview in which Picasso said that he did not care whose style influenced his work so long as it was not his own. Picasso's comment is in alignment with Hillman's view of therapy: both approaches are wary of succumbing to the stasis that can result when one is directed not by an unbridled imagination capable of leading into brand-new terrain but instead by a preconception of the patterns and terrain one "ought" to pursue simply because they constitute one's anticipated "personal style."

From this perspective, knowing one's self requires that knowers confront their most familiar, favorite mask: the seemingly omnipresent and nucleic "me" around which all ideas and emotions are assumed to revolve. When confronted, this me is shown to be nothing more than a veil, a patchwork of impressions condensed into a hazy sense of comfortable familiarity; we see this image as an accurate and complete depiction of ourselves, when in fact all we have done is highlight a particular, momentarily fixed version. At this point, Hillman emphasizes the need to push beyond such camouflage and locate the next underlying guise that also represents (and hides) our self—an impression that, in turn, conceals yet another mask, and another, ad infinitum.

Such a perspective could understandably produce some anxiety; talk of multiple personas can seem only a step away from the trauma of schizophrenia. Yet for Hillman the answer is not to ignore this inability to locate our central selves, our core psyches, but, rather, to confront this infeasibility head on, armed with one tool: the active imagination. In other words, we need not remain at the edge of the poststructuralist abyss, bemoaning our inability to grab hold of any finite me; such angst can be bypassed when we understand that our only recourse is to continue our process of creating, confronting, and re-creating the fictions that make up our lives (or vice versa). To write (or paint or perform or compose) is to fashion not so much our identities but bridges that connect various facets of our experience within an incomprehensibly dense and unmapped personal landscape. The goal may be not only to hypothesize the contours of such a psychic terrain but to revel in the act of serving as the architects (or cartographers) of our own imaginations. Writing *is* an architectural medium: writing language into form, which in turn "writes" the mind that thinks into form.

I do not mean to imply that teachers need to outlaw the concept of personal voice—only that we should understand the limitations of this popular label. When we rely on this term, we also carry with us its antithesis, a notion of the "false voice." Our opinion of what constitutes effective as opposed to ineffective voice has more to do with the conventions and expectations of our social institutions than it does with our supposedly innate ability to discern when a student uses, say, a unique and honest voice as opposed to some other language that inaccurately represents his or her intentions. We need to become highly suspicious of our motivations whenever we begin to believe the injurious myth of the "natural" voice. The poet Charles Bernstein offers some challenging insights on the problematic notion of the "natural":

> What I want to call attention to is that there is no natural writing style; that
> the preference for its supposed manifestations is simply a preference for a
> particular look . . . & often a particular vocabulary (usually perceived as per-
> sonal themes); that this preference (essentially a procedural decision to work
> within a certain domain . . .) actually obscures the understanding of the work
> which appears to be its honoured bases; & especially that the cant of "make it
> personal" & "let it flow" are avoidances—by mystification—of some very
> compelling problems that swirl around truthtelling, confession, bad faith, false
> self, authenticity, virtue, etc.   (*Content's Dream* 45)

To encourage a writer to write within a so-called natural form can be as
limiting as forcing a writer to adopt unequivocally any of the often prescriptive
formulas and delineated codes found in dozens of rhetorics and readers currently circulating within the profession.

Before discussing how, exactly, composition instructors might implement
widely ignored and esoteric rhetorics alongside those more expected within
our academic curricula, we must anticipate the argument that a prismatic
atmosphere of multiple genres and voices might lend itself more to chaos
and confusion than to any enhanced possibilities for effective writing. Here
Hillman's insights can be of further value. Hillman talks of cognition as
polycentric, our awareness of which can only come about once we have
confronted our egocentricity as no more than a partial portrait of our personalities; until we recognize our fractured makeup, our creative endeavors run the
risk of having only the most predictable and permissible of results. Though
our common inclinations are often to remain with the familiar—creation
along paths marked less by their challenging innovation than by adherence
to conformity—understanding the stagnation inherent in the notion of a
solitary, terminal voice can permit us to open up to the myriad contradictions,
inconsistencies, and opposing tensions that make up the reality of our daily
existence. Hillman comments:

> Instead of trying to cure pathological fragmentation whenever it appears, we
> would let the content of this fantasy cure consciousness of its obsession with
> unity. By absorbing the plural viewpoint of "splinter psyches" into our con-
> sciousness, there would be a new connection with multiplicity and we would
> no longer need to call it disconnected schizoid fragmentation. Consciousness,
> and our notion of consciousness, would reflect a world view that is diverse and
> unsettled.   (*Re-visioning* 41–42)

Presented as is, such a philosophy of composition could still seem hopelessly
schizophrenic to students (and colleagues), which is why we must once more
underscore the obvious: that the notion of a central style is a falsity, a creative

dead end. We all contain a transient maze of personalities, a fact quickly ascertained when we think of the numerous voices we adopt and discard in speaking to various audiences. Subtle and drastic differentiae manifest themselves in our discourses with everyone we encounter: My style of speech and choice of vocabulary differ widely among my close friends, while my rhetoric among less intimate friends differs in yet other ways. I speak with my parents in radically different patterns and in still others with my grandmothers, aunts, and uncles. I talk to my sister in ways that are unlike the ways in which I speak with the rest of my relatives. Then there are my in-laws, to whom I speak with yet other voices, which vary depending on whether the in-laws are in my wife's immediate family, or cousins closer to my age, or aunts and uncles who command a different kind of respect. With my wife, the voices I use are of a form unique to our relationship. I speak with my students with another set of loose, usually unconscious guidelines, which can vary according to whether the students are adolescents, freshmen, seniors, or postgraduates. Then there are very young children, salespeople over the phone, store clerks, clergymen and women, immediate superiors, presidents of universities, officers of the law, members of the opposite sex, mechanics, infants, professionals and colleagues I wish to impress—the list is endless. Further complicating the issue are the host of moods that affect my voice—when I'm irritable, dead tired, complacent, hungry, or insecure and defensive. If we add to all these voices the intensely private ways lovers speak to each other, the peculiar ways people talk to animals, and the style one adopts when talking to oneself, then the complex quilt we call personality is discovered to be utterly unfixed. Add in the even greater range of voices floating around us within the media—the news anchor's rehearsed ad-libs, the obnoxious radio deejay, the sitcom villain, the self-indulgent wail of the rock star, the folksy tone of the local newspaper's feature editor, the vacant politician—and then further compound this landscape with the scope of personas encountered in literature, film, painting, and other narrative arts, and it becomes amazing that any of us can keep track of who we are among this relentlessly noisy crowd.

If I have belabored the point that we are all donning and casting aside an unbridled assortment of masks—depending on whether we are hollering at the cat, conversing intimately with someone we love, experiencing moments of religious or philosophical contemplation, or laughing raucously at something silly—it is to demonstrate how flexible this network is and how effortlessly we switch gears in this automatic process. Despite this deluge of personas, we manage exceedingly well to process, and in turn construct, an extraordinary amount of information on a daily basis, usually unaware of the different theatrical and mythical roles we jump in and out of during such activity. By pointing these roles out to our students, we might find it easier to encourage them to experiment with additional voices by calling on the same resources they use to process, and thus perpetuate, the immense variety of discourses they encounter every day.

The radical implications of Hillman's interpretation of fiction can potentially extend themselves into every genre, any field of study. Through Hillman's eyes one can argue that all history, and even memory itself, is a shifting web of fictive threads: photographs are fictions, the CBS evening news is a fiction, the priest's sermon is a fiction, and this essay, too, is a fiction, as is any reader's interpretation of this essay. Yet the term *fiction* here need not have negative connotations: a fiction is not a lie but, rather, an additional perspective or another version of some argument—a version made powerful by its willingness to leave itself open to question and further change. Fictions are narratives of potential energy; we draw from them to continue molding our own "truths" and impressions. Consequently, we need to reexamine our common habit of separating fiction from so-called fact. In the light of this habit, the insistence of English departments on differentiating factual, or expository, writing from creative, or fictive, writings calls out for reinterpretation.

Most English departments continue to imply that expository prose occupies a realm of inquiry and introspection fundamentally alien from the one poets and novelists inhabit; the assumption is that writers of expository prose work with factual data, not fictions. From Hillman's perspective, however, these barriers crumble: all writings are fictions, whether essays, sonnets, dissertations, or one-act plays. The difference between sestinas and research papers is a matter of technique and craft, not of the content or absence of something akin to truth. Whether one calls writing poetry or prose, essay or fiction, these terms are merely vehicles for the same pool of ideas that compose our realities. Richard A. Lanham, in *Literacy and the Survival of Humanism*, tells teachers:

> Put aside the moralistic polarity and study how, in fact, style works in the world, relates to and molds human behavior. Study styles, not preach about and at them. Any pedagogy that hopes to work must educate intuitive judgments, not try to avoid them or legislate about them.   (103)

Since much of the writing produced by students in composition and literature courses falls under the implicit or stated heading of expository prose, including most professional writings by teachers and scholars in this field, it makes sense to investigate how our constructions of so-called critical prose can be modified from Hillman's perspective. If we take his idea to its limits, there is no reason why we cannot create classroom environments where students and colleagues write and read critical essays as if they were poetry and vice versa.

Hillman talks significantly about "poiesis," which he defines as "simply 'making,' " the transition from imagination into words (*Healing* 4). Critical interpretation, whether applied to literature or our own texts, is poiesis, a "collaboration between fictions, a revisioning of the story into a more intelligent, more imaginative plot, which also means the sense of mythos in all the parts of the story" (*Healing* 17–18). Hillman's idea is to approach analysis (that is, critical expository prose) as mimesis. Since we often respond to paintings and music not as translators in search of summaries but as creators of new imaginative reactions, why not try the same approach with the critical essay? "Imaginative art forfeits interpretation and calls instead for a comparable act of imagination," writes Hillman—in other words, not to abandon interpretation but to redefine it (*Healing* 29). The thrust here is in favor of perpetual enactment, a recognition that historicizing is the only way to make ourselves take shape. In a sense, composition can be likened to the creating of a musical score. Just as literature can be seen as so much sheet music that is never captured or defined but only perpetually reinterpreted, so too can we view our own explorations into composition as those of musicians making completely new scores, whether we are the original composers (writers) or players in the orchestra (readers). Either way, a unique piece is always formed. By adopting this viewpoint, we come to recognize that we need not remain simply the interpreters of literature but can become the makers of our own literatures.

Numerous twentieth-century writers—from Gertrude Stein to Nicole Brossard, Charles Olson to Jacques Derrida—have been praised for their striking originality, their courage to forfeit standard tones of academic professionalism in favor of challenging prose shaped in unparalleled ways. As teachers of composition, we can entice our students to attack language with the same air of imaginative nonconformity, as much as we teach them to compose writings in accordance with institutional expectations. We can, in Ezra Pound's words, "make it new" by both embracing and resisting convention.

In fact, these two directives—teaching the language(s) of the academy on the one hand and reinterpreting composition as poiesis on the other—can merge together to produce effective ends. Consider, for example, how many students write their papers in a pseudoacademic discourse they do not understand, often forcing themselves to forgo the investigation of valuable tangential trains of thought for the sake of conformity. In anticipation of this problem, we can invite students to emphasize the fictive quality of their writings and arguments in order for them to seek ways of bringing in further views, information, and commentary. Just as so-called literary journalists like Tom Wolfe, John McPhee, and Joan Didion, or more recent writers of the personal essay, incorporate anecdotes and other obviously subjective asides in their reportage, students too can be shown that the expository essay need not always be a collection of raw data packaged into the polished stuff of critical analysis and argument. Rather, writing causes the process of interacting with one's own fictions as they are realized.

By temporarily releasing students from the anxiety of producing critical arguments completely supported by "facts," we invite them to postpone, at least early in the composing process, their concern over how to support their ideas. Instead, they may begin cultivating stories and fictions, both anecdotal and imaginary, by following tangents, experiencing different voices, playing with different genres—all, perhaps, within the same text. When we grant students more freedom to indulge their imaginations in their texts, all writing becomes creative writing. If we take this position to its extreme, we can quickly see the difficulties of constantly perpetuating an academic distinction between creative writing and critical expository prose.

What does this proposal mean, exactly, for the writing instructor? It means drastically rethinking the operation and goals of the writing classroom. It involves understanding why specific rhetorics are encouraged while others are censored in academic curricula and then altering this imbalance. It means questioning why we enforce certain writing pedagogies at the cost of others. Ultimately, composition studies would be viewed as far more than a field concerned primarily with functional and academic literacy: composition could be seen as nothing less than an intellectual process, at once scholarly and poetic, through which feasibly all academic disciplines converge as the writer critically probes the perplexities of authorial voice, and all the inherent fictions implied therein, through an intense, interdisciplinary framework.

Of course, arguments like these give rise to some major questions. Is it enough to delegate the teaching of composition to a semester or two of instruction, where students come into contact with at best only a few philosophies of composition? If composition instruction means encouraging students to seek a gamut of rhetorical styles and genres emanating from different academic and nonacademic movements, then instruction in numerous discourses must be made available within academic divisions. This availability in turn would necessitate the hiring of instructors who specialize in alternative, overlooked rhetorical philosophies.

A balanced English department, for instance, might have faculty members proficient in teaching not only versions of classical argumentation and the rhetoric of personal narrative but also various discourses resistant to assumptions embodied in many Eurocentric, patrifocal academic ideologies. Such an English department might offer workshops and seminars on the postmodern essay, experimenting with "feminine" composition, the poetics of Native American discourse, and Asian expository prose. Other course offerings might include journalistic prose, literary journalism, technical writing, composition for business-oriented students, modes of scientific writing, as well as classes for ESL students and others markedly deficient in what their respective universities choose to define as "standard" English.

This polycentric curriculum would not be solely a characteristic of English departments. History departments could offer classes highlighting separate means of writing about history: from classical, "objectivist" research, to new historicism, to the avant-garde brand of historical research found in works by Susan Howe and Paul Metcalf. Philosophy departments could encourage students to write according to Aristotelian logic in some classes and the rhetoric (or antirhetoric) of Zen in others, while the rebellious, experimental play of poststructuralist philosophers might be emulated in more advanced courses. African American studies could feature courses in which students investigate possibilities for writing with so-called Afrocentric tropes—the discourse of blues, jazz, "the dozens," orature, signifying, and so forth.

Such university-wide curriculum would see composition studies as something like an immense spider plant. The center of this plant—composition studies taught within English and humanities departments—would be the site of extreme interplay among all modes of writing: classical argumentation, avant-garde poetics, diaries, journals, fiction, screenplays, technical prose, scientific papers, oral manifestos—the works. Shooting out from this core would be numerous smaller "plants"—related, but independent. These secondary branches for composition study would take root within other academic departments: the history department that teaches various means of writing about history, the religious studies department offering different approaches toward writing about world religions, and so on. In essence, a thriving symbiotic relation would exist in which composition studies—a unique, hybrid discipline of exceptional variety and kaleidoscopic proportions—influences, and is influenced by, a more specialized, variegated attention to composition in other academic departments. This proposal echoes concerns within the writing-across-the-curriculum movement, but in a broader sense: multiple philosophies of rhetoric crisscrossing one another in a flexible, interdisciplinary network and strengthening the field as a whole in the process.

While this agenda is intriguing, it is more than a little idealistic at this point in the development of our discipline. The current argument between academic and personal writing—still very much a source of contention in our profession—remains cloaked within the rather conservative assumption that numerous alternative discourses, lying outside the realm of either academic or personal-expressionist ideologies, fail to warrant inclusion within this polar debate. Given this situation, how readily would professionals in the field embrace the multirhetorical, relativistic stance outlined above?

And yet, for teachers sympathetic to some of the ideas expressed in this essay, it is difficult to be content with the few options now available for instructors of composition; the duality between current-traditional instruction

and "liberal," process-oriented pedagogies offers a static polarity unrepresenta-
tive of the exciting wealth of alternatives developed by intellectuals within
and outside academe. Until English classes begin to reflect the need for
polycentric composition instruction, we must find ways of teaching a multiplicity of rhetorics within the introductory composition courses and advanced
expository writing classes already at our disposal.

To transform the writing classroom into an arena conducive to creative
exploration across a scope of conflicting rhetorical styles, we must achieve
several primary goals. First, students have to learn that the effects (and affects)
of discourse, written and oral, merely reflect different communities and that
the aims of the classroom are twofold: to teach students how to interact
effectively with the discourse(s) of the academy, while simultaneously instill-
ing a greater understanding of opposing means of making knowledge through
writing that is prevalent in communities often ignored within the academy.
It is paramount, obviously, to stress how academic and professional environments validate and condemn different writing methodologies; nothing is
gained by failing to teach students how to use language in ways that will
grant them acceptance into the different professional communities they wish
to enter. But if teachers stress only academic means of communication in the
classroom, they do a gross disservice by rendering interdisciplinary, culturally
diverse discourses invisible and thus nonexistent.

In the light of this consideration, students could be encouraged throughout
a semester-long introductory writing course to compose arguments and texts
in a variety of rhetorical styles. First, students would have to become proficient
in ways of creating essays that will gain respect in their individual academic
disciplines. I once tried this approach in an introductory expository writing
class in which students spent a large part of the semester working on lengthy
research papers, proceeding through numerous drafts. Students chose their
own topics, which had to remain grounded somewhat in their major academic
discipline. (I met individually with students whose majors were undecided
to help them come up with topics to their liking, usually centered in the
humanities.) In these papers, students had to demonstrate evidence of considerable research (documenting all references and bibliographies in accordance
with the accepted styles of their individual fields), as well as incorporate an
equal amount of their own insights and supported opinions. Thus they worked
on essays that attempted to balance the statistical, research-oriented accumulation of data expected in many disciplines with the introspective, personally
motivated argument often expected in other classes. In essence, I tried to
combine classical, or formal, academic discourse, and that which is more
expressionist in style, mirroring the two generic poles most common within
their college curriculum.

Throughout the semester, I also had the same students read and discuss a
range of essays, each written in a unique rhetorical style: students read a
scholarly article from a scientific journal, editorials from the *New York Times*,

one of Frederick Douglass's narratives, a brief work by André Breton, and critical prose from writers like Michelle Cliff, E. D. Hirsch, Jr., HD (Hilda Doolittle), Ishmael Reed, David Antin, Robert Grenier, Dennis Tedlock, and Rachel Blau DuPlessis. The students then wrote shorter essays imitating the particular "rhetoric of the week": the analytic objectivism of the scientific essay, the so-called personal essay, surrealistic automatic writing, experimental rhetorics inspired by contemporary feminist and postmodern essayists, and so on. In addition, students also spent some time writing journal entries, keeping dialogic notebooks, and investigating ways in which other multicultural communities write and communicate. (They discussed, for example, how prevalent African American rhetorical tropes differ from, say, Eurocentric modes of discourse.)

Finally, I sprinkled my own preferences throughout the course, which students examined in conjunction with the other discourses encountered in the class. I find it impossible to maintain any wholly neutral stance throughout the course whereby I refrain from influencing students according to my own idiosyncratic preferences, but I don't think such a stance is desirable to begin with. Besides introducing students to all these other writings, I want to underscore what I consider valuable too (a main reason I went into teaching in the first place). For example, I stressed the importance of taking fictions seriously. Even though the course focused primarily on expository prose, I encouraged students to pursue all manner of fictions (actual dreams, daydreams, fantasies, contrived stories) at relevant points in the course in order to come into contact with the wealth of material stored in their imaginations, material that is essential in their construction of essays, their formulation of opinions and new ideas. Hillman equates the interminable search for new fictions with digestion, claiming that history itself is a "digestive operation" (*Healing* 27). The raw facts, or nutrients, of history do not become experienced until they are conceptualized, contemplated, and reinterpreted—that is, eaten. Digestion, or critical inquiry, is the process by which our memories, histories, and opinions become alive, influential. Consequently, the writing classroom becomes an incubator for the students' stories and fictions, which can then, if necessary, be translated into discourses more commonly understood by institutions as expository prose, so that students can communicate more effectively within their academic environments.

Lastly, I emphasize that writing, all of it, is a poetic activity. It is not poetic in any romantic or precious sense but poetic in that discourse is ultimately a search for something new, an entrance into "the *rhetoric* of poiesis . . . the persuasive power of imagining in words, an artfulness in speaking and hearing, writing and reading" (Hillman, *Healing* 4). Or as George Quasha writes:

Psychological freedom is compositional; the private mind composes itself and inhabits an artspace. And psychological understanding becomes a problematic of composing in language, where each moment calls for its own poetics. So psychic attunement in reading does not call for assigning interpretive meanings to the text, which then reflect meanings back to our lives; it is not a detective's hunt for the secret of the text but a discovery, in [Henry] Corbin's words, that "the text itself is a secret," a knowing through the text that opens out into our lives.   (xi)

It is this possibility of criticism being indistinct from poetry, or creative writing, that I try to convey to my students. The barriers between genres and disciplines perpetuated by social institutions often run the risk of channeling creative efforts into stifling results, and ultimately, students must choose which forms they will follow or disregard—those decided by institutions, those of their own making, or some combination of the two.

As paradoxically fractious but cohesive, our field places us in an interesting position. Anyone involved in composition studies is concerned, to some degree, with the business of writing. And more people are realizing that writing doesn't exist in a vacuum, that oral discourse—dialogic and performative—is an inseparable facet of composition. But beyond these considerations, what are the boundaries we choose to enforce? Which writing practices can we justifiably ignore? What cultural discourses can we disregard, especially when more and more of our institutional rhetoric advocates just the opposite? On what grounds can we advance any parameters that leave out so much more than they include?

When I think about the possibilities of composition, its interdisciplinary ramifications, Gertrude Stein comes to mind. Influenced by physicists and philosophers like Henri Bergson and William James, she went on to become one of the foremost composition theorists of the twentieth century—a woman whose fascination with words kept her joyously aware of what it meant to live with language in a "continual present" (518). I also think about John Cage, whose musical compositions of silence and found tones led him to make some of the most innovative written essays and lectures of the twentieth century—works enriched by his fascination with Zen, botany, autobiographical anecdotes, and the alphabet. Or I recall Benjamin Lee Whorf, whose genius in anthropology and linguistics helped him to compose a new form for describing the mysterious correlation between discourse and temporality. Whorf posited concepts of Hopi time and language that, though not necessarily representative of how Hopi Indians communicate, nevertheless add yet another dimension to our understanding of what it means to utilize discourse as a social or artistic medium. I think of the French Oulipo movement, that band of mathematicians and scientists who devised amazing algorithmic formulas by which they could produce written texts that never reached closure or conclusion. Or I recall the work of women like Monique Wittig and Rachel

Blau DuPlessis, who seek through written language the ability to compose a space for themselves—a space that for so long has been rhetorically nonexistent. And I remember the Russian constructivists and futurists of the early twentieth century, writers who experimented in fusions of the visual and the linguistic with revolutionary results.

These composition theorists have in common their incessant need to experiment with writing at its most primal degree. I strongly believe that we need to discover ways of channeling that same sense of exploratory excitement into our writing classrooms. We must rethink composition as a hybridized field, a sieve attracting satellite disciplines and transposing them in fascinating, unexpected directions. We can achieve this goal by perceiving our field through multiple angles, by making our talk of the universe of discourse more closely reflect the multivocality that constitutes any universe. We can begin critically rethinking the problematic concept of personal voice in favor of embracing multiple fictive voices, diving headfirst into rhetorics strange and new to us until we recognize a richer palette of discourse alternatives. Finally, from a pragmatic point of view, I think such an excess of variety would have a greater chance of getting more students interested in the art of writing.

Obviously we need to teach students how to anticipate the various assumptions and expectations of their future professors and potential employers. But if composition instruction remains at this level, writing is little more than a craft to be "mastered" for functional ends. If we are sincere about writing as a means of examining, and hence making, the richly dense realm of our multiple personalities, then composition instruction must encourage students to move beyond the functional, the conventional, the traditional and into forms of their own making. Language is an alterable medium to be manipulated and constructed, not simply a pattern of rules and obligations delineated according to formulaic tenets, as found in current-traditional assumptions as well as in the more subtle but equally prescriptive motivations implicit in liberal-expressionist teachings. Our teaching of discourse should at least attempt to reflect the discourses alive and well in the world; otherwise, we are enforcing particular ideologies under ethnocentric guises of normalcy, appropriateness, and universality. Just as Hillman's therapeutic technique invites clients to wrestle with a multitude of fictive interpretations, composition studies might become healthier by capitalizing in extreme degrees on the pluralism implicit in our discipline—acknowledging and generating a chorus of harmonic rhetorical fictions.

Harvard University

ETHNOGRAPHY AND THE STUDY OF LITERACY: PROSPECTS FOR SOCIALLY GENEROUS RESEARCH

David Bleich

IN *The Making of Knowledge in Composition*, Stephen North identifies two classes of composition workers—researchers/scholars and practitioners, with the researchers/scholars creating "theory" for practitioners to "apply." The appliers far outnumber the theorists, but the theorists have more power and prestige. North sees the practitioners as custodians of a kind of knowledge used by all members of the field but not taken seriously by theorists in their formal work. He calls this local knowledge "lore" and describes it as "the accumulated body of traditions, practices, and beliefs in terms of which Practitioners understand how writing is done, learned, and taught" (22). A key problem posed by North's book is how we as members of the composition discipline/profession can integrate all kinds of knowledge in our profession—those emerging from the variety of theoretical "methods" along with the local knowledge of working teachers.

Ethnography, like composition, is a relatively new field of inquiry, and it has an analogous modern history: for the past century or so, it has been practiced by many people who called it different generic names—history, autobiography, journal writing, diary, travel account—while also affiliating it with the narrower and more academically prestigious discipline of anthropology. At about the same time that composition research began its current period of growth, ethnography developed a more autonomous identity. The phrase of anthropologist Clifford Geertz, "thick description," is repeatedly cited by ethnographers who have used a more personally involved style in researching their chosen culture or population. Geertz's description of the ethnographer's work as "writing" or inscribing (as opposed to reporting or conveying information) was urged by postmodernist developments in language philosophy and theory. The field of ethnography as we understand it today may also be expressed as "writing culture," the term James Clifford and George Marcus use in the title of their 1986 ethnographic essay collection.

The connection between ethnography and language philosophy helps to explain why those of us studying the teaching of writing have found in ethnography a cognate field of inquiry, a field promising enrichment and change for the many "practitioners" who do ethnographic work that is not recognized as such for the political reasons North outlined.

How do the relations and overlapping of ethnography and literacy bear on the foregoing issue? That is, how can composition or literacy studies grow as a discipline and as a profession, prosper in and contribute to the English departments with which it is affiliated, and make use of the varieties of theoretical methods as well as the accumulated lore partially known and shared by thousands of writing teachers? The situation of academic ethnography is political, but some ethnographic studies of school classrooms are helpful correctives. Focusing attention on the classroom as an institution (a culture? a community?) can loosen the boundary between theorists and teachers, and between academic ethnographic work and the work of writing in classrooms.

Ethnography, in spite of its reputation today as a progressive field, is, in practice, often marked by styles and standards of work understood as "academic" for at least a millennium and probably longer than that. After an initial informal skimming of Clifford and Marcus's *Writing Culture* in my graduate seminar on teaching first-year college English, the students and I decided to include it in our collective reading list. This book seemed to promise an introduction to new styles of thought associated with the study of other cultures by privileged Westerners. We expected that learning about other cultures from an anthropological perspective would help us respond to those cultures in our own classrooms and render our own familiar Western academic culture less apparently "standard." But we started thinking about Clifford's introduction, which offers, as a reason for the volume's including only one essay by a female author, the idea that "feminist ethnography . . . has not produced either unconventional forms of writing or a developed reflection on ethnographic textuality as such." A member of the seminar then read, in an issue of *Signs*, an essay by Frances E. Mascia-Lees, Patricia Sharpe, and Colleen Ballerino Cohen, who observe with frustration that Clifford actually uses Marjorie Shostak's *Nisa: The Life and Words of a !Kung Woman* as the centerpiece of his essay "On Ethnographic Allegory" and that he comments on how it is both feminist and "original in its polyvocality." The *Signs* authors conclude that Clifford "prefers to write about feminists rather than inviting them to write for themselves" (13; see also Clifford 107).

This important introductory point in the *Signs* essay leads to the main argument, which deals with how and why postmodernist styles of ethnographic work still have not acquired certain fundamental, politically enlightened and egalitarian traits that they otherwise seem to endorse. The essay opposes the attempt by Clifford and Marcus to subsume feminism under postmodernism. The authors argue that feminism announces its politics and pursues an open political program, while postmodernist scholarship, even in its interdisciplinarity, continues the culturally masculine tradition of defining subject matters whose agendas depend on the suppression of politics. The authors cite one feminist anthropologist, Judith Stacey, who doubts that ethnographic work characterized by privileged scholars finding out about other, less privileged cultures is viable altogether: recording and representing observations *for an audience of other privileged readers*, regardless of how polyvocal these records and representations are, remains a project that serves its own privileged class. The authors claim that ethnographic work must change its purpose and conception so that it is in some significant way a *contribution to the welfare of the community or society being studied*. Such research, which I have identified as "socially generous research," is no longer mainly a discovery project but, rather, an initiative that contributes to the empowerment of the subject community and to the mutuality of this community and the research community: "framing research questions according to the desires of the oppressed group" and "choosing to do work that 'others' want and need" (Mascia-Lees, Sharpe, and Cohen 33).

The *Signs* authors are not responding solely to the one work by Clifford and Marcus. Their essay disputes a prevailing style of ethnographic research. David Fetterman's guidebook *Ethnography: Step by Step*, which tries to introduce ethnographic techniques to those who have not yet learned about them, advises ethnographers to approach their projects as follows:

> Ethnographers attempt to be unobtrusive, to minimize their influence on the natural situation. Their purpose is to describe another culture as it operates naturally. However, ethnographers are honest. They recognize that their presence is a factor in this human equation. Thus, rather than present an artificial and antiseptic picture, ethnographers openly describe their roles in events during fieldwork. The ethnographic presence tells the reader how close the ethnographer is to the people and to the data. The technique can contribute additional credibility to the researcher's findings. These embedded self-portraits simultaneously serve as a quality control, documenting the degree of contamination or influence the ethnographer has on the people under study.
>
> At the same time, the ethnographer should not dominate the setting, nor should the ethnographer's signature be in every word or on every page. The researcher need not include every parenthetical thought to demonstrate intellectual prowess. In describing a culture, the focus of the writing should be on the topic. . . . Ethnographers leave both explicit and implicit signatures on their work. . . . An artfully crafted ethnographic presence can convey the depth and breadth of the ethnographer's experience in the field.   (116–17)

This passage represents the presuppositions of Fetterman's book fairly well. Characteristic of the new ethnography are the assumptions that ethnographers are aware of their own presence in the scene of research and that they should take this presence into account. (The foregoing two paragraphs appear in a section entitled "Ethnographic Presence.") These assumptions make sense as far as they go, and they are observed by Clifford and Marcus. But consider certain other phrases that may well pose problems. For example, "the natural situation" refers to the social situation that exists without an ethnographer present, and it may or may not be "natural." When an outside researcher is present, however, it becomes a *different* situation, and I doubt that it is possible to decide *how much* influence the researcher has, much less to find ways of *minimizing* it. (Sometimes, as I discuss later, one does not want to tinker with the researchers' roles at all.) Rather, the research site must be reconceived, particularly since the researcher, already a member of a more privileged society, is using that privilege to do the research in the first place. (This is the point made by Stacey and cited by Mascia-Lees, Sharpe, and Cohen.) Fetterman assumes that the situation or the setting *can remain independent* in some sense, so long as the presence of the researcher is accounted for. But Stacey and the *Signs* authors are not thinking only about the individual researcher. They are challenging the individualistic basis on which ethnography has proceeded, a basis implicitly accepted by the guidelines in Fetterman's book. When Fetterman writes that "the ethnographer should not dominate the setting," he implies that individual vigilance, ethical bearing, and each researcher's credible "signature" are enough to create mutual respect, to validate the research, and to authorize the research situation.

Fetterman, like Clifford and Marcus, assumes that an ethnographic approach to a community, a culture, or a society need not be questioned as a knowledge-seeking initiative. All three authors assume the political legitimacy of members of privileged societies who use their superior wealth to enter, or travel to, less privileged societies in order to bring home a new understanding of these societies. Although ethnographic work is done in our own society, sometimes among social and economic equals, the ethnographer Fetterman describes nevertheless adopts the stance of intellectual detachment and observational privilege. When such researchers go to indigent or suffering societies, it makes little sense to say that they are "participant-observers." But even when no apparent inequality exists, such as when a university faculty member does ethnographic studies of upper-middle-class schools, the researcher still makes use of his or her hierarchical relation to the subject of study. That is, even politically sympathetic ethnographers seem to require for themselves *some* elevated position relative to the studied culture. Thus, in traditionally styled ethnographic projects, the *standard of objective, detached observation is invoked to conceal the problematic social disparity between researcher and researched.* The rationalization of this concealment is no different from the time-honored rationalization for all intrusive or invasive research procedures: to "seek the truth."

The so-called search for truth is so fully bound up with the traditional, socially masculine research style of the physical sciences that it is hard for many people to understand what the *Signs* authors are worried about. Consider Fetterman's characterization of ethnographic presence as "a factor in this human equation." Or his reference to the researcher's subject materials as "data." Or his thinking of the ethnographer's self-portraits as "quality control." Or his concern for the "degree of contamination" of the culture under study. I see Fetterman as similar to Clifford and Marcus: yes, all three use scientific terms as metaphors; yes, Fetterman consciously shifts to the artistic term *signature* to refer to the researcher's presences. But these shifts in language do not change the research model Fetterman describes and Clifford and Marcus use: the objective, individualistic, scientific one that has been increasingly criticized by feminist epistemologists and those who are challenging the traditional "knowledge is power" approach to scientific work.

North and the *Signs* authors have related concerns. Mascia-Lees, Sharpe, and Cohen see ethnographic work as not fulfilling its promise as long as such work is assimilated to the traditional objective (knowledge-power) paradigm of science. North is concerned that serious research in the new field of composition has been similarly associated with this paradigm. He hopes that the knowledge of practitioners can be assimilated to the body of understanding about literature, writing, and the teaching of writing. This new synthesis, he implies, will help change the political status of the field as a whole; the subject itself will question the traditional relation of knowledge and power.

Usually, practitioners as North describes them—working teachers primarily concerned with the quality of the classroom experience—do research along the lines that Stacey and the *Signs* authors propose:

> [A]t least in some phenomenological sense, Practitioners could be said to be facing new practical problems, and so making such "new" contributions all the time. That is, they work with students who can be said to change from day to day, even hour to hour. The student for whom one prescribes a regimen of sentence-combining today is not exactly like any student ever assigned it before, and will not even be quite like today's "herself" tomorrow.   (33)

That is, because the *welfare* of students is never omitted from the practitioners' interests, the knowledge that teachers have is more like lore than like formulated knowledge. Teachers with the quality of classroom experience on their minds lean toward *including themselves as members of the class.* Thus, they are not simply "participant-observers" as described by Fetterman and as commonly understood by many researchers; they are, rather, *interested parties,* a group (teachers) whose own interests largely coincide, in the classroom, with the interests of another group (students). The research or inquiry is not a primary interest but a cointerest, so to speak, with teaching. The *Signs* authors criticize Clifford and Marcus for their primary interest in the privileged audience that reads the resulting ethnographies. The near exclusion of women from Clifford and Marcus's list of authors is a problem in itself. But this exclusion goes hand in hand with the assumed exclusion of the objects of study from the audience for the ethnographic announcement. Not to have feminist anthropologists contribute their own work is a symptom of narrowness in conceptions of research; Clifford and Marcus's research was not conceived of as a contribution to the culture under study. Thus, ethnography and composition research have similar challenges at this time: to include in the research initiative the responsibility to serve the population that would otherwise only be considered as "data."

There are many ways to pursue this responsibility. Just as teachers of classroom teachers made the earliest reader-response research inquiries, so teachers and those interested in preuniversity education have taken more socially generous ethnographic initiatives. A recent volume on classroom ethnography, edited by Catherine Emihovich, has several essays pertinent to this discussion, two of which I consider here.

David Bloome's essay "Locating the Learning of Reading and Writing" is partly academic, partly ideological, and partly practical. As an academic piece, the essay tries to reconceptualize the classroom, to think of its different identities as an institution and a research site, as a place where important things are continuously taking place, and, therefore, as a place that might welcome the involvement of researchers. Ethnographic study of the day-to-day workings of classrooms has led Bloome to reject the deficit and difference conceptions of nonachieving students, as well as the effectiveness concept of teaching. Each of these concepts comes from an individualist ideology: students fail because of a *cultural deficit* or because their culture is different and they cannot catch on; teaching techniques are ineffective because they do not respond to specific needs. These views of classroom failure isolate large-scale low achievement in single causes and imply that some formulaic method can be found, either for students or teachers or both, to reliably produce well-integrated, highly motivated students and schools.

As a practitioner, a teacher of teachers, Bloome presents his research as a way for both students and teachers to gain a new platform, for both to proceed through classroom inquiries more interrogatively and less declaratively, for their voices to appear more prominently in the academic discussions about schools, and for the unique identity of each classroom to become an element in any research project in that classroom. Bloome poses a set of problems for those doing research on the teaching of literature:

> 1. How is the meaning of a story or other written text negotiated during instruction? How is the meaning of a story influenced by what occurs in the classroom? How does the meaning and meaning-making process vary across situations?

2. What are the interactional consequences of students' different interpretations of written texts? How do the interactional consequences vary across situations?

3. What is the social meaning of students' use of written language?

(102)

This series of questions is at once academic, ideological, and practical. For example, one could think of an outsider asking and trying to answer the first set of questions by simply observing classroom behavior. But more important, the teacher and the students in the class could ask the questions either as more formal "research" questions or just as ways to continue the study of literature. I make similar claims for the second and third sets of questions. In my work over the past twenty-five years, repeated inquiries, both in and out of class, into the first two sets of questions have led me to raise the third question more prominently in my teaching and scholarship, as I am doing in this essay. As Tom Fox discusses and demonstrates in his recent *Social Uses of Language in the Classroom*, students function in class by asking about the "social meaning" of their written and oral language. These questions, along with the many others Bloome proposes, show the potential of ethnographic work to invoke two or more perspectives at once: to pose research questions that serve the teaching situation, to pose teaching questions that serve the research situation, and to pose both sorts of questions that, in turn, serve other interests in society as well, such as parents, employers, or legislators.

Bloome explains his sense of the ethnographic perspective in a way that seems similar to North's practitioner's perspective:

From an ethnographic perspective, the location of reading and writing is not in individuals, but rather in the social context of events involving or related to written language. Similarly, learning to read and write is also located in the social context, in how it changes and develops over time and across events. . . .

While researchers have been able to provide a series of findings about the nature of classroom culture and classroom language, these findings are descriptive in nature. While they explain what happens within the events described, they do not provide causal explanations. Further, ethnographic findings do not provide sweeping generalizations applicable to all classrooms. Rather, they provide theoretical insights which raise questions that are applicable to all classrooms. (110–11)

As Bloome presents it, ethnographic research depends on practitioners' experiences and perspectives. Particularly with literacy whose learning is necessarily "located" in social contexts, the ethnographic researcher has to enlist the subjects of study as partners, as posers of questions, as people who can see and change their own experiences through interaction with "outside" but politically interested teacher-researchers. Furthermore, the local character of ethnographic knowledge helps to give it its practical role: if no ideology says that a finding must be universal, that what was true of this classroom must be true of all others, one can relax with this finding's more clearly reliable contribution to the local situation, and one might then claim that this local "truth" resulted from socially generous research.

University researchers such as Clifford and Marcus, but also many of those in literary studies and other academic subjects, find it all too easy to forget that they are teachers in one or more local situations; university teachers fluently assume the role of detached observer in both teaching and research rather than the role of interested party in both. Part of the reason for the strength of individualist ideology in the university has to do with the power and prestige of science and its historical advocates, practitioners, and characteristic subject matters. J. L. Lemke's contribution to the Emihovich volume is entitled "The Language of Science Teaching." By observing and recording the conversations between teachers and students in a variety of science classrooms, Lemke, a university faculty member and physicist, was able to document the ideological pressures on language use in the classroom, as well as the less-than-salutary classroom role in which he was placed as a result of this ideology.

Lemke observes, first of all, that in most science classrooms, the "language of the classroom always reflects the unequal power relations among the participants and not just their unequal mastery of the thematics of science" (221). A key language indicator of these relations is the way questions are asked in all classrooms:

> What sort of social power is it that lets some people get away with asking questions to which they already know the answers? Try it with a friend, or your supervisor, and see what happens. Who has the right, or power, to *test* someone else, to set criteria, or say that is the best answer?   (222)

Lemke is referring to the Socratic technique that is used even in the most successful classrooms. He notes that students usually answer such questions with an uncertain interrogative: "What two elements could be represented by such a diagram? Jennifer." "Hydrogen and helium?" (223). Jennifer's answer reflects at the same time fear of the teacher and fear of the subject matter. Lemke comments:

> The emotional tastes and preferences society inculcates in women, and in many poorer and lower-middle-class groups, neatly ensures that they will be the least likely to pursue an interest in a subject presented as a cold, impersonal one. We glimpse here one of the many important processes by which social relations of predominance are reproduced.   (234)

In other words, even the seemingly benign conversational style of the active teacher in most classrooms enacts and promotes a damaging ideological value:

the hegemony of science and its mostly white male population. Furthermore, what Lemke sees as taking place through the fear of technical and scientific matters is also true of students at both secondary and university level when any subject comes under academic authority: intimidation by faculty members who use the most advanced academic language to teach their subjects. Related to what the *Signs* authors discuss is that contemporary—postmodern—literary criticism, as documented in the *New York Times* by Richard Bernstein, justifies its use of obscure jargon by comparing itself to the science disciplines. What does Lemke think of scientific language that is under the ideological guidance of science?

> Most basically, I think it is expected to avoid the *humanness* of everyday language: no personification, no mention of specifically human attributes, actors, or types of action; no metaphors that call up human, emotionally loaded images. The result is familiar to all of us: the cold, impersonal world of science that seems so alien to the more personal, human world in which we are familiarly comfortable. . . . No matter that this image is contrary to the real life of working science, which is as personal as any other part of social life. Even when it deviates from this "ideal" of scientific language, as it often does, classroom language still works to maintain the separation from everyday speech.   (231–32)

Lemke's ethnographic studies of the science classroom demonstrate, then, that science's ideological reach is detectable in schools and classrooms, which become, as a result, unwitting and often unwilling collaborators with values that many teachers oppose. *This collaboration takes place through the habits, styles, and standards of oral and written literacy.*

In science, as in our own discipline, there is a "chain of command." Lemke cites an episode in a science classroom in which the subject is the relation between heat and light energy: A female student questioned the teacher's assertion that the ground (the earth) "creates" heat energy from the light it absorbs from the sun. The student felt it inaccurate to say that the ground *creates* the heat energy since it has already been absorbed as light. Lemke is kinder in his remarks about the teacher than I thought he might have been, noting that the teacher finally does explain, after reminding the student about the law of energy conservation she learned in the previous grade, that the ground *changes* the light energy into heat energy, which is what was meant by the word *creating*. It seems from the passage that the student did in fact remember the law of energy conservation and that this memory was the basis of her question. Lemke documents the teacher's nervousness. When the teacher says to the student, "Well I don't know if [the law of energy conservation] is true anymore," Lemke remarks, "[H]e looks at me when he admits he may not have the rule quite right himself" (229). The teacher seems to have been correctly caught on an important point of language use: *create* is not the appropriate term to describe the ground's *conversion* of light into heat, especially since the conservation law says something like "energy can neither be created nor destroyed." In citing the rule, therefore, he feels uncertain about it and looks at the physicist (Lemke) who happens to be observing that day. Lemke observes, "The chain of authority from scientist to teacher to student, at least as seen by the teacher, becomes briefly visible" (229).

Lemke spends a good deal of his essay documenting that the "code" of classroom talk "gives the teacher, in principle, total dominance of the lesson" (235). He notes that this code is often broken, and classroom asides are usually permitted. Even though students often call out and are recognized, even though they are not required to "respond" as the only form of participation, the practice of students responding to the teacher's questions is still "the rules." What kind of rules require this regular "breaking" in order to stay intact? Ideological rules, Lemke offers, because an ideology perpetuates itself by escaping challenge of its rules in their periodic relaxation. A principal part of the ideology is "the presumption that classroom learning is essentially an *individual* process between separate, isolated students and the teacher" (236). The ideology is universally followed during test taking, when all talking is forbidden. In fact, the structure of testing and grading enforces the individualism in education. One questions tests and grades less in science than in humanities. But strong pressure exists, even in the humanities, to continue the individualistic style through the enforcement of measurable, testable standards of writing and language use. Such enforcement would touch on all humanistic subjects and would be a new means to control political initiative. There is thus a degree of urgency in our desire to make use of what we are learning from ethnographic studies of classrooms.

Ethnographic work on language and literacy in the classroom shows the ways in which new approaches to literacy studies can affect a broad range of subject matters and teaching styles. Of special interest in these approaches is the combining of research and teaching in ways that could enrich university life and education for the majority of students and teachers. I confine myself here, however, to the English classrooms where I and others in my "class" work. Until about ten years ago, my classrooms were hierarchically organized with the students being the unprivileged majority and the teacher—myself— in an authoritarian position, pretty much as Lemke describes. In issues of writing and interpretation, the students' knowledge, no matter how it was achieved, finally had to be authorized by me, the teacher: because I was the one who signed the grade sheet, good writing and intelligent reading were neither more nor less than what I said they were.[1] The need for grades, moreover, made it both difficult and unlikely for students to teach either one another or me or for them to become ethnographic researchers on their own. There was no machinery for considering student readings and writings (perhaps best referred to as "literacies" or "literacy styles") as new or alternative perspectives pertinent not to the students' certifiability but to their communities of interest, in and out of the classroom. It was not possible, in other words, for students to develop self-authorized or collectively authorized investigations into literacy styles since the teacher was the "final" authority.

Since I had been listening to (and reading) discussions of ethnographic work, it seemed clear that university classrooms, and especially those in which I participated as teacher, were almost ideal locations for ethnographic research—for students as much as for teachers. I began to propose classroom projects and assignments in which students would do ethnographic research on their own and on others' literacy styles, and these research projects were always *reflexive*. Students would study *one another's* work with an eye toward teaching one another and learning from one another at the same time. I did not, however, think it necessary to announce, "We are now going to do *ethnographic* work," or to give the rules and then expect students to follow those rules. Instead, I did what North describes practitioners doing: seeing what suits this particular class and proposing the substance of the study. In the example that follows, students reviewed their own and their partners' readings of several short stories, raising questions such as those I cited from Bloome's recent essay.

In the fall of 1988, I taught a course entitled Narrative Literature at the University of Rochester. I did not announce any special approach in this course except that students would work in groups of three or four and that part of their subject matter, along with the short stories and the one novel they read, would be their group members' responses to the literature. Each student wrote a weekly response and a final project that compared the responses of group members and the student's own responses. These analyses were determined in large part by the kind of relationships that grew among the group members. A distinctive feature of this class of twenty students was that only one of them was female, while the text for the course was the *Norton Anthology of Literature by Women*. Although neither feminism nor ethnography was given as the topic of the course, class and group discussions repeatedly concerned gender, race, and class, issues the students also considered when reading one another's essays on the assigned materials. I wrote a few essays as well and distributed them to the class for analysis and discussion. No work was graded. Students doing all the work in a reasonably conscientious manner got a B; students distinguishing themselves in some way got an A. Two students who were not able to do the work withdrew.

Ms. S, the only woman in this class, wrote these introductory remarks to her final project:

> Before I begin to deal with the subjects of myself and my group members, our interaction in class and our writing, I'd like to describe some of the time I spent in class as I experienced it. I feel that it is an integral part of this project,

and that this study of my perception of my group members and their writing will be more clear to the reader if I begin this paper by telling something about myself.

This paper is the product of this semester's work, the culmination of my experience of this unusual class. In preparing to write it I have analyzed my own writing, noting that in many ways it reflects on my situation in the classroom in being the only woman in a class of over twenty men. This situation was completely new to me, and was all the more bizarre because the stories which we were asked to read and respond to had all been written by women. At times I felt as though what I was saying in class and writing in my papers was taken by my fellow students as representative of a female viewpoint; indeed, there were times when I myself represented it as such.

My experience of being the only woman in the class was educational and interesting. At first I found it novel; I was often singled out because of it. Later on I began to find it tiresome to be called upon to give the female perspective on whatever social issue was being discussed. There was also something tiring about looking across the tables at twenty male faces, however nice, every time I was in class. It seemed to me that there was a glaring contrast between the words of the women whose stories we read and the male opinions expressed in class. Even when feminist ideas were expressed, they seemed to have arrived through a filter of male vision. . . .

Within our group my being a woman made for some different reactions to the stories—as Mr. B later pointed out in the paper in which he analyzed my essays, I was more likely to respond to the threat of rape because I was a woman. The first thing I remember about Mr. B is our discussion in class of the word "freshman" as one that excludes women, and Mr. B's remark (made in the characteristic humor with a smile that apologizes for doing anything for a laugh—but nevertheless telling) that if I ever called him a "freshperson" I would get the back of his hand.

Members of Ms. S's subgroup included Mr. B, referred to above, and Mr. A. The major part of Ms. S's essay is a description of how her two group members developed during the semester, with only some reference to herself. I think that the situation in this class—the details of its population and reading matter in particular—led Ms. S to address political issues in an ethnographic style in her work. Other students, functioning according to majority psychology, did not introduce their analyses with a description of the classroom circumstances and atmosphere, which they may have assumed had little bearing on their work. Two points are noteworthy: first, a classroom minority is likely to notice the intraclass politics much more quickly than the majority does; and second, the ethnographic style and perspective of writing is a good way to *call attention to* these political conditions. Conversely, if it is part of the teaching program to include considerations of gender, race, and class in the study of literacy, an ethnographic research format is more appropriate than, say, the essay-writing model usually used in English classes.

In spite of the class's decorum, good humor, and seriousness throughout the semester, both the subject of sexism in the literature and the gender configuration of the class posed strong challenges for all. Like most young men unaware of how sexism works and of its part in the ideology they take for granted, many class members expressed an almost unending series of sexist and homophobic opinions, noted in Ms. S's restrained remark about "the words of the women whose stories we read and the male opinions expressed in class." Obviously, my own efforts to oppose these remarks appeared to Ms. S as feminism "through a filter of male vision." As a woman, Ms. S really was alone. Nevertheless, part of what empowered her did not actually appear in her account: first, she was an Israeli; second, she was Jewish like me, the teacher; third, she was the offspring of a professor; fourth, she was not to be shouted down by other class members; fifth, she knew how to hold her own in a public argument in which mutual interruption was common. In her final paper, she took the opportunity to present the sexist situation in class by describing, in almost embarrassing detail, the opinions of her group members. As her introduction shows, Ms. S retained her tone of analytical calm and so transformed her response to this "bizarre" experience into what I would consider a piece of scientific work.

One of the more prominent themes in both the class's sense of itself and Ms. S's ethnography is Mr. B's sense of humor, which announced its arrival on the first day of class with the "back of his hand" remark. Even though it was funny (and to the extent that I laughed, I participated in its sexism, in spite of the opinions I otherwise advocated), it was gratuitous since it was not personally provoked by anything Ms. S said. It took about nine weeks for Mr. B to understand that this style of joking was antisocial as well as personally offensive to Ms. S.

In her essay, Ms. S analyzes two responses that reveal Mr. B's humor as defensively sexist:

> Mr. B described how he avenged himself on a girl who had treated his feelings for her lightly by doing the same. In fact, he plotted a seduction scene and then walked out on the girl just when she was expressing her feelings for him. The following is Mr. B's description of walking out on [his former girlfriend]:
>
> > "Not on your life," I exclaim, accompanying this with a pathetic laugh. You must understand, this was the supreme moment of my existence, the exact point in my life which I had worked since birth to make happen. . . . In my glory, I stumbled out of the room and into the hallway.
>
> In my first written analysis of Mr. B's and Mr. A's papers, I wrote that I believed B used this kind of humor to put distance between himself and his emotions. It seems to me now that his grandiose description of "the supreme moment" of his existence was put there as a way in which to show the readers that B now realizes that he was being rather foolish. However, I think that

Mr. A and I would have taken far more kindly to this scene had B written "I realized how stupid I was," or something equally simple, instead of trying to be impressive.

After analyzing another such instance in which Mr. B treats a serious incident—his grandmother being mugged—with inappropriate humor, Ms. S reports a change in Mr. B's style of writing in this class:

> Once B became aware (through extensive group discussions) that his sense of humor, rather than amusing his readers, defeated the purpose of the assignments, he stopped interjecting wry wit into his writings and the result was a great improvement in their emotional content.

In the cause of regulating Mr. B's antisocial and sexist humor both in his writing and in class discussions (Ms. S cited other of Mr. B's public wisecracks), Ms. S and Mr. A were political allies. Mr. A was not derisive or sarcastic and was much less reluctant to express and report his feelings seriously. Yet he was no less sexist in the attitudes that emerged.

Ms. S comments on several instances in Mr. A's essays that bring out this attitude. For example, Ms. S writes, Mr. A describes "a sixteen-year-old girl [he had] 'tricked' into having sex with him by deceiving her about his feelings for her. . . . He also refers to females as 'emotionally weaker' in this paper, a statement that I strongly disagree with, and which seems sexist to me." At another point, she remarks that Mr. A "seemed to feel much, much worse about laughing at the boy's tie than about his pressuring N and P to have sex with him."

Ms. S's essay does a thorough job of representing A's and B's work fairly and fully, distinguishing between the two students as personalities with unique social and literacy styles yet portraying their sexism steadily. Ms. S involves herself in her analysis by briefly discussing A's and B's perception that she overidentified with rape victims and feared rape too much. She disputes this claim—that her fear is too great—but whether the men's perception is correct matters less than Ms. S's awareness of always being in a room with many men, many of whom laughed at jokes that made fun of women.

Ms. S's classroom ethnography brings out yet another political issue. In reading through her essay, I noticed that she did not deal with the heterosexism that most of us in the class probably participated in. No gay class member announced himself as such, although someone might have spoken up but for the joking at the expense of gay men. In one instance in Ms. S's essay, she and I probably collaborated in not opposing heterosexist attitudes. Ms. S is discussing Mr. A's response to Joanna Russ's "When It Changed," a story about a planet where only women have been living for six hundred years and where women reproduce only women by the "merging of ova." Ms. S comments:

> Because of his social conditioning and because of his personality, the idea of a society without men was difficult for him to grasp; also in this way he avoided the issues of the lesbian relationship and of the sexual threat presented by the men from earth. I believe that "When It Changed" attempts to cause its readers to identify with a woman in a lesbian relationship, but A was unable to accomplish this. Instead A identifies with "the husband."

Thus, Ms. S correctly claims that Mr. A cannot recognize a love-sex relationship between women. She uses the term *lesbian* to describe this relationship, and she describes the men from earth who arrive as a "sexual threat" rather than as a threat of tyranny, the way they are presented in the story. I believe she uses the term *lesbian* in part because I had used it in my oral commentary on the story. It was not until my discussion in this class that I began thinking that I may have given a heterosexist reading of the story. Russ does not describe the society as lesbian. My use of the term represents my reading of the society as "other" relative to my society—a perception probably created by the habit of assuming universal heterosexuality. If the society as a whole has no men, the terms *lesbian* and *homosexual* may not carry their usual references, since there is only one biological kind in the story. Yet in class no one challenged my use of the term *lesbian* to describe the population of "Whileaway."

Ms. S's essay is much richer than this discussion of it indicates. I believe that it is the beginning of an authentic piece of ethnography, since Ms. S's observations emerged from an *interested perspective* that was not academically regulated. Mr. B is a WASP, Mr. A a Hispanic, Ms. S an Israeli Jew. In her essay, Ms. S directly or indirectly discloses material that invites further thought on the social psychology of the group itself, on the literature the group read, on the whole class, and on the interaction of cultural styles that her small subgroup played out. The language of each person played an increasingly important role as the group continued to function. It was related to their work in class, to their cultural values, to their gender values, and to their interpersonal interaction.

Ms. S's work counts as an instance of socially generous research. Ms. S was "just" another student to Mr. B and Mr. A. Yes, she was doing an assignment. Nevertheless, Ms. S's account of the total classroom scene clearly shows she had reasons beyond the assignment for writing such an essay. It was a piece of research, but it also was a communication to her group members and to me. It was in part a critique of the class, of the teacher, and of the university circumstances in which she worked. While it has mostly local reference, the questions her work raised could give other teachers and students a different view of their own classroom situations; important questions could be raised earlier on in some classes if other students and teachers learned of Ms. S's findings and options. I don't know that we need to dispute whether Ms. S's work corresponds to some ideal of ethnography in order to appreciate how much this approach to classroom work in literacy enriches the classroom experience as well as the subject matter.

What Ms. S achieved, however, teaches us teachers and researchers more about how our professional orientations are changing, and ought to continue to change, under the influence of an ethnographic consciousness. If we understand Ms. S as student/researcher/teacher, we may see her as a new model of academic identity that may ease some of North's painful hand-wringing at the end of his book. He seems genuinely and deeply perplexed about how our profession will resolve the traditional problems of a community divided between literary and writing cultures.

Part of North's trouble is related to his belief in the social rigidity of professional boundaries. In this context, I notice that Ms. S immediately challenged the premise of my assignment and looked at the big picture. She did not know that she was making an "ethnographic" move. Conversely, therefore, consciously making an ethnographic move also may be an attempt to view the big picture *just because* of one's implication in this total scene. North's continuing respect for, and perhaps even loyalty to, the professional boundaries even as he is surveying the big picture helps to generate the verbal unrest at the end of his book. A similar problem faces teachers and teacher-researchers searching for a more unified sense of the many professional choices they can make.

The ethnographic move is disruptive, or at least it is perceived to be by the majority who are honoring the traditions of teaching and learning in which they have themselves been taught. When Ms. S takes the initiative to cite the overall circumstances of our class *because it serves the interests of her total project*, it is not simply an ethnographic move but an ideological one. By and large, ideological disruption is not considered a legitimate move for students or, I can attest, for teachers either. From another perspective, however, it is not disruptive at all. In fact, the ethnographic move actually preserves the most important individual options while still enlarging research toward political and social consciousness. Every teacher hopes students will show initiative. We consider initiative to be a sign of a "good" student, one engaged on a path toward independent thought. But we live in a period where not only the premises of schooling but the premises of family as well are regularly questioned. Just as our offspring often surprise us to the point of alarm in their wishes to authorize their own experience and perceptions, students ought to have that same space for initiative. From a traditional standpoint, Ms. S was acting as an individual student attempting to do an assignment. I honor that attempt because her contribution was valid. But it is equally important for us as teachers to recognize her ethnographic move as directed both toward the total scene of this classroom and toward the ideologies of teaching and society. She is teaching us that traditional constraints are too rigid. It is not enough merely to accredit her work. It is incumbent on us to *change* our approaches and attitudes because we are crediting her in the bureaucratic sense. We need to view such initiatives both as *teaching* and as *socially generous research*. I contribute this essay to this volume as an instance and a documentation of how ethnographic work changes the classroom by changing the social relations of teaching and learning.

University of Rochester

NOTE

[1] This situation held true mostly for the students' *analyses* of their literary response statements. Because the statements themselves were not graded and because their substance did not count in grading, the students quickly learned to take liberties and write with conviction.

NOT A CONCLUSION: A CONVERSATION

HAVING invested considerable energy in establishing the indeterminate and interpenetrating relations between composition studies and other areas, the editor and the authors of this volume agreed that the usual sort of conclusion would be inappropriate. Rather than a summary or a synthesis, further dialogue and questions seemed to be in order. Accordingly, each author read and responded to another's essay, and the editor wove excerpts from those responses into the following discussion, adhering to a thematic pattern of organization that permits greater interaction among contributors.

GERE: One issue common to several of these essays is the nature of language, which is not surprising given the centrality of textuality in hermeneutic thought. Although no one describes language as entirely transparent, a variety of perspectives emerge, and the authors question one another's treatment of the subject. Writing in response to Kurt Spellmeyer's essay, for example, Judith Halden-Sullivan observes that although Spellmeyer interrogates history, he does not interrogate the language that fosters a return to the hermeneutic circle or language's interrogation of the human mode of being. A set of questions therefore arises.

HALDEN-SULLIVAN: What is it that human beings are "always inside"? Why does this essential question evade discussion? How sufficient is the current assessment of language as a "mediator"? In what ways is this reluctance to experience language our historical blindness? How fully can composition theorists account for the connection between language and the world and for the connection between human beings and the "truth" of their historical worlds that language makes present?

In promising a "reconstruction" of other people's self-understanding, a historical impossibility, and the ideal "unobstructed communication" it affords, Spellmeyer disregards the hermeneutic circle and brackets language in the same way early composition theorists bracketed history. He hints at a nostalgia for control—for scientific validation through "case studies, statistical samplings, and participant surveys" of what evades such quantification: the ineffable character of language in relation to human beings who exist at *its* disposal. I applaud Spellmeyer's pursuit of "the possibility of a knowledge without domination and a commonality without coercion," but I would initiate it by hermeneutic reflection on that which manifests a self, a context, a history: the being of language and the language of being.

GERE: Issues of textual production and interpretation figure centrally in Spellmeyer's considerations, so Spellmeyer does call some dimensions of language into question. This interrogation leads, in turn, to a consideration of language's role in composition classes. In particular, we need to ask what hermeneutics and other poststructuralist perspectives on language can contribute to composition instruction. Barbara Gleason raises this issue in her response to David Bleich and points to potential limitations of poststructuralist theories of language.

GLEASON: There are potential conflicts between poststructuralist assumptions about language, the self, reading, and writing on the one hand and a writing teacher's aim on the other. The writing teacher (and the teacher-researcher) must assume that student writers have some degree of free will, individual autonomy, and personal responsibility, all of which bear closely on the question of what it means to develop as a writer, that is, to gain an awareness of language or to develop a sense of one's own authority. Poststructuralist philosophies provide little insight into the issues of individual freedom and control that writing teachers routinely confront.

GERE: The issue of individual freedom and control with regard to language has many dimensions for composition studies. One of these is the role of poetics in writing instruction, which Rosemary Gates discusses in her essay. In responding to Gates, Derek Owens points to constraints operating in the professional writing of composition studies. Owens raises doubts about the poetics Gates describes. Even though he shares Gates's view that composition studies should embody attitudes toward language that encourage experimental writing, he argues that responding to institutional structures leads composition studies to do the opposite.

OWENS: In composition, Gates says, the formation of word and image is self-consciously poetic. Well, I agree (that is, I think it ought to be), but to my eyes folks in composition studies aren't exactly climbing all over one another to push this philosophy to its limits—not in their own prose, anyway. I read *College English* and *College Composition and Communication* and the *Journal of Advanced Composition* and other journals with as much regularity as I can, but I do so mostly for retrieval of information, a professional sense of obligation to keep abreast of developments in the field (always an impossibility, but my guilt is assuaged a bit in the attempt). But if it's fascinating writing I'm after, writing that is also self-reflexively concerned about the act of composition, I read *TYUONYI*, or *HOW(ever)*, or *ACTS*, or any number of other journals that seek the new. My point is that if, in theory, composition is a natural outgrowth of the compositionist's innate love of language and its creative potential, one would expect our professional publications and conference presentations to be sites for the kinds of cutting-edge writings one would associate with such impulses. But there are no Vladimir Mayakovskys, Gertrude Steins, Kurt Schwitters, and Jackson MacLows lining up to work in our profession. If anything, the jargon often associated with our work does a fine job of making sure it doesn't attract poets.

Gates says that composition permits subversion of dichotomies, demands flexibility, includes diversity in its equation. Again, in principle, it could—should—be this way; I couldn't agree with her more. But we're still tied down by institutional constraints that smother inventiveness. I don't dare to take enormous risks in the essays I write for publication. (I'm untenured—what if my work isn't "safe" enough for some review committee down the line? What journals would accept the types of experimental texts I'm encouraging anyway?) I end up writing essays that are at least as fanciful as they are pragmatic, hoping to infect a few others with the same need for variety instilled in me, while in the meantime trying my best to balance in the classroom the literacy demands of the academy with other, more eclectic ones. We are bound and gagged by rules of style quietly imposed by dissertation committees, editorial boards, college mission statements, and the departmental memo. We can argue for a theory of composition that is based on poesies, but only if our rhetorics don't actually do what they ask for.

All this isn't so much a critique of Gates's piece—in general I align myself with the attitudes that support her argument. I just think her essay is more a challenge for sympathetic readers than any accurate measure of what composition is today. If "inflexible standardization is the arteriosclerosis of language," as Charles Bernstein tells us (*Politics* 236), then the rhetoric of the institution is too often our collective hemlock; and all too often we settle for it. When the day comes that the prose in *College English* is as visually and texturally challenging as the texts we are asking for, then a serious concern for poetry will have crept into our discipline. Until then, we need to continually remind ourselves of the thick hypocrisies laced throughout this profession. Let's keep our fingers crossed; I sincerely hope Gates's challenge takes root.

GERE: Although Owens raises some important questions about the language in which composition studies transacts its business, he takes a somewhat overstated stance, particularly when he describes composition scholars as "bound and gagged" by colleagues. Furthermore, in creating dichotomies between the so-called jargon of composition and prose that is "visually and texturally challenging," he re-creates some of the boundaries between production and interpretation that philosophical approaches to language aim to reduce.

Kurt Spellmeyer complicates these issues in his response to Brenda Deen Schildgen's essay. Although he avoids the overstatements of Owens, Spellmeyer raises many of the same questions as he distinguishes between the conservative and creative views of language in Aristotle's work. Spellmeyer laments the suppression of interpretive knowledge by educators and acknowledges that language in composition classes may prevent students from seeking truth.

SPELLMEYER: I strongly concur with Schildgen's conclusion that Aristotle follows Plato's lead in regarding production and interpretation as divisible only at the greatest cost to both. Like Platonic dialectic, Aristotelian rhetoric demands from its practitioners the continuous reinvention of knowledge—of form and content together. However egregiously Aristotle's successors may have misconstrued him, *he* always recognized the degree to which speech is simultaneously a practice (an effort to persuade) and a reflection on practice (an interpretive, ad hoc assessment of the "available means of persuasion in '*each particular case*' " [*Rhetorica* 1355b]). Still, Aristotle is not Plato, and I am somewhat inclined to think that Schildgen underplays the differences between them. Whereas Plato's Socrates often acts as though there were no conventions at all and suggests that anything might be said at any time—or that, indeed, the entire civilization of Athens might be rebuilt from the ground up—Aristotle typically overemphasizes the immobility of the status quo. The same conservative impulse that leads him to presume that most free Athenian males will agree about basics of civic life (notwithstanding more than three decades of war and internecine scheming) carries him too deftly, in the *Politics*, past the vexing institution of slave labor (esp. bk. 1, chs. 4, 5).

Among Aristotle's successors, however, the conservative impulse tends to win out, and the interpretive dimension of speech falls away until we find, around 1930, the now conventional textbook rules for writers: five-paragraph themes, sentence patterns, the so-called rhetorical modes, and injunctions against wordiness, terseness, ambiguity, and so forth. Things look far more hopeful now, with this pallid "rhetoric" on the decline and hermeneutics on the rise. Yet I feel obliged to pose several hard and less hopeful questions, which complicate both Schildgen's essay and my own. Why, we might ask, have generations of educators suppressed with such holy zeal the interpretive, open-ended character of knowledge? Why does formalism still prove so irresistibly appealing, not only to teachers and scholars, but also to political pundits, people in business, and parents who cannot write very well themselves but want their children to do better? Now that teachers have begun to understand the fundamentally dialectical character of knowledge and language, will they be able—even as they witness highly public attacks every week or so on freshman programs that stray beyond the "basics" of style and mechanical correctness—to act on their new knowledge? Or will they find that speech and writing are destined to remain the social practices through which students are *least* free to pursue something like a living truth?

GERE: Even though Spellmeyer acknowledges the possibility that language may not enable a search for truth, he assumes that "teachers have begun to understand the fundamentally dialectical character of knowledge and language," which may be somewhat optimistic. While poststructural ideas have currency among composition scholars, it does not follow that teachers have assimilated these ideas. Gleason raises this issue in her response to Bleich's essay. In considering the theoretical positions taken by teacher-researchers, she questions whether they see writing as the "materialization of symbolic behavior."

GLEASON: While the pervasiveness of poststructuralist thought in composition is patently obvious, many ethnographic classroom studies clearly are not informed by poststructuralism. Much of this work is neither couched in the language of poststructuralism nor bolstered by the authority of relevant scholars. While this situation does not address the issue of whether poststructuralist thought should inform ethnographic research, it does invite us to reflect on what actually is occurring. To what extent do classroom ethnographers embrace notions of the self suggested in poststructuralist literature (the self as "subject" positioned within, and fundamentally constrained by, language)? And to what extent are teacher-researchers prepared to understand writing as the materialization of symbolic behavior? Is this philosophical position (with all its implied assumptions about knowledge, language, and culture) a primary focus for teachers of literacy?

GERE: Another way to describe Gleason's concern is to question whether teacher-researchers distinguish between discursive and epistemic subjects. John Trimbur develops this distinction in his response to James A. Berlin's essay. Investigating the tension in Berlin's essay between structuralist and culturalist representations of the subject, Trimbur explores how discursive formations and lived experience each represent the subject, the former as critique and the latter as possibility.

TRIMBUR: One way to read Berlin's essay is for the tension, noted by Stuart Hall in "Cultural Studies: Two Paradigms," between structuralist and culturalist representations of the subject—as a discursive formation or a lived experience. The issue of where the subject comes from—the semiosis of Althusserian interpellation or the communal practices of what Raymond Williams calls a "way of life"—has been a persistent and productive preoccupation of British cultural studies. I can see traces of this tension in Berlin's alternation between what I'll call a discursive subject and an epistemic subject.

This alternation is expressed in the now conventional poststructuralist formulation that the subject is written as much as it writes, produced as much as it produces, and artifact as much as agent. Two different figures of the subject collide in the space of such statements. From the perspective of what Berlin calls "the ways discursive formations are related to power," we have a discursive subject, a socially constructed, textually situated, culturally coded subject position. At the same time, however, as Berlin notes, the construction of the subject from a play of discourses "does not preclude the possibility of individuality and agency." Even at the moment of subjectification, an excess overflows the cultural text—an epistemic subject acting "in and through . . . discourses" that figures in the productivity of signifying practices.

I call attention to the tension between these two figures of the subject because it reveals an important point of critical perspective: how can cultural studies of writing represent power as productive? The discursive subject is a constrained figure, contained by the givenness of its own textuality. It pictures the subject as the object of textual power. Berlin's epistemic subject, by contrast, uses textual power to make sense of the world and to inscribe its motives in the collective cultural text. We have, on the one hand, a discourse of critique and, on the other, a discourse of possibility.

I don't want to suggest that these two figures and discourses can—or should—be unified. It is the tension that is crucial and that can reveal how contradictory the various approaches to the study and teaching of writing actually are. Instead of the flat, one-dimensional taxonomies we are accustomed to in composition studies, the tension Berlin identifies can help us to see, for example, that expressivist rhetorics not only invoke a "privatized notion of power" but also contain radically democratic impulses to "work for the equitable distribution of the power to speak and write among all groups in a society."

GERE: The term *lived experience* suggests another theme running through many of these essays. Both the nature of lived experience and ways of representing it, particularly in the postmodern dispensation of nonreferential language, come into question. Halden-Sullivan points to the difficulties inherent in thinking of composition as an interpretive social science, difficulties that center on the impossibility of reconstructing people's self-understanding.

HALDEN-SULLIVAN: Spellmeyer's analysis ends on a dissonant note with his recommendation for "hermeneutic research"—an oxymoron, given the antagonism between the phenomenological character of hermeneutics and the scientific predisposition of research—and his description of this research's intent:

> Composition as an interpretive social science would enlist the various research traditions in the project of reconstructing, always admittedly from an outsider's viewpoint, the self-understanding of its subjects, but instead of doing so for the purposes of therapy, it would seek to promote unobstructed communication between readers and texts, writers and writers, writers and teachers.

Composition as an "interpretive social science" takes on a task defined as impossible in any hermeneutic investigation—"reconstructing, from an outsider's viewpoint, the self-understanding of its subjects."

GERE: As long as Halden-Sullivan remains within the hermeneutic perspective, she cannot, I believe, resolve this difficulty. One alternative lies in the direction of ethnographic research, an approach advocated in Bleich's essay. In responding to Gleason's essay, Bleich further explains his belief in the importance of attending to lived experience (something fostered by ethnography as he describes it) and raises concerns about the phenomenological investigations Gleason describes. Although he acknowledges the value of attempting to engage subjective energies in the classroom, Bleich questions phenomenology's capacity to do this.

BLEICH: As I began to teach writing with increasing involvement, and as I began to teach prospective secondary and university teachers, I became less trusting of the usefulness of a philosophy whose every text showed hardly the briefest gesture toward the authority of people's actual experiences. Husserl and Freud were almost exact contemporaries, and both were similarly accomplished; one reason people today know Freud and not Husserl is that Freud's theories are inseparable from his cases, his accounts of people's lived lives. Until phenomenological reflection finds a locus in real, "narratable" experience, in the programs of social and political enlightenment, and in the development of history, I feel skeptical of its own viability as an enterprise for thinking people, even those, like ourselves, who spontaneously respect and make use of our subjective lives.

As individuals, I believe we have already assimilated the insight of phenomenology into our private thoughts. At the same time, I think the social realization of phenomenology must lie in our collectively turning to the disciplined study of our actual experiences and to the discernment of the implications, personal and political, in our teaching relationships. Do I want to reflect at any length on "error"? No, I would prefer to find ways of spreading my excitement about language use to my colleagues and students. Do I want to reduce my history and identity to "prejudices"? No, I want to celebrate the identity of each of us as individuals and as members of societies, peoples, and cultures. Do I want to accept what I think is the traditional androcentric intellectual move of looking for universals in everything? No, I would rather wait and see what we all, in our respective zones of social life, do accept and then think of those things in their own contexts.

GERE: Thinking about lived experience in terms of universals resembles the social science concern with generalizing from experimental studies. In both, the impulse is toward defining a truth that extends beyond contingency, context, and political constraints. Bleich recognizes the incompatibility of universalizing lived experience in a context of indeterminacy.

BLEICH: Although I am definitely glad to learn how Louise Phelps has been approaching her own development as a thinker, for us to universalize her categories (even relative to herself alone) is to do them an injustice. Maybe others have such categories; maybe they don't. Maybe they would be useful to others and maybe not.

GERE: Bleich's critique of universalizing lived experience would be even more compelling if it considered the issue of power. How does power operate in this universalizing? Brenda Deen Schildgen considers this dimension in her response to the essay by Richard J. Murphy, Jr. For her, the danger of assuming that lived experiences are universally shared is essentially political. While she agrees with Michael Polanyi that the tacit knowledge preserved and conveyed by stories has considerable power and she believes that Polanyi offers a serious challenge to scientific claims of objectivity, Schildgen argues that stories of lived experiences are always mediated by interpretation and that this interpretation cannot be separated from questions of power.

SCHILDGEN: Implicit in this "story" approach to learning and its embrace of "tacit knowledge" are two potentially dangerous assumptions, both capable of leading to pedagogical tyranny. These assumptions are that Polanyi's "tacit knowledge" is not formed by ideological or sociological prejudices and that social-cultural experience is universally shared. Both assumptions are ideologically, politically, and socially flawed. A self-conscious methodology, as I believe may be more current in the composition classroom, attempts to locate and examine the exercise of tacit knowledge.

First, I agree that we apply tacit knowledge, what Hans-Georg Gadamer would call "prejudice" or "foreconceptions" when we engage in teaching students or teachers, as in the examples in Murphy's essay. With Gadamer and Habermas, however, and in the self-conscious memories of my own teaching experiences, I have realized how prejudiced the exercise of tacit knowledge can turn out to be. Like Gadamer, I argue that we need to scrutinize the sources of this tacit knowledge, to become aware of how unconscious and unspoken foreconceptions rule the attitudes we adopt and the recommendations we make as a consequence. A methodical approach to learning, understanding, and interpreting, particularly as they emerge in a writing course or in the training of teachers, requires teachers to be self-conscious and to recognize the vulnerability of their own tacit convictions once these are brought to consciousness, expressed in language, and shared with others.

My second argument with Murphy is his assumption that stories communicate without the mediation of interpretation. Stories are colored by many presuppositions and are simultaneously open to many interpretations because of the presuppositions of readers or listeners. The tacit assumptions and the unrecognized presuppositions that place those stories in our memories are the sources of pleasure and learning but also of potential tyranny. We must bring these sources of tacit knowledge to consciousness in order to recognize that they might rule the classroom atmosphere we create.

Finally, tacit knowledge, prejudice, and foreconceptions are the threads that weave these stories, and to accept them without recognizing their inherent ideological convictions is at best to ignore the creative possibilities of their differences while silencing their underlying pluralism and diversity. At worst, it is to ignore tyrannical prejudices—against people, ideas, and cultures—that are masked by tacit knowledge. Scrutiny of foreconceptions brings unspoken prejudices to consciousness and makes dialogue, communication, and recognition of differences possible. When this silent knowledge speaks with self-awareness and a recognition of its own difference, authentic conversation can begin.

GERE: Schildgen's caution about the prejudices inherent in tacit knowledge brings another political question to the foreground. If we fail to scrutinize the unconscious assumptions of tacit knowledge, we run the risk of merely installing a substitute for the tyranny of objectivism rather than undercutting that kind of unmediated power altogether. Despite her sensitivity to this problem, Schildgen appears unconcerned about casting composition classes in rather monolithic terms. Murphy, writing in response to Schildgen's essay, notes that she describes "the" composition classroom as if it were everywhere and always the same. Perhaps the genesis of this view lies in Schildgen's concern with "method," to which she assigns considerable importance even though it remains underdeveloped in her comments here. Murphy questions this approach in insisting on the individuality of students, teachers, and composition classes.

MURPHY: One day, students meet in my classroom to read their best writing aloud. Vince Davis chokes on his own words, lurches over to the window, his back to the rest of us, and sobs with grief. Another day, Audrey Wilson reads about the grandmother who taught her to sew. She confesses later that she made the dress she was wearing, in silent honor of her grandmother.

Among other things that make the teaching of writing difficult is the absolute idiosyncrasy of every class, student, and paper. However accustomed I become to certain patterns of work, to certain features of assignments that seem particularly effective, I cannot trust them. I like teacher-student conferences and think they help both students and me. Students sign up, but I find myself disconcertingly unable to carry on any sort of useful talk with some of them. I schedule writing groups and try to organize them purposefully. But even when the students participating in such groups are fully prepared and committed, their discussion of one another's writing is sometimes hopelessly thin. No one seems able to address either literary or ideological questions; sometimes students do not discuss the writing at all. I cannot predict.

Schildgen's essay rightly claims that in reading students' writing we are engaged in an interpretive act. And to understand that writing, not to mention our students and ourselves, I agree that we must do what Schildgen says Gadamer describes: recognize our foreconceptions, enter into dialogue, and accept the subjectivity of the other (the same things this exchange among authors is asking us to do). But sometimes Schildgen's essay seems to suggest that all composition classrooms are the same—that they all have the same underlying presuppositions; that "current composition theory and practice" are homogeneous enough to be said to "redefine" rhetoric. My experience tells me otherwise, not just because my classroom is different from Schildgen's or from my colleague's next door or from my own classroom next semester (or yesterday), but because in teaching writing we are engaged in a personal act that belies generalization.

I think Schildgen agrees. She writes that "universalist pretensions" are contradicted by the classroom experience of "most self-reflective teachers." I want to insist on the particularity of that experience. Gadamer may help us better understand that our reading of student texts is interpretive. But I think we will better understand teaching in general only if we do not forget that it is fundamentally individual and personal. In that sense at least, the composition classroom does not exist.

GERE: Murphy's insistence on the particularity of composition classrooms is affirmed by the ethnographic research Bleich describes, and, as we have seen, Bleich argues for the particularity of lived experience. Yet, the authority of that experience can be called into question. Gleason, for example, in her response to Bleich's essay, notes a potential conflict between the theories underlying ethnography and the need for student writers to develop a sense of authority as they learn. She seems to suggest, however, that part of this authority may develop when students are encouraged to become more self-conscious about their progress as writers.

GLEASON: Bleich calls attention to an underlying cause for the popularity of ethnographic perspectives on literacy. Because of the implied concern for allowing voices to be heard (especially, here, the voices of women), however, it is surprising to see so little mention of those whose work has substantially enriched our understanding of classroom ethnography and teacher research and of ethnographic perspectives on literacy—for example, Shirley Brice Heath, Dixie Goswami, Lucy Calkins, and Janet Emig. Perhaps most widely recognized for her humanistic stance on inquiry is Mina Shaughnessy, whose work foreshadowed essential themes in classroom ethnography. To the extent that Shaughnessy approached her student population with an interest in their cultural knowledge and expectations, she paved the way for researchers with more recognizably ethnographic methods and language.

This expanded sense of the term *ethnography* (as attitude) invites questions about its multiplicity of meanings. In contrast to the traditional connotation of method, Bleich refers to ethnography as a "field" with implied poststructuralist leanings ("writing culture," writing understood as all materialization of symbolic behavior). For Bleich, the epistemological thrust of this new ethnography aligns it more closely with the concerns of writing teachers: "The connection between ethnography and language philosophy helps to explain why those of us studying the teaching of writing have found in ethnography a cognate field of inquiry."

What I find more persuasive is Bleich's argument that recent, more phenomenological approaches to ethnography make it particularly compatible with classroom studies of literacy. The best evidence is the descriptive study in which Bleich portrays his own perceptions as well as those of his students in a class on narrative literature. Certainly, it is worthwhile for students to reflect on their own learning and on classroom situations. The possibility that students may benefit substantially from focusing on their own experiences more than justifies this approach as a viable way for teachers to gain greater insight into their students' learning and into their own roles in the context of classroom instruction.

GERE: Gleason's insistence on the value of allowing multiple voices to be heard, particularly the voices of women, brings the question of gender into consideration. Despite their avowed concern with multiplicity, few of the commentators in this dialogue address the issue of gender. Although Bleich's essay concerns itself with women's subjectivity, Bleich does not foreground gender in his comments. Certainly many of the prejudices Schildgen warns against have their basis in gender, and we cannot separate gender from the issue of power as Trimbur frames it. In a response to George Dillon's essay, Irene Papoulis looks at gender-power relations in another way. By exploring how a seemingly neutral term such as *reasonable* can have one meaning for women and another for men, Papoulis complicates Dillon's assertion that academic discourse can promote critical reflections that lead to greater autonomy and justice.

PAPOULIS: As a feminist, I read Dillon's article with mixed feelings. I admire his use of Habermas's "ideal speech situation" paradigm as a philosophical foundation for his pedagogical approach, but at the same time I wonder about the possible implications of his methods for women students.

Both Dillon's repetition of the word *reasonableness* as a goal for dealing with controversy and his advocacy of "grain of truth extraction" seem directed more toward men than toward women. While I have no desire to claim that male and female behaviors in our culture are in any way monolithic, I think it is useful to generalize about the kinds of tendencies each gender exhibits. With regard to argumentation, it seems to me that the habit of being overly polemic or vituperative is far more common to men than it is to women. It is not news to most women that we would do well to withhold our own perspectives in an attempt to understand those of others. Many of us have been trained from an early age to do so, with a consequent stunting of our ability to assert our own deeply felt beliefs.

For that reason, people who can brazenly, and eloquently, assert an unpopular perspective often have a great deal to teach writers, often women, who tend to be self-denying in their responses to texts. Being overly reasonable can become a shield against one's own ideas, and sometimes an emotional response is much more useful than a rational one, even if one's goal is to communicate with one's adversaries. The excerpt from Lewis Lapham's piece, for example, which Dillon and his students found excessive, seems to me to be convincingly argued precisely because of its passion. Extracting a grain of truth from that piece, as Dillon wants his students to do, is impossible without severely undermining the power of its persuasive images. In concentrating on censuring Lapham for his "rallying tone and emotional arm-waving" and "sweeping and grandiose generalizations," Dillon's student could have been blocking her own impulse to respond in a more subjective, and perhaps more interesting and engaged, way to Lapham's prose.

I would like to think of reasonableness, then, not necessarily as a goal toward which all students would do well to move but instead as something that some students emphatically need more of. Other students, women in particular, might do well to be less reasonable and more concerned with their own emotional and even polemical responses to texts. Such unconciliatory responses could stimulate those students to move away from the role of complacent mediator, a role that could atrophy their ability to generate original responses to controversial topics. Dillon hints at a worry about the danger of being too conciliatory in his discussion of the students who responded to Shelby Steele's essay; I wonder what he would have said had he explored his wariness there in more detail.

GERE: In arguing that terms such as *reasonable* can block women students from their own responses, Papoulis extends Gleason's point about the need for students to develop self-awareness by focusing on their own experiences. This insistence on self-awareness represents one way of looking at subjectivity. Another perspective emerges as Gates responds to Owens's essay. Gates urges that the distinction between the persona presented in writing and the situated subject be maintained, and in so doing she echoes Trimbur's distinction between lived experience and discursive formations.

GATES: I see several problems with reading James Hillman as if he were treating the function of ego personality in human interrelationships. Voices in writing are a representation of oneself to other selves with respect to certain topics, materials, situations, and purposes. Those voices are not a direct representation of the self. They may express an aspect of personality through a persona, but they are not the same as the self. The traditional models of personality describe a consistency of behavior in the situations of one's life. The parts of oneself do not act autonomously, except in cases of multiple personality, which is a disorder causing great problems in a person's life. The disordered, conflictual personality is held up as a model to teach students through writing. Furthermore, multiple personalities cannot be developed at will; they are formed in early childhood as a creative, effective, and normal psychological response to continuous, severe, overwhelming trauma. We are not able to create personality in the facile and consciously deliberate way suggested, that is, as a mere active, conscious fiction making. We may indeed have many personas and voices, and these can contribute to an enriching expansion of self as long as there is an integration in the ego personality.

Perhaps a distinction needs to be made between Hillman's "soul" and the use in Owens's essay promoting multiple personalities as a viable ego functioning. The problem here is in failing to distinguish among voice, personality, and persona. For example, Owens says: "We all contain a shifting

maze of personalities, a fact quickly ascertained when we think of the numerous voices we adopt and discard in speaking to various audiences." In what
sense can a theory of personality as a maze of personalities be a fact? Voices,
rhetorics, and styles are not personalities. And theories of mind, soul, and
personality are just that—theories—and they will remain so because there is
no way to see directly into the mind. I think the tack Owens takes in
denouncing the term *natural voice* as dangerous is a misunderstanding, since
most of us who have written on the topic do not mean that voice is not in
any way constructed. We only mean that, in learning to write, students must
begin from a place where they are comfortable, and they must at least search
first for the clear and full expressions of themselves through their command
of language instead of leaping ahead to imitate a style they neither understand
nor control.

Hillman suggests that we need to know and develop our souls. This was
Plato's ideal, and even rhetoric was to contribute to it. I think that the
exploration and development of soul are as important now as they were
two millennia ago. Perhaps Hillman's work might suggest definitions and
directions for soul making at the close of the current millennium.

GERE: "Even rhetoric," as Gates puts it, can play a role in expanding
subjectivities. Indeed, both the philosophical turn as expressed in hermeneutics and phenomenology and the postmodern articulation of subjectivity depend on rhetorical principles that, as Spellmeyer explains, can be traced to
Aristotle. Maintaining the distinction between lived experience and discursive
formations or between what Gates calls rhetorical persona and soul enables
students to become subjects of their own experiences, to interrogate their
own lives. In considering the way that Trimbur foregrounds the political-
intellectual project of cultural studies, Berlin observes that the practices
Trimbur encourages will enable students to evaluate their own experience, to
see in reading and writing possibilities for political and personal transformation.

BERLIN: I would add to Trimbur's statements the consideration that a
rhetorical turn will require a reformed pedagogical practice (a consideration
he has elsewhere repeatedly addressed), which may itself present difficulties.
Students will become encouraged, as Paolo Freire reminds us, to be the
subjects rather than the objects of their experience. The classroom will start
with their own responses to everyday experience—to the school, the workplace, the media—but these responses will have to be interrogated to determine where genuine negotiation and resistance are taking place and where
accommodation disguised as negotiation is instead present. (For example,
most students I have encountered at Purdue are convinced that they are totally
unaffected by advertisements, at first refusing to consider that their response
is probably neither complete resistance nor complete capitulation.) The

teacher will have to help students problematize their characteristic responses and see the points of conflict and contradiction therein. It is true that classroom difficulties in the United States are different from those in Freire's Brazil. Far from seeing themselves as incapable of reading and interpreting culture, students from the United States commonly regard themselves as free agents who are completely in charge of the conditions of their experience. While Freire had to convince Brazilian workers that they were capable of seizing greater control of their own destinies, we have to remind our students that they are not as free and independent as they have been led to believe. After all, the notion of the sovereign, self-present subject is commonly used in the United States as an ideological device to make students feel personally responsible for the conditions of their experience, in this way obscuring the role of the economic, social, and political in the shaping of human events. Teachers of critical literacy in the United States commonly experience resistance when they ask students to consider the material and signifying practices that work to limit agency, particularly from students of the dominant class but also from those who have been taught to identify most strongly with this group. These students have learned to see their privileges (both real and anticipated) as the result of effort and hard work, the rewards of the meritocracy at its best. Realizing that the conditions of one's experience—the limits imposed by one's class, race, or gender, for example—can prove resistant to the greatest degree of determination and hard work is a threatening notion to those who want to believe that everyone gets his or her just deserts in a land of complete freedom and unlimited opportunity. I introduce this matter simply as a reminder of the difficulties that teachers of critical literacy can expect to encounter, difficulties that will, I think, be resolved through developing new conceptions of the teacher-student relationship.

GERE: These new conceptions of the teacher-student relationship will not be easily achieved or monolithic in their formation. They will emerge from creative tensions, from contradictory approaches. Unlike what Trimbur calls "the flat, one-dimensional taxonomies we are accustomed to in composition studies," they will incorporate conflicted perceptions. This anthology suggests some starting points because it describes some of the sites of interactions within composition studies, interactions that demonstrate the permeability of what we call disciplines. As we continue to explore questions about language, discourse, subjectivity, and the relations between them, we will create the spaces in which new concepts of teachers and students can grow.

WORKS CITED

Althusser, Louis. *Lenin and Philosophy*. New York: Monthly Review, 1971.

Apel, Karl-Otto. *Towards a Transformation of Philosophy*. Trans. Glyn Adey and David Frisby. London: Routledge, 1980.

Arieti, Silvano. *Creativity: The Magic Synthesis*. New York: Basic, 1976.

Aristotle. *The Basic Works of Aristotle*. Ed. Richard McKeon. New York: Random, 1941.

————. *De Anima*. Trans. A. J. Smith. *Basic Works* 533–603.

————. *Ethica Nichomachea*. Trans. W. D. Ross. *Basic Works* 927–1112.

————. *Politica*. Trans. Benjamin Jowett. *Basic Works* 1113–1316.

————. *Rhetorica*. Trans. W. Rhys Roberts. *Basic Works* 1317–1451.

Atwill, Janet. "Refiguring Rhetoric in Art: The Concept of Techne and the Humanist Paradigm." Diss. Purdue U, 1989.

Babb, Howard S., ed. *Essays in Stylistic Analysis*. New York: Harcourt, 1972.

Bartholomae, David. "Freshman English, Composition, and CCCC." *College Composition and Communication* 40 (1989): 38–50.

————. "Inventing the University." *When a Writer Can't Write: Studies in Writer's Block and Other Composing Problems*. Ed. Mike Rose. New York: Guilford, 1985. 134–65.

————. "The Study of Error." Graves 311–27.

Baudelaire, Charles. *"The Painter of Modern Life" and Other Essays*. Trans. and ed. Jonathan Maynes. New York: Da Capo, 1964.

Bauer, Dale M. "The Other 'F' Word: The Feminist in the Classroom." *College English* 52 (1990): 385–96.

Baumlin, James S., and Tita French Baumlin. "Psyche/Logos: Mapping the Terrain of Mind and Rhetoric." *College English* 51 (1989): 245–61.

Bazerman, Charles. *Shaping Written Knowledge: The Genre and Activity of the Experimental Article in Science*. Madison: U of Wisconsin P, 1988.

Belenky, Mary Field, et al. *Women's Ways of Knowing*. New York: Basic, 1986.

Berger, Arthur Asa. *Signs in Contemporary Culture: An Introduction*. Salem: Sheffield, 1989.

Berger, Peter L., and Thomas Luckmann. *The Social Construction of Reality*. New York: Doubleday, 1967.

Berlin, James A. "Rhetoric and Ideology in the Writing Class." *College English* 50 (1988): 477–94.

————. *Rhetoric and Reality: Writing Instruction in American Colleges, 1900–1985*. Carbondale: Southern Illinois UP, 1987.

————. "Rhetoric Programs after World War II: Ideology, Power, and Conflict." *Rhetoric and Ideology: Compositions and Criticisms of Power*. Ed. Charles W. Kneupper. Arlington: Rhetoric Soc. of America, 1989. 6–19.

Berman, Marshall. *All That Is Solid Melts into Air*. New York: Simon, 1982.

Bernstein, Charles. *Content's Dream*. Los Angeles: Sun, 1986.

————. *The Politics of Poetic Form: Poetry and Public Policy*. New York: Roof, 1990.

Bernstein, Richard. "Academic Left Finds the Far Reaches of Postmodern." *New York Times* 8 Apr. 1990, sec. 4: 5.

————. "When Parentheses Are Transgressive." *New York Times Magazine* 29 July 1990: 16.

Bernstein, Richard J. *Beyond Objectivism and Relativism: Science, Hermeneutics, and Praxis*. Philadelphia: U of Pennsylvania P, 1983.

Berthoff, Ann E. "The Problem of Problem Solving." Winterowd, *Contemporary Rhetoric* 90–96.

Bizzell, Patricia. "Cognition, Convention, and Certainty: What We Need to Know about Writing." *Pre/Text* 3 (1982): 213–43.

————. "College Composition: Initiation into the Academic Discourse Community." *Curriculum Inquiry* 12 (1982): 191–207.

————. "The Ethos of Academic Discourse." *College Composition and Communication* 29 (1978): 351–55.

Bleich, David. *The Double Perspective: Language, Literacy, and Social Relations*. New York: Oxford UP, 1988.

Bloome, David. "Locating the Learning of Reading and Writing." Emihovich 87–116.

Bolinger, Dwight. *Language: The Loaded Weapon*. London: Longman, 1980.

Braddock, Richard, Richard Lloyd-Jones, and Lowell Schoer. *Research in Written Composition*. Champaign: NCTE, 1963.

Brantlinger, Patrick. *Crusoe's Footprints: Cultural Studies in Britain and America*. New York: Routledge, 1990.

Britton, James. *Language and Learning*. Harmondsworth: Penguin, 1970.

Britton, James, et al. *The Development of Writing Abilities*. London: Macmillan, 1975.

Brodkey, Linda. "Modernism and the Scene(s) of Writing." *College English* 49 (1987): 396–418.

————. "On the Subject of Class and Gender in 'The Literacy Letters.' " *College English* 51 (1989): 125–41.

Bruffee, Kenneth A. "Social Construction, Language, and the Authority of Knowledge: A Bibliographical Essay." *College English* 48 (1986): 773–90.

————. "Writing and Reading as Collaborative or Social Acts." *The Writer's Mind: Writing as a Mode of Thinking*. Ed. Janice N. Hays et al. Urbana: NCTE, 1983. 159–69.

Butcher, S. H. *Aristotle's Theory of Poetry and Fine Art*. 1911. New York: Dover, 1951.

Callahan, Raymond E. *Education and the Cult of Efficiency*. Chicago: U of Chicago P, 1962.

Carini, Patricia F. *The Art of Seeing and the Visibility of the Person*. Grand Forks: U of North Dakota P, 1979.

Clifford, James. "On Ethnographic Allegory." Clifford and Marcus 98–121.

———. *The Predicament of Culture: Twentieth-Century Ethnography, Literature, and Art*. Cambridge: Harvard UP, 1988.

Clifford, James, and George E. Marcus, eds. *Writing Culture: The Poetics and Politics of Ethnography*. Berkeley: U of California P, 1986.

Coleridge, Samuel Taylor. "Kubla Khan." *Major British Poets of the Romantic Period*. Ed. William Heath. New York: Macmillan, 1973. 474–75.

Coles, Nicolas, and Susan V. Wall. "Conflict and Power in the Reader Responses of Adult Basic Writers." *College English* 49 (1987): 298–314.

Coles, Robert. *The Call of Stories*. Boston: Houghton, 1989.

Connors, Patricia E. "The History of Intuition and Its Role in the Composing Process." *Rhetoric Society Quarterly* 20 (1990): 71–78.

Cooper, Lane. *The* Rhetoric *of Aristotle*. New York: Appleton, 1932.

Cooper, Marilyn, and Michael Holzman. *Writing as Social Action*. Portsmouth: Boynton, 1989.

Corbett, Edward P. J. *Classical Rhetoric for the Modern Student*. New York: Oxford UP, 1971.

Daiker, Donald A., and Max Morenberg, eds. *The Writing Teacher as Researcher: Essays in the Theory and Practice of Classroom Research*. Portsmouth: Boynton, 1990.

Dallmayr, Fred R. "Prelude: Hermeneutics and Deconstruction: Gadamer and Derrida in Dialogue." Michelfelder and Palmer 75–92.

Dautermann, Jennie. "Negotiating Meaning in Hospital Discourse Communities: An Observation of Writing in the Work Place." Diss. Purdue U, 1991.

de Certeau, Michel. *The Practice of Everyday Life*. Berkeley: U of California P, 1984.

Derrida, Jacques. "A Discussion with Jacques Derrida." *Writing Instructor* 9 (1989–90): 7–18.

———. *Of Grammatology*. Trans. Gayatri Chakravorty Spivak. Baltimore: Johns Hopkins UP, 1974.

———. *Speech and Phenomena and Other Essays of Husserl's Theory of Signs*. Trans. David B. Allison. Evanston: Northwestern UP, 1973.

———. "Three Questions to Hans-Georg Gadamer." Trans. Diane Michelfelder and Richard Palmer. Michelfelder and Palmer 52–57.

Dillon, George. *Rhetoric as Social Imagination: Explorations in the Interpersonal Function of Language*. Bloomington: U of Indiana P, 1986.

Donahue, Patricia, and Ellen Quandahl, eds. *Reclaiming Pedagogy: The Rhetoric of the Classroom*. Carbondale: Southern Illinois UP, 1989.

Dreyfus, Hubert, and Paul Rabinow. "What Is Maturity? Habermas and Foucault on 'What Is Enlightenment?' " *Foucault: A Critical Reader*. Ed. David Couzens Hoy. Oxford: Blackwell, 1986. 109–21.

Eagleton, Terry. *Literary Theory: An Introduction*. Minneapolis: U of Minnesota P, 1983.

———. *Walter Benjamin; or, Towards Revolutionary Criticism*. London: Verso, 1985.

Ede, Lisa, and Andrea Lunsford. *Singular Texts/Plural Authors*. Carbondale: Southern Illinois UP, 1990.

Elbow, Peter. *Embracing Contraries: Explorations in Learning and Teaching*. Oxford: Oxford UP, 1986.

———. "Reflections on Academic Discourse: How It Relates to Freshmen and Colleagues." *College English* 53 (1991): 135–55.

———. *Writing without Teachers*. New York: Oxford UP, 1973.

———. *Writing with Power*. New York: Oxford UP, 1983.

Elbow, Peter, and Pat Belanoff. *A Community of Writers: A Workshop Course in Writing*. New York: McGraw, 1989.

———. *Sharing and Responding*. New York: Random, 1989.

Emig, Janet. *The Composing Processes of Twelfth Graders*. Research Rept. 13. Urbana: NCTE, 1971.

———. "Inquiry Paradigms and Writing." *The Web of Meaning: Essays on Writing, Teaching, Learning, and Thinking*. Ed. Dixie Goswami and Maureen Butler. Upper Montclair: Boynton, 1983. 157–70.

Emihovich, Catherine, ed. *Locating Learning: Ethnographic Perspectives on Classroom Research*. Norwood: Ablex, 1989.

Ericcson, K. Anders, and Herbert A. Simon. "Verbal Reports as Data." *Psychological Review* 87 (1980): 215–51.

Ewen, Stewart. *All Consuming Images: The Politics of Style in Contemporary Culture*. New York: Basic, 1988.

Faigley, Lester. "Competing Theories of Process: A Critique and a Proposal." *College English* 48 (1986): 527–42.

———. "Judging Writing, Judging Selves." *College Composition and Communication* 40 (1989): 395–413.

Fay, Brian. *Critical Social Science: Liberation and Its Limits*. Ithaca: Cornell UP, 1987.

Fetterman, David M. *Ethnography: Step by Step*. Newbury Park: Sage, 1989.

Fiske, John. *Television Culture*. London: Routledge, 1987.

———. *Understanding Popular Culture*. Boston: Unwin, 1989.

Flower, Linda, and John R. Hayes. "A Cognitive Process Theory of Writing." *College Composition and Communication* 32 (1981): 365–87.

———. "Problem-Solving Strategies and the Writing Process." *College English* 39 (1977): 449–61.

Flynn, Elizabeth. "Composing as a Woman." *College Composition and Communication* 39 (1988): 423–35.

Foley, Douglas. *Learning Capitalist Culture: Deep in the Heart of Tejas*. Philadelphia: U of Pennsylvania P, 1990.

Forster, E. M. *Aspects of the Novel*. New York: Harcourt, 1927.

Foster, Hal. *The Anti-aesthetic: Essays on Postmodern Culture*. Port Townsend: Bay, 1983.

———. *Recodings: Art, Spectacle, Cultural Politics*. Seattle: Bay, 1985.

Fox, Thomas. *Social Uses of Language in the Classroom*. Norwood: Ablex, 1990.

Fraser, Nancy. "Rethinking the Public Sphere: A Contribution to the Critique of Actually Existing Democracy." *Social Text* 25–26 (1990): 56–80.

Freire, Paolo. *Pedagogy of the Oppressed*. New York: Herder, 1970.

Freud, Sigmund. "Constructions in Analysis." *Standard Edition* 23: 255–69.

———. "Dreams." *Standard Edition* 15.2: 83–233.

———. *An Outline of Psycho-analysis*. Ed. and trans. James Strachey. New York: Norton, 1989.

———. *The Standard Edition of the Complete Psychological Works of Sigmund Freud*. Ed. and trans. James Strachey. 24 vols. London: Hogarth, 1953–74.

Gadamer, Hans-Georg. *Reason in the Age of Science*. Trans. Frederick G. Lawrence. Cambridge: MIT P, 1981.

———. *Rhetorik und Hermeneutik*. Göttingen: Vandenhoeck, 1976.

———. "Text and Interpretation." Trans. Dennis Schmidt and Richard Palmer. Michelfelder and Palmer 21–51.

———. *Truth and Method*. New York: Crossroad, 1986.

Gardner, Howard. *Frames of Mind: The Theory of Multiple Intelligences*. New York: Basic, 1983.

Gates, Rosemary L. "Applying Martin Greenman's Concept of Insight to Composition Theory." *Journal of Advanced Composition* 9 (1989): 59–68.

Geertz, Clifford. *The Interpretation of Cultures*. New York: Basic, 1973.

———. *Local Knowledge: Further Essays in Interpretive Anthropology*. New York: Basic, 1983.

Genung, John Franklin. *The Working Principles of Rhetoric*. Boston: Ginn, 1900.

Gere, Anne Ruggles. *Writing Groups: History, Theory, and Implications*. Carbondale: Southern Illinois UP, 1987.

Giddens, Anthony. *Central Problems in Social Theory*. Berkeley: U of California P, 1979.

Gillespie, Diane. "Claiming Ourselves as Teachers." *Change* 21 (1989): 56–58.

Gilligan, Carol, et al., eds. *Making Connections*. Cambridge: Harvard UP, 1990.

Goldman, Stuart. "That Old Devil Music." *National Review* 24 Feb. 1989: 28+.

Goswami, Dixie. "Teachers as Researchers." Graves 347–58.

Goswami, Dixie, and Peter R. Stillman, eds. *Reclaiming the Classroom: Teacher Research as an Agency for Change*. Portsmouth: Boynton, 1987.

Grassi, Ernesto. *Rhetoric as Philosophy: The Humanist Tradition*. University Park: Pennsylvania State UP, 1980.

Graves, Richard L., ed. *Rhetoric and Composition: A Sourcebook for Teachers and Writers*. 3rd ed. Portsmouth: Boynton, 1990.

Greenman, Martin A. "Intuition and the Limits of Philosophical Inquiry." *Metaphilosophy* 18 (1987): 125–35.

Grossberg, Lawrence. "Putting the Pop Back into Postmodernism." *Universal Abandon: The Politics of Postmodernism*. Ed. Andrew Ross. Minneapolis: U of Minnesota P, 1988. 167–90.

Guthrie, W. K. C. *Aristotle: An Encounter*. Cambridge: Cambridge UP, 1981. Vol. 6 of *A History of Greek Philosophy*. 6 vols.

Habermas, Jürgen. "The Hermeneutic Claim to Universality." *Contemporary Hermeneutics: Method, Philosophy and Critique*. Ed. Josef Bleicher. London: Routledge, 1980. 181–211.

———. "The Idea of the University: Learning Processes." *The New Conservatism*. Trans. Shierry Weber Nicholsen. Cambridge: MIT P, 1989. 100–27.

———. *Lifeworld and System: A Critique of Functionalist Reason*. Trans. Thomas McCarthy. Boston: Beacon, 1987. Vol. 2 of *The Theory of Communicative Action*. 2 vols.

———. "Modernity—An Incomplete Project." Foster, *Anti-aesthetic* 3–15.

———. *Moral Consciousness and Communicative Action*. Trans. Christian Lenhardt and Shierry Weber Nicholsen. Cambridge: MIT P, 1990.

———. *Reason and the Rationalization of Society*. Trans. Thomas McCarthy. Boston: Beacon, 1984. Vol. 1 of *The Theory of Communicative Action*. 2 vols.

———. *The Structural Transformation of the Public Sphere: An Inquiry into a Category of Bourgeois Society*. Trans. Thomas Berger, with Frederick Lawrence. Cambridge: MIT P, 1989.

———. *Zur Logik der Sozialwissenschaften*. Frankfurt: Suhrkamp, 1970.

Hairston, Maxine. "Comment and Response." *College English* 52 (1990): 694–96.

Hall, Stuart. "Cultural Studies: Two Paradigms." *Media, Culture and Society*. Vol. 2. London: Open UP, 1986. 57–72.

———. "Notes on Deconstructing the Popular." Ed. Raphael Samuel. *People's History and Socialist Theory*. London: Routledge, 1981. 227–40.

Halliday, M. A. K. "Poetry as Scientific Discourse: The Nuclear Sections of Tennyson's 'In Memoriam.' " *Functions of Style*. Ed. David Birch and Michael O'Toole. London: Pinter, 1988. 31–44.

Hamilton, Barbara Bova. "The Rhetoric of a Judicial Document: The Presentence Investigation, Document Design, and Social Context." Diss. U of Southern California, 1987.

Hardy, Barbara. *Tellers and Listeners*. London: U of London, 1975.

Harrienger, Myrna. "Issues of Discursivity, Subjectivity, and Empowerment: Elderly Ill Women." Diss. Purdue U, forthcoming.

Harste, Jerome C., Virginia Woodward, and Carolyn R. Burke. *Language Stories and Literacy Lessons*. Portsmouth: Heinemann, 1984.

Harvey, David. *The Condition of Postmodernity: An Enquiry into Cultural Change*. Oxford: Blackwell, 1989.

Heath, Shirley Brice. *Ways with Words: Language, Life, and Work in Communities and Classrooms*. Cambridge: Cambridge UP, 1983.

Heba, Gary. "Inventing Culture: A Rhetoric of Social Codes." Diss. Purdue U, 1991.

Hebdige, Dick. *Subculture: The Meaning of Style*. London: Methuen, 1979.

Heidegger, Martin. *Being and Time*. Trans. John Macquarrie and Edward Robinson. New York: Harper, 1962.

———. *On the Way to Language*. Trans. Peter D. Hertz. San Francisco: Harper, 1971.

———. *Poetry, Language, Thought*. Trans. Albert Hofstadter. New York: Harper, 1971.

Heilbrun, Carolyn G. *Writing a Woman's Life*. New York: Ballantine, 1988.

Hill, Adams Sherman. *The Principles of Rhetoric and Their Application*. New York: American, 1878.

Hillman, James. *Healing Fiction*. Tarrytown: Station Hill, 1983.

———. *Re-visioning Psychology*. New York: Harper, 1975.

Hillocks, George. *Research on Written Composition*. Urbana: NCTE, 1986.

Himley, Margaret. "A Reflective Conversation: 'Tempos of Meaning.'" *Encountering Student Texts: Interpretive Issues in Reading Student Writing*. Ed. Bruce Lawson, Susan Sterr Ryan, and W. Ross Winterowd. Urbana: NCTE, 1989. 5–19.

———. *Shared Territory: Understanding Children's Writing as "Works."* New York: Oxford UP, 1991.

Hoggart, Richard. *The Uses of Literacy*. Boston: Beacon, 1961.

Horner, Winifred G., ed. *Composition and Literature: Bridging the Gap*. Chicago: U of Chicago P, 1983.

Hurlbert, C. Mark, and Michael Blitz, eds. *Composition and Resistance*. Portsmouth: Boynton, 1991.

Husserl, Edmund. *Ideas: Introduction to a Pure Phenomenology*. Trans. W. R. Boyce Gibson. New York: Collier, 1962.

Hutcheon, Linda. *A Poetics of Postmodernism: History, Theory, Fiction*. New York: Routledge, 1988.

Jakobson, Roman. "Linguistics and Poetics." *Essays on the Language of Literature*. Ed. Seymour Chatman and Samuel R. Levin. Boston: Houghton, 1967. 296–322.

Jakobson, Roman, and Morris Halle. *Fundamentals of Language*. The Hague: Mouton, 1956.

Jameson, Fredric. "Postmodernism; or, The Cultural Logic of Late Capitalism." *New Left Review* 146 (1984): 53–92.

———. *Prison House of Language*. Princeton: Princeton UP, 1972.

Johnson, Richard. "What Is Cultural Studies Anyway?" *Social Text* 16 (1986–87): 38–80.

Kazmierczak, Jill. "The Roles of Teaching and Learning." Unpublished paper, 1988.

Kinneavy, James. *A Theory of Discourse*. Englewood Cliffs: Prentice, 1971.

Kirk, G. S., and J. E. Raven. *The Presocratic Philosophers*. Cambridge: Cambridge UP, 1975.

Klein, Julie. "Across the Boundaries." *Social Epistemology* 4 (1990): 267–80.

Knoblauch, C. H. "Rhetorical Constructions: Dialogue and Commitment." *College English* 50 (1988): 125–40.

Knoblauch, C. H., and Lil Brannon. *Rhetorical Traditions in the Teaching of Writing*. Upper Montclair: Boynton, 1984.

Kockelmans, Joseph J. "Language, Meaning, and Ek-sistence." *On Heidegger and Language*. Ed. and trans. Kockelmans. Evanston: Northwestern UP, 1972. 3–32.

———. *On the Truth of Being: Reflections on Heidegger's Later Philosophy*. Bloomington: Indiana UP, 1984.

Labov, William. *Language and the Inner City: Studies in Black English Vernacular*. Philadelphia: U of Pennsylvania P, 1972.

———. *The Study of Nonstandard English*. Urbana: NCTE, 1970.

Lakoff, George, and Mark Johnson. *Metaphors We Live By*. Chicago: U of Chicago P, 1980.

Lanham, Richard A. *Literacy and the Survival of Humanism*. New Haven: Yale UP, 1983.

Lapham, Lewis. "A Political Opiate." *Harper's Magazine* Dec. 1989: 43–48.

Lauer, Janice. "Heuristics and Composition." Winterowd, *Contemporary Rhetoric* 79–89.

Lauer, Janice, and J. William Asher. *Composition Research: Empirical Designs*. New York: Oxford UP, 1988.

Lauer, Janice M., and Andrea Lunsford. "The Place of Rhetoric and Composition in Doctoral Studies." *The Future of Doctoral Studies in English*. Ed. Andrea Lunsford, Helene Moglen, and James F. Slevin. New York: MLA, 1989. 106–10.

Lay, Mary M. "Interpersonal Conflict in Collaborative Writing: What We Can Learn from Gender Studies." *Journal of Business and Technical Communication* 3.2 (1989): 5–28.

Leitch, Vincent B. "Cultural Studies." *The Johns Hopkins Guide to Literary Criticism and Theory*. Ed. Martin Kreiswirth and Michael Groden. Baltimore: Johns Hopkins UP, forthcoming.

Lemke, J. L. "The Language of Science Teaching." Emihovich 216–39.

Loder, Kurt. "Face the Music." *Rolling Stone* 4 May 1989: 57 + .

Lunsford, Andrea. "Composing Ourselves: Politics, Commitment, and the Teaching of Writing." *College Composition and Communication* 41 (1990): 71–82.

Lyotard, Jean-François. *The Postmodern Condition: A Report on Knowledge*. Trans. Geoff Bennington and Brian Massumi. Minneapolis: U of Minnesota P, 1984.

Macrorie, Ken. *Twenty Teachers*. New York: Oxford UP, 1984.

Martin, Harold. "The Aims of Harvard's General Education A." *College Composition and Communication* 9 (1958): 87–99.

Mascia-Lees, Frances E., Patricia Sharpe, and Colleen Ballerino Cohen. "The Postmodernist Turn in Anthropology: Cautions from a Feminist Perspective." *Signs* 15 (1989): 7–33.

Melanchthon, Philip. "On the Life of Aristotle, 1537." *Philip Melanchthon: A Melanchthon Reader.* Trans. Ralph Keen. New York: Lang, 1988. 71–77.

Michaels, Leonard, and Christopher Ricks. *The State of the Language.* Berkeley: U of California P, 1980.

Michelfelder, Diane P., and Richard E. Palmer, eds. *Dialogue and Deconstruction: The Gadamer-Derrida Encounter.* Albany: State U of New York P, 1989.

Miller, Carolyn. "A Humanistic Rationale for Technical Writing." *College English* 40 (1979): 610–17.

Miller, Mark Crispin. "Cosby Knows Best." *Boxed In: The Culture of TV.* Evanston: Northwestern UP, 1988. 69–75.

Miller, Susan. *Rescuing the Subject: A Critical Introduction to Rhetoric and the Writer.* Carbondale: Southern Illinois UP, 1989.

Moffatt, Michael. *Coming of Age in New Jersey: College and American Culture.* New Brunswick: Rutgers UP, 1989.

Moffett, James. *A Student-Centered Language Arts Curriculum.* Boston: Houghton, 1968.

———. *Teaching the Universe of Discourse.* Boston: Houghton, 1968.

Morley, Dave. "Texts, Readers, Subjects." *Culture, Media, Language: Working Papers in Cultural Studies, 1972–79.* Center for Contemporary Cultural Studies. London: Hutchinson, 1980. 163–76.

Myers, Greg. "Reality, Consensus, and Reform in the Rhetoric of Composition Teaching." *College English* 48 (1986): 154–74.

———. "The Social Construction of Two Biologists' Proposals." *Written Communication* 2 (1985): 219–45.

North, Stephen. *The Making of Knowledge in Composition: Portrait of an Emerging Field.* Portsmouth: Heinemann, 1987.

Nunberg, Geoffrey. "Slang, Usage-Conditions, and l'Arbitraire du Signe." *Parasession on the Lexicon.* Ed. Donka Farkas, Wesley Jacobson, and Karol W. Todrys. Chicago: Chicago Linguistic Soc., 1978. 301–11.

Ohmann, Richard. "Prolegomena to the Analysis of Prose Style." Babb 35–49.

Papoulis, Irene. " 'Personal Narrative,' 'Academic Writing,' and Feminist Theory: Reflections of a Freshman Composition Teacher." *Freshman English News* 18.2 (1990): 9–12.

Pattison, Robert. *On Literacy: The Politics of the Word from Homer to the Age of Rock.* New York: Oxford UP, 1982.

Perl, Sondra, and Nancy Wilson. *Through a Teacher's Eyes: Portraits of Writing Teachers at Work.* Portsmouth: Heinemann, 1986.

Perry, William G. *Forms of Intellectual and Ethical Development in the College Years.* New York: Holt, Rinehart, 1970.

Phelps, Louise Wetherbee. *Composition as a Human Science*. New York: Oxford UP, 1988.

———. "Images of Student Writing: The Deep Structure of Teacher Response." *Writing and Response: Theory, Practice, and Research*. Ed. Chris M. Anson. Urbana: NCTE, 1989. 37–67.

———. "Rhythm and Pattern in a Composing Life." Waldrep 241–57.

Plato. *Phaedrus*. Trans. W. C. Helmbold and W. G. Rabinowitz. New York: Bobbs, 1956.

Polanyi, Michael. *Personal Knowledge*. Chicago: U of Chicago P, 1969.

Porter, James E. "Ideology and Collaboration in the Classroom and in the Corporation." *Bulletin of the Association for Business Communication* 5.32 (1990): 18–22.

Pratt, Mary Louise. "Ideology and Speech-Act Theory." *Poetics Today* 7 (1986): 59–72.

Quasha, George. "Publisher's Preface." Hillman, *Healing* ix–xii.

Raban, Jonathan. *Soft City*. London: Macmillan, 1974.

Radway, Janice. *Reading the Romance: Women, Patriarchy, and Popular Literature*. Chapel Hill: U of North Carolina P, 1984.

Remmers, H. H., et al. *Concerning Freshman Composition—Tangibles and Intangibles of Achievement*. Lafayette: Purdue UP, 1934.

Ricoeur, Paul. *Hermeneutics and the Human Sciences*. New York: Cambridge UP, 1981.

———. *The Rule of Metaphor*. Trans. Robert Czerny, Kathleen McLaughlin, and John Costello. Toronto: U of Toronto P, 1977.

Rorty, Richard. "Deconstruction and Circumvention." *Critical Inquiry* 11 (1984): 1–23.

Rosaldo, Renato. *Culture and Truth: The Remaking of Social Analysis*. Boston: Beacon, 1989.

Rosen, Harold. *Stories and Meanings*. Sheffield, Eng.: NATE, 1985.

Rosenblatt, Louise M. *Literature as Exploration*. 1938. New York: MLA, 1983.

Russell, David R. "Romantics on Writing: Liberal Culture and the Abolition of Composition Courses." *Rhetoric Review* 6 (1988): 132–48.

Salvatori, Mariolina. "The Dialogical Nature of Basic Reading and Writing." *Facts, Artifacts, and Counterfacts: Theory and Method for a Reading and Writing Course*. Portsmouth: Boynton, 1986. 137–66.

Schilpp, Paul Arthur, ed. *Albert Einstein: Philosopher-Scientist*. Evanston: Library of Living Philosophers, 1949.

Scholes, Robert. *Textual Power: Literary Theory and the Teaching of English*. New Haven: Yale UP, 1987.

Shaughnessy, Mina. *Errors and Expectations: A Guide for the Teacher of Basic Writing*. New York: Oxford UP, 1977.

Sherman, Cindy. *History Portraits: Cindy Sherman*. New York: Rizzoli, 1991.

Shor, Ira. *Culture Wars: School and Society in the Conservative Restoration, 1969–84*. Boston: Routledge, 1986.

Shores, David L., ed. *Contemporary English: Change and Variation*. Philadelphia: Lippincott, 1972.

Shostak, Marjorie. *Nisa: The Life and Words of a !Kung Woman*. Cambridge: Harvard UP, 1981.

Spencer, Herbert. *The Philosophy of Style*. Ed. Fred Newton Scott. 2nd ed. Boston: Allyn, 1892.

Squires, Geoffrey, Helen Simons, Malcolm Parlett, and Tony Becher. *Interdisciplinarity*. London: Nuffield Foundation, 1979.

Steele, Shelby. "Black and White: Race and Blame." *Harper's Magazine* June 1988: 45–53. Rpt. in *Current* Nov. 1988: 4–10.

———. Speech. Education for a Pluralist Society Conference. Seattle, 2 Feb. 1991.

Stein, Gertrude. "Composition as Explanation." *Selected Writings of Gertrude Stein*. Ed. Carl Van Vechten. New York: Modern Library, 1962. 513–23.

Sternglass, Marilyn. *The Presence of Thought: Introspective Accounts of Reading and Writing*. Norwood: Ablex, 1989.

Strunk, William, Jr., and E. B. White. *The Elements of Style*. 3rd ed. New York: Macmillan, 1979.

Tathem, Campbell. "Mythotherapy and Postmodern Fictions: Magic Is Afoot." *Performance in Postmodern Culture*. Ed. Michel Benamou and Charles Caramello. Madison: Coda, 1977. 137–57.

Taylor, Warren. "Rhetoric in a Democracy." *English Journal* 27 (1938): 851–58.

Therborn, Goran. *The Ideology of Power and the Power of Ideology*. London: Verso, 1980.

Todorov, Tzvetan. "Présentation." *Rhétorique et Hermeneutique Poétique* 23 (1974): 289–90.

Trimbur, John. "Consensus and Difference in Collaborative Learning." *College English* 51 (1989): 602–16.

———. "Cultural Studies and Teaching Writing." *Focuses* 1.2 (1988): 5–18.

———. "Essayist Literacy and the Rhetoric of Deproduction." *Rhetoric Review* 9 (1990): 72–86.

Trimmer, Joseph. "Telling Stories about Stories." *Teaching English in the Two-Year College* 17 (1990): 157–64.

Turner, Victor. *On the Edge of the Bush: Anthropology as Experience*. Ed. Edith L. B. Turner. Tucson: U of Arizona P, 1985.

Van Manen, Max. *Researching Lived Experience: Human Science for an Action Sensitive Pedagogy*. London, Ont.: Althouse, Univ. of Western Ontario, 1990.

Venturi, Robert. *Learning from Las Vegas*. Cambridge: MIT P, 1977.

Waldrep, Thomas. *Writers on Writing*. Vol. 1. New York: Random, 1985. 2 vols. 1985–88.

Waldrop, Rosmarie. *The Reproduction of Profiles*. New York: New Directions, 1987.

Wallas, Graham. *The Art of Thought*. New York: Harcourt, 1926.

Wallis, William. "Four Initial Exercises for the Composing Self." CCCC Convention. St. Louis, March 1990.

Warnke, Georgia. *Gadamer: Hermeneutics, Tradition, and Reason*. Palo Alto: Stanford UP, 1987.

Weinsheimer, Joel C. *Gadamer's Hermeneutics: A Reading of* Truth and Method. New Haven: Yale UP, 1985.

Wendell, Barrett. "The Elements and Qualities of Style." *English Composition*. New York, 1891. 1–40. Rpt. *Literature, Society, and Politics: Selected Essays*. Ed. Robert T. Self. St. Paul: Colet, 1977.

Wera, Eugene. *Human Engineering: A Study of the Management of Human Forces*. New York: Appleton, 1921.

White, Hayden. *Tropics of Discourse: Essays in Cultural Criticism*. Baltimore: Johns Hopkins UP, 1982.

Will, George. "The Journey up from Guilt." *Newsweek* 18 June 1990: 68.

Williams, Joseph M. "The Phenomenology of Error." *College Composition and Communication* 32 (1981): 152–74.

Williams, Raymond. *The Politics of Modernism: Against the New Conformism*. London: Verso, 1989.

Williamson, Don. Editorial. *Seattle Times* 5 Feb. 1991: A8.

Willis, Paul. *Learning to Labour: How Working Class Kids Get Working Class Jobs*. New York: Columbia UP, 1981.

Wimsatt, W. K., Jr. "Diction." Babb 206–17.

Winterowd, W. Ross. *Contemporary Rhetoric: A Conceptual Background with Readings*. New York: Harcourt, 1975.

———. *The Rhetoric of the "Other" Literature*. Carbondale: Southern Illinois UP, 1990.

Worsham, Lynn. "The Question concerning Invention: Hermeneutics and the Genesis of Writing." *Pre/Text* 8 (1987): 197–244.

Yeats, W. B. *The Collected Poems of W. B. Yeats*. 1956. New York: Macmillan, 1979.

INDEX

Althusser, Louis, 130
Antin, David, 173
Apel, Karl-Otto, 24, 29
Arieti, Silvano, 149
Aristotle, 2, 10–11, 13, 25–26, 28, 29,
    30, 31, 55, 78, 109, 113, 115,
    195–96, 205
Arnold, Matthew, 15
Asante, Molefi Kete, 161
Asher, J. William, 115
Atwill, Janet, 110
Augustine, 116

Bain, Alexander, 28
Bakhtin, Mikhail, 108
Balzac, Honoré de, 119
Barthes, Roland, 114
Bartholomae, David, 20–21, 22, 63, 114
Baudelaire, Charles, 119, 120
Baudrillard, Jean, 118
Bauer, Dale M., 87
Baumlin, James S., 28
Baumlin, Tita French, 28
Bazerman, Charles, 114
Becker, Alton, 45
Belanoff, Pat, 64–65, 139, 142–43
Belenky, Mary Field, 133–35, 136, 138,
    139, 140, 144, 146
Bennett, William, 108
Berger, Arthur Asa, 115
Berger, Peter L., 29
Bergson, Henri, 174
Berlin, James A., 5, 63, 108, 197–98, 205
Berman, Marshall, 119, 120
Bernstein, Charles, 165, 195
Bernstein, Richard, 184
Bernstein, R. J., 29
Berthoff, Ann E., 45, 64
Bizzell, Patricia, 20–21, 114
Blair, Hugh, 116
Bleich, David, 4, 5, 112, 194 198, 199,
    202, 203
Blitz, Michael, 111
Bloom, Allan, 108
Bloome, David, 181–82, 186
Bolinger, Dwight, 34, 43
Braddock, Richard, 1
Brannon, Lil, 73

Brantlinger, Patrick, 103
Breton, André, 173
Britton, James, 74, 147
Brodkey, Linda, 21, 114
Brossard, Nicole, 169
Bruffee, Kenneth A., 22, 23, 24, 25, 107,
    114
Buck, Gertrude, 106
Burhans, Clinton, 76
Burke, Carolyn R., 131
Burke, Kenneth A., 2, 13, 113, 115
Bush, George, 90
Butcher, S. H., 11

Cage, John, 174
Calkins, Lucy, 202
Callahan, Raymond E., 20
Carini, Patricia F., 66
Chomsky, Noam, 2
Cicero, 2, 116
Cliff, Michelle, 173
Clifford, James, 24, 29, 176–77, 178,
    179, 180–81, 183
Cohen, Colleen Ballerino, 177, 178, 179
Coleridge, Samuel Taylor, 148
Coles, Nicolas, 22
Coles, Robert, 81
Connors, Patricia E., 149
Cooper, Lane, 10–15, 16, 17, 26, 28
Cooper, Marilyn, 112
Corbett, Edward P. J., 2
Cosby, Bill, 91, 93
Culler, Jonathan, 99

Daiker, Donald A., 113
Dallmayr, Fred R., 43
Dante Alighieri, 55
Dautermann, Jennie, 115
de Certeau, Michel, 128
Derrida, Jacques, 40, 41, 43, 60–61, 71,
    169
Dewey, John, 78, 106
Dickens, Charles, 119
Didion, Joan, 169
Dillon, George, 4, 5, 115, 203, 204
Donahue, Patricia, 109–10
Dostoevsky, Fyodor, 119

Douglass, Frederick, 173
Dreyfus, Hubert, 85
Duchamp, Marcel, 164
DuPlessis, Rachel Blau, 161, 173, 174–75

Eagleton, Terry, 99–100, 102, 103, 107
Ede, Lisa, 114
Einstein, Albert, 149, 154
Elbow, Peter, 41, 64–65, 73, 95, 135, 139, 141, 142–43, 145
Eliot, T. S., 124
Emig, Janet, 1, 60, 63, 73, 113, 147, 202
Emihovich, Catherine, 181
Ericcson, K. Anders, 63
Ewen, Stewart, 115

Faigley, Lester, 50, 63, 106
Faulkner, William, 17
Fay, Brian, 29
Fetterman, David M., 178–80
Fiske, John, 115, 129
Flaubert, Gustave, 17
Flower, Linda, 2, 20–21, 22, 24, 29, 53, 113
Flynn, Elizabeth, 114
Foley, Douglas, 29
Forster, E. M., 150, 154
Foster, Hal, 122, 123, 124
Foucault, Michel, 114
Fox, Thomas, 182
Fraser, Nancy, 132
Frazer, J. G., 16
Freire, Paolo, 205–06
Freud, Sigmund, 11, 29, 136–40, 141, 142, 143–44, 145, 150, 152, 162–63, 199

Gadamer, Hans-Georg, 30, 31–32, 33–34, 35–37, 38, 39, 40, 41, 42–43, 77–78, 200, 201
Gardner, Howard, 62
Gates, Henry Louis, Jr., 161
Gates, Rosemary L., 5, 151, 194–95, 204, 205
Geertz, Clifford, 16, 25, 176
Genung, John Franklin, 13, 29
Gere, Anne Ruggles, 38, 114
Giddens, Anthony, 29
Gillespie, Diane, 81
Gilligan, Carol, 133, 145
Gins, Madeline, 161
Gleason, Barbara, 5, 194, 196, 197, 198, 203, 204
Goethe, Johann Wolfgang von, 11

Goldman, Stuart, 88–89
Goswami, Dixie, 66, 113, 202
Graff, Gerald, 99
Grassi, Ernesto, 31
Graves, Richard L., 81
Gray, Jim, 74
Greenman, Martin A., 150–51, 153
Grenier, Robert, 172
Gresham, Thomas, 88
Grossberg, Lawrence, 127, 130
Guthrie, W. K. C., 28

Habermas, Jürgen, 5, 24–25, 41, 84–86, 95, 122, 132, 200, 203
Hairston, Maxine, 116
Halden-Sullivan, Judith, 5, 193, 198
Hall, Stuart, 127, 129, 197
Halle, Morris, 150
Halliday, M. A. K., 150
Hamilton, Barbara Bova, 115
Hardy, Barbara, 81
Harrienger, Myrna, 115
Harste, Jerome C., 131
Harvey, David, 119, 121, 122, 125
Hayes, John R., 2, 20–21, 22, 24, 29, 53, 113
HD (Hilda Doolittle), 173
Heath, Shirley Brice, 29, 113, 202
Heba, Gary, 115
Hebdige, Dick, 102, 115, 127
Heidegger, Martin, 44, 45, 46, 47–50, 52, 53, 55, 60
Heilbrun, Carolyn G., 81
Heraclitus, 49
Herder, Johann Gottfried von, 86
Hill, Adams Sherman, 13, 14
Hillman, James, 160, 162–63, 164–65, 166, 168–69, 173, 175, 204, 205
Hillocks, George, 43
Himley, Margaret, 66–67, 70
Hirsch, E. D., Jr., 108, 173
Hoggart, Richard, 127
Holzer, Jenny, 125
Holzman, Michael, 112
Hook, J. N., 76
Horner, Winifred G., 1
Howard, Ebenezer, 121
Howe, Susan, 161, 171
Hugo, Victor, 119
Hurlbert, C. Mark, 111
Husserl, Edmund, 60–61, 63, 69, 70, 199
Hutcheon, Linda, 155, 156

Jackson, Shirley, 74
Jakobson, Roman, 150, 151–52, 154, 156

James, William, 174
Jameson, Fredric, 99, 119, 125, 126
Johnson, Mark, 1
Johnson, Philip, 123–24
Johnson, Richard, 100–02, 112–13, 130
Joyce, James, 124
Jung, Carl, 164

Kant, Immanuel, 86
Kazmierczak, Jill, 82–83
Keats, John, 58
Kinneavy, James, 147
Kirk, G. S., 49
Klein, Julie, 3
Knoblauch, C. H., 63, 73
Kockelmans, Joseph J., 47, 52, 53, 54
Kroeber, Alfred L., 16, 28
Kruger, Barbara, 125

Labov, William, 34, 43
Lacan, Jacques, 28
Lakoff, George, 1
Lanham, Richard A., 168
Lapham, Lewis, 89–90, 203–04
Lauer, Janice, 45, 64, 112, 115
Lay, Mary M., 115
Le Corbusier, 121, 123
Lee, Spike, 55
Leitch, Vincent B., 101
Lemke, J. L., 183–85
Lentricchia, Frank, 99
Lessing, Gotthold Ephraim, 86
Lincoln, Abraham, 12
Lloyd-Jones, Richard, 1
Locke, John, 86
Loder, Kurt, 88–89
Luckmann, Thomas, 29
Lunsford, Andrea A., 112, 113, 114, 118
Lyotard, Jean-François, 150, 153

MacLow, Jackson, 194
Macrorie, Ken, 73, 74
Madhubuti, Haki, 161
Mallarmé, Stéphane, 164
Manet, Edouard, 119
Mapplethorpe, Robert, 13
Marcus, George E., 176–77, 178, 179,
    180–81, 183
Martin, Harold, 107
Marx, Karl, 120
Mascia-Lees, Frances E., 177, 178, 179
Mayakovsky, Vladimir, 194
McPhee, John, 169
Melanchthon, Philip, 31
Merleau-Ponty, Maurice, 60

Metcalf, Paul, 171
Michaels, Leonard, 34
Mill, John Stuart, 86
Miller, Carolyn, 114
Miller, Mark Crispin, 91–93
Miller, Susan, 2, 112
Milton, John, 55
Moffatt, Michael, 29
Moffett, James, 1, 147
Mohr, Marion, 73
Morenberg, Max, 113
Morley, Dave, 128
Murphy, Richard J., Jr., 4, 5, 199, 200,
    201, 202
Murray, Donald, 61, 73
Myers, Greg, 114

Newton, Isaac, 86
Nixon, Richard, 108
North, Stephen, 1, 3, 75–77, 78, 79, 80,
    176, 177, 180, 182, 186, 191
Nunberg, Geoffrey, 43

Odell, Keith, 81–82, 83
Ohmann, Richard, 107, 129, 157
Olbrechts-Tyteca, Lucie, 89
Olson, Charles, 169
Owens, Derek, 5, 194, 195, 204–05

Papoulis, Irene, 5, 135, 203, 204
Pattee, Frederick Lewis, 106
Pattison, Robert, 64
Perelman, Chaim, 89
Perl, Sondra, 66
Perry, William G., 134
Phelps, Louise Wetherbee, 67, 68–69, 70,
    71, 77–79, 80, 117–18, 199
Piaget, Jean, 1, 152
Picasso, Pablo, 124, 164
Pike, Kenneth, 45
Plato, 31, 116, 195–96, 205
Polanyi, Michael, 5, 72–73, 74–75,
    79–81, 83, 199, 200
Porter, James E., 116
Pound, Ezra, 122, 169
Pratt, Mary Louise, 153

Quandahl, Ellen, 109–10
Quasha, George, 173

Raban, Jonathan, 121
Rabinow, Paul, 85

Radway, Janice, 127
Raven, J. E., 49
Reagan, Ronald, 108
Reed, Ishmael, 173
Remmers, H. H., 16, 18–20
Richards, I. A., 116
Ricks, Christopher, 34
Ricoeur, Paul, 30, 31, 60, 78
Rorty, Richard, 150, 152
Rosaldo, Renato, 24, 29
Rosen, Harold, 81
Rosenblatt, Louise M., 53
Russ, Joanna, 189
Russell, David R., 104

Said, Edward, 99
Salvatori, Mariolina, 22
Sartre, Jean-Paul, 60
Schildgen, Brenda Deen, 5, 56, 195, 196,
    199, 200, 201, 203
Schilpp, Paul Arthur, 150
Schnabel, Julian, 124
Schoer, Lowell, 1
Scholes, Robert, 20, 99
Schwitter, Kurt, 194
Scott, Fred Newton, 28, 106
Scudder, Vida Dutton, 106
Searle, John, 153
Sharpe, Patricia, 177, 178, 179
Shaughnessy, Mina, 34, 42, 74, 114, 202
Sherman, Cindy, 122–23, 125, 132
Sherrington, Charles, 11
Shor, Ira, 126
Shores, David L., 34
Shostak, Marjorie, 29, 177
Simon, Herbert A., 63
Skinner, B. F., 29
Socrates, 196
Spellmeyer, Kurt, 5, 193, 195, 196, 198,
    205
Spencer, Herbert, 28
Spivak, Gayatri, 99
Squires, Geoffrey, 1, 3
Stacey, Judith, 178, 179, 180
Steele, Shelby, 93, 95, 204
Stein, Gertrude, 124, 169, 174, 194
Steinbeck, John, 74
Sternglass, Marilyn, 63, 71
Stillman, Peter R., 66, 113
Strunk, William, Jr., 29

Tathem, Campbell, 159
Taylor, Warren, 106
Tedlock, Dennis, 173
Therborn, Goran, 103
Todorov, Tzvetan, 30
Toulmin, Stephen, 2
Trimbur, John, 5, 100, 107, 108, 114,
    197, 204, 205, 206
Trimmer, Joseph, 81
Turner, Victor, 9, 10, 24, 27
Tyler, Moses Coit, 106
Tylor, E. B., 16

Van Manen, Max, 62, 67
Venturi, Robert, 123, 124

Wagner, Otto, 121
Waldrep, Thomas, 68
Waldrop, Rosmarie, 159
Wall, Susan V., 22
Wallas, Graham, 149, 150
Wallis, William, 65
Warhol, Andy, 164
Warnke, Georgia, 36, 38, 42, 43
Weinsheimer, Joel, 31
Wendell, Barrett, 13–15, 17, 26, 27
Wera, Eugene, 19, 27, 28
White, E. B., 29
White, Hayden, 23
Whitehead, A. N., 80
Whitman, Walt, 164
Whorf, Benjamin Lee, 174
Will, George, 89, 90, 91, 93
Williams, Joseph M., 68, 70
Williams, Raymond, 119, 127, 197
Williamson, Don, 95
Willis, Paul, 29, 127
Wilson, Nancy, 66
Wimsatt, W. K., Jr., 157
Winterowd, W. Ross, 115
Wittgenstein, Ludwig, 29, 121
Wittig, Monique, 161, 174
Wolfe, Tom, 169
Woodward, Virginia, 131
Worsham, Lynn, 45–46, 50, 51, 53, 54
Wright, Frank Lloyd, 121, 123

Yeats, William Butler, 15
Young, Richard, 45